# LONDON '92-'93 ON $45 A DAY

by Dan Levine

**PRENTICE HALL TRAVEL**

NEW YORK • LONDON • TORONTO • SYDNEY • TOKYO • SINGAPORE

**FROMMER BOOKS**

Published by Prentice Hall General Reference
A division of Simon & Schuster Inc.
15 Columbus Circle
New York, NY 10023



ISBN 0-13-334681-1
ISSN 1055-5331

Design by Robert Bull Design
Maps by Geografix Inc.

Manufactured in the United States of America

**FROMMER'S LONDON '92–'93 ON $45 A DAY**
Editor-in-Chief: Marilyn Wood
Senior Editors: Judith de Rubini, Pamela Marshall, Amit Shah
Editors: Alice Fellows, Paige Hughes, Theodore Stavrou
Assistant Editors: Suzanne Arkin, Peter Katucki, Lisa Renaud, Ellen Zucker
Contributing Editor: Michael Cain
Managing Editor: Leanne Coupe

# CONTENTS

## 6 WHAT TO SEE & DO IN LONDON 107



## 7 STROLLING AROUND LONDON 136



## 8 SHOPPING A TO Z 151

## 9 LONDON NIGHTS 163



## 10 EASY EXCURSIONS FROM LONDON 183



## APPENDIX 203



## INDEX 206

# LIST OF MAPS

## LONDON



## LONDON WALKING TOURS



## EXCURSION AREAS

## INVITATION TO THE READERS

In researching this book, I have come across many wonderful establishments, the best of which I have included here. I am sure that many of you will also come across wonderful hotels, inns, restaurants, guesthouses, shops, and attractions. Please don't keep them to yourself. Share your experiences, especially if you want to comment on places that have been included in this edition that have changed for the worse. You can address your letters to:

Dan Levine
*Frommer's London '92–'93 on $45 a Day*
c/o Prentice Hall Travel
15 Columbus Circle
New York, NY 10023

## A DISCLAIMER

Readers are advised that prices fluctuate in the course of time and travel information changes under the impact of the varied and volatile factors that affect the travel industry. Neither the author nor the publisher can be held responsible for the experiences of readers while traveling. Readers are invited to write to the publisher with ideas, comments, and suggestions for future editions.

## SAFETY ADVISORY

Whenever you're traveling in an unfamiliar city or country, stay alert. Be aware of your immediate surroundings. Wear a moneybelt and keep a close eye on your possessions. Be particularly careful with cameras, purses, and wallets, all favorite targets of thieves and pickpockets.

# CHAPTER 1

# INTRODUCING LONDON



Whoever told you that London is too expensive didn't read this book. It is not exactly cheap, but one of the best things about London is that so much of this world-class city is accessible to budget-minded tourists. Most of London's top attractions are either free or priced well below comparable sights Stateside. All of London's most important museums and galleries are free, as are the main sections of such major attractions as Westminster Abbey and the Houses of Parliament. The Changing of the Guard at Buckingham Palace is free, as is attendance at the often acerbic Speaker's Corner every Sunday in Hyde Park. The theater in London is still cheaper than in New York, and inexpensive seats are regularly available to the opera, ballet, and symphony. Dozens of bed-and-breakfasts and restaurants listed in this guidebook will keep you within your budget; and most offer a whole lot more character than any budget motel or diner Stateside.

Whether you're window-shopping in the West End or sightseeing in The City, this book will convince you that even today, spectacular London is enjoyable on a budget.

London attracts more American visitors than any other city in Europe. Tourists are drawn by world-class museums, top shops, unparalleled theater, and a pulsating nightlife. Famous sights, a strong sense of tradition, and the mystique of the monarchy are also compelling attractions. Combine all this with affordable hotels and restaurants and an efficient public transportation network, and London's popularity is no mystery.

In general, English people are slow to break the ice, but once it's broken, they respond with kindness and humor. Pop into any pub and you will discover both warm hospitality and good conversation.

London is a city bathed in history—but many tourists are disappointed when they arrive in this modern city, where all too often the only things marking the past are the little blue plaques commemorating former residences. Don't despair: The past is alive and well in London—you just have to know how to look for it. With few notable exceptions, history in the capital is more pronounced *socially* than it is *architecturally*. Indeed, the British class system is the most striking relic of the nation's past, though as a visitor it's

## WHAT'S SPECIAL ABOUT LONDON

**The Flea Markets**
- ☐ Particularly Portobello Road and Camden High Street, which seem to go on forever and offer a full day of fun.

**Food and Drink**
- ☐ Harrods Food Hall, the only food market I know that could double as a museum.
- ☐ Pubs—architecturally or culturally, there is truly nothing here more unique, special, and ubiquitous.

**Museums**
- ☐ The British Museum, world-famous and the standard by which world-class museums are judged.
- ☐ The Museum of the Moving Image, one of the city's newest, is as enjoyable as a top movie.

**Spectacles**
- ☐ Covent Garden Market, an upbeat marketplace and meeting space in the heart of the West End, perpetually packed and revealing London's lightest side.
- ☐ Speaker's Corner, where comedians, anarchists, religious fanatics, and would-be politicians compete for your ear every Sunday.

**Attractions**
- ☐ The Tower of London, combining fascinating history with awesome architecture, colorful pageantry, and good humor.
- ☐ Big Ben and the Houses of Parliament, symbols of London and of the country's long-lived democracy.

**Special Events**
- ☐ Chelsea Flower Show, the rose of England's garden shows, on the grounds of the breathtakingly beautiful Chelsea Royal Hospital.
- ☐ Notting Hill Carnival, one of Europe's largest street festivals, featuring Caribbean music, food, and fun.
- ☐ Wimbledon Lawn Tennis Championships, the most prestigious event in tennis, warrants a special trip.

**Evening Entertainment**
- ☐ Great theater—no other city in the world offers such a wide variety of high-quality productions. Best of all, London's theater enjoys good government support, making ticket prices quite affordable.

sometimes easy to miss. The royal family does not exist solely as a tourist attraction; rather, it is at the head of the aristocracy, and remains a potent symbol of the importance the British still place on breeding. In government, more than three quarters of the members of the House of Lords are hereditary peers. They are not elected to this upper house of parliament; they inherit their seats as a birthright. The actual buildings of Buckingham Palace and the Houses of Parliament are each less than 150 years old—but along with the Changing of the Guard, the Ceremony of the Keys, the Lord Mayor's Show, and other pageantry parades, these buildings represent something much older.

When you are in London, you are in one of the world's most exciting cities. Take advantage of its terrific offerings and unique opportunities. Explore the narrow alleyways of The City, enjoy lunch in a local pub, attend a free concert in a church, and strike up a conversation with the locals. Even though the British Empire is no more, its former capital still flourishes with more than its fair share of cultural activities, entertainment houses, special events, and, of course, history. Have fun!

# 1. CULTURE, HISTORY & BACKGROUND

It's always thrilling to arrive in London and suddenly notice that everyone is speaking with an accent. You knew they would be, of course, but somehow, when all the people around you are lengthening their vowels, you smile because you know they're not faking it. You've made it. You really are in England. The Brits' fancy names for everyday objects seem so charming. It's not just *what* they say, like "lift" for elevator and "torch" for flashlight, but *how* they say it; everyday speech somehow seems so formal.

Once you get used to the accent, however, a deeper and more meaningful realization sets in: Even though they speak English, the English people are part of a completely foreign culture. It is this understanding that is perhaps the most rewarding aspect of visiting England. Culturally, London is just as foreign to North Americans as Berlin, Brussels, or Madrid. Yet you speak the language. And almost without effort you are communicating with a foreign nation, in a tongue you know well.

### IMPRESSIONS

*When a man is tired of London, he is tired of life; for there is in London all that life can afford.*

—Samuel Johnson

*. . . we would rather see London laid in ruins and ashes than that it should be tamely and abjectly enslaved.*

—Sir Winston Churchill, 1940

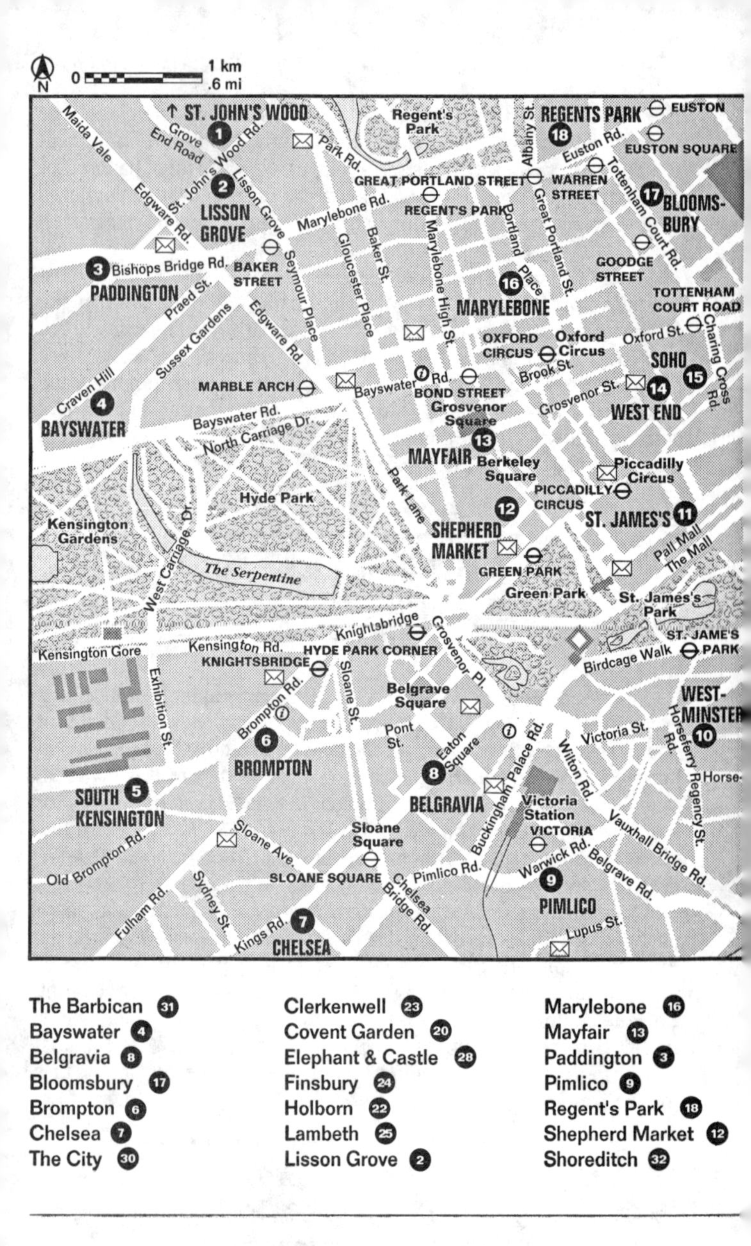


## GEOGRAPHY/PEOPLE

It's easy to forget that London is the capital of an island nation. England is separated from continental Europe by a channel, and it has benefited and suffered from its relative isolation from the rest of the world. By both protecting the British Isles from foreign aggres-

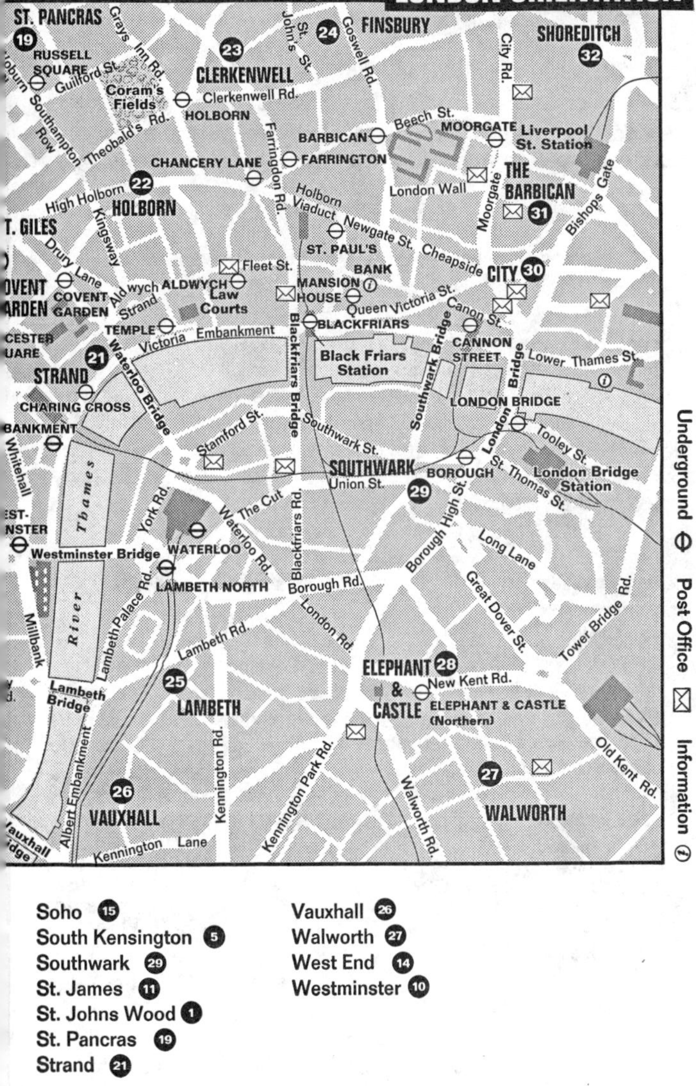


sions and acting as a barrier to communication, the English Channel has long been both help and hindrance.

England's close proximity to the rest of Europe is reflected in many cultural similarities. But the nature of island life, and the wide swath of water that separates Britain from its neighbors, has also fostered a culture that is markedly different from those that flourish on the Continent.

## IMPRESSIONS

*London is the epitome of our times, and the Rome of today.*
—Ralph Waldo Emerson

*London itself perpetually attracts, stimulates, gives me play, a story and a poem without any trouble, save that of moving my legs through the streets.*
—Virginia Woolf, 1928

---

The English people's fierce independence and penchant for politeness finds comparison not with the French or Germans, but with the Japanese—other islanders with limited space and geographically defined borders. England's separate development has resulted in distinctly unique foods, fashions, customs, and even religion. Eel pies, bowler hats, pints in pubs, and the Church of England are all utterly English, and an integral part of a unique culture.

### DATELINE

- **43** Londinium settled by Roman invaders. Bridge built across the Thames.
- **410** Roman grip weakens and Saxons seize London.
- **1066** William I (the Conqueror) crowns himself king. Construction of Tower of London begun.
- **1215** Magna Carta signed by King John.
- **1348** Half of London's population killed by Black Death (bubonic plague).
- **1381** 100,000 peasants occupy London in massive revolt.
- **1397** A wealthy merchant, Richard

*(continues)*

## HISTORY/POLITICS

### HISTORY

By any measure, London is a very old city. Excavations have proved that there were primitive settlements here as far back as 2500 B.C. Although scholars debate the origin of London's name, popular belief is that it derived from the Celtic words "Llyn Din," meaning "lakeside fortress." Origins notwithstanding, most historians agree that the British isles began to fall under Roman control in A.D. 43, and the conquerors called the town by the Thames "Londinium."

A bridge was built at a suitably solid spot, and the town began to flourish around the north bank of the bridgehead. It wasn't until the later part of the second century, after years of attack by surrounding tribes, that the Romans built a massive wall of Kentish ragstone around the city. Within a century, the population swelled to 15,000 and Londinium became a bustling center of trade and industry.

Roman Britain started to crumble around the end of the third century. Citizens were overtaxed, buildings fell into disrepair, and Saxon invaders from northern Germany started to encroach into southern England. At the same time Rome itself came under siege and, in A.D. 410, the majority of London's Roman troops departed to protect their emperor.

Over the next 400 years various Germanic tribes, collectively called Anglo-Saxons, began to settle in the country. By A.D. 871 the tribes united to become England, and Alfred the Great was crowned the country's first Saxon king. From 1042, England was ruled by Edward the Confessor ("Confessor" being a stop on the road to canonization). Now sainted for the deed, Edward rebuilt Westminster Abbey and transferred the court and government out of the City of London to what is now known as the City of Westminster.

When William, Duke of Normandy (the Conqueror), crowned himself king in 1066, he maintained the rights previously gained by the city dwellers, and allowed the City of London to continue electing its own leaders as it had for centuries—a practice which continues to this day. Favored barons were granted land, where they built huge fortified stone houses known as "burhs." Although none of those mansions stand today, streets such as Bucklersbury and Lothbury tell us where they stood.

By the end of the 14th century, London's population exceeded 30,000. Suburbs beyond the city walls expanded, and dozens more came into being. Due to a lack of central planning, roads developed haphazardly, creating the confusion of streets that still exists today.

Aside from his having six wives, the 16th-century reign of Henry VIII is most noted for the dissolution of England's monasteries. Both envious and threatened by the wealth and power they exerted, the king took control of the many buildings owned by the church, including Whitehall Palace and Hampton Court, the former homes of Cardinal Wolsey. King Henry built St. James's Palace on the land of an old leper hospital, and enclosed what is now Hyde Park, Green Park, and St. James's Park for his private gardens.

**DATELINE**

Whittington, elected Lord Mayor.

- **1401** Water pipes bring water from Tyburn.
- **1455** The Wars of the Roses start.
- **1461** Edward of York is crowned king.
- **1476** England's first printing press is installed near Westminster Abbey.
- **1483** King Richard III imprisons (and presumably murders) crown-rival nephews Edward V and his brother.
- **1485** Tudor dynasty begins when Henry VII defeats Richard at Bosworth.
- **1509** Henry VIII made king. Marries first of six wives.
- **1536** Church of England established, with king at head.
- **1553** Mary Tudor made queen. Lady Jane Grey, the "Nine Days Queen," is executed.
- **1558** Elizabeth I enthroned. Shakespeare writes and arts flourish.
- **1588** Spanish armada defeated.
- **1600** London expands to include areas south of the Thames.
- **1605** Guy Fawkes's Gunpow-

*(continues)*

Elizabethan London marked the development of English theater and the building of open-air playhouses. Ironically, city fathers (they were all men) in the second half of the 16th century felt that theaters attracted the wrong element, and banned them from The City. Many of the best-known playhouses, including Shakespeare's Globe, opened in the borough of Southwark, across the river Thames.

Although the city had never been entirely free from plague, the disease didn't rise to epidemic proportions until 1665, when more than 100,000 Londoners—a fifth of the population—died. The Great Plague didn't abate until a second catastrophe hit the city the following year.

The Great Fire of 1666, fanned by strong easterly winds, burned over 10,000 homes and virtually destroyed the entire City of London. After the fire, houses were rebuilt with stone and brick, and architect Christopher Wren was commissioned by the king to reconstruct St. Paul's Cathedral along with dozens of The City's churches.

The 18th century saw the building of the Empire, and marked England's transformation into a world-class financial and military power. London was the primary beneficiary of Britain's new prosperity, as evidenced by the construction of Grosvenor, Bedford, Hanover, and Soho squares. This was the great era of Georgian architecture, and its influence spilled over into the applied arts, including furniture, silver, and glass. Two new bridges—Westminster and Blackfriars—were built, streets were upgraded, and hospitals and services were improved. The newfound wealth gave rise to activities of leisure and brought about a cultural renaissance. Cafés opened, pubs flourished, and the fine arts gained prominence under the leadership of William Hogarth and Sir Joshua Reynolds.

Queen Victoria ascended the throne in 1837 and reigned for 64 years, the longest tenure in English history. The new 19th-century middle class believed learning was

### DATELINE

der Plot to blow up King James I and Parliament is foiled.

- **1642–60** Oliver Cromwell leads Parliamentary forces during Civil War.
- **1649** King Charles I executed at Banqueting House.
- **1660** Monarchy restored under Charles II.
- **1665** 100,000 Londoners, one-quarter of the city's inhabitants, killed by Great Plague.
- **1666** Great Fire burns much of the city.
- **1675** Construction of Sir Christopher Wren's St. Paul's Cathedral begun.
- **1685–89** James II is deposed after attempts to impose absolute rule. Monarch's powers limited by new Bill of Rights.
- **1694** Bank of England established by City merchants.
- **1730** Fleet River covered over.
- **1780** Roman Catholics are persecuted in Gordon Riots.
- **1800s** London's population tops 1

*(continues)*

an integral part of prosperity. Theater became respectable, and the Regent's Park Zoo flourished. London University was founded, and free municipal public libraries came into being. The National Gallery in Trafalgar Square was completed in 1838, while the British Museum's new buildings in Bloomsbury were finished in 1847.

London suffered from repeated bombings during World War II. Trenches were dug in public parks, tube stations doubled as bomb shelters, and gas masks were issued to the entire population. The British resolve to stand up stoically against the Germans is still a source of local pride.

Successive waves of immigrants, satellite television, and modern office buildings have literally and figuratively changed the face of contemporary London. But scratch the surface and you'll find a complex city that is an amalgam of all the eras that have come before. The city's cultural life is strongly based on manners and mores evolved from the past. Pageantry parades, parliamentary procedure, and the unrelenting class system are all vestiges of the country's long history. Most Britons are uncertain about what the arrival of the European Community will bring. Whatever the future holds, the city will surely continue to grow and evolve, forever writing new chapters in the colorful book that is London.

## FAMOUS LONDONERS

**Sir Arthur Conan Doyle** (1859–1930) Creator of Sherlock Holmes, the world's most famous sleuth, Conan Doyle felt that his popular mysteries obscured his more serious historical novels. A professed spiritualist, his posture as an upstanding figure of the establishment, maintaining British traditions, won him knighthood in 1902.

Residence: Not as you'd think at 221b Baker Street, but 12 Tennison Road, S.E.25.

Accomplishments: One of the most successful writers of his time, author of *The*

**DATELINE**

million. Industrial revolution transforms the city with docks, railways, canals, tunnels, and river embankments.

- **1847** Bloomsbury's British Museum opens.
- **1851** Hyde Park hosts the Great Exhibition.
- **1858** Covent Garden's Royal Opera House opens.
- **1863** The first Underground connects Paddington to The City.
- **1882** Law Courts built in the Strand.
- **1894** Tower Bridge opens.
- **1907** Central Criminal Court (the Old Bailey) is constructed.
- **1914–18** World War I. London bombed from planes and airships.
- **1939–45** World War II. Air raids and rocket attacks destroy a substantial part of the city. 30,000 killed, 50,000 injured.
- **1948** London hosts Olympics.
- **1951** Royal Festival Hall opens.
- **1953** Queen Elizabeth II is crowned.
- **1960s** Concrete

*(continues)*

Adventures of Sherlock Holmes* and of numerous novels that are still widely read and written about.

**Charles Dickens** (1812–1870) Master portraitist of Victorian London's cruelty and social ills in his many books, from his first, *Sketches by Boz,* to his last, *The Mystery of Edwin Drood.* Dickens lived in London only from 1837 to 1839, but in that time he produced some of his best-loved works. Great caricaturist and creator of such familiar characters as Mr. Pickwick, Uriah Heep, Miss Havisham, and Ebenezer Scrooge.

Residence: 48 Doughty Street, W.C.1.

Accomplishments: *The Pickwick Papers, Nicholas Nickleby,* and *Oliver Twist,* all written in Dickens's London home.

**William Hogarth** (1697–1764) Artist and brilliant depicter of London's social and political life in such series as *The Harlot's Progress* and *Marriage à la Mode.*

Accomplishments: His works hang in the Tate Gallery, Sir John Soane's Museum, and other galleries around the city.

**Samuel Johnson** (1709–1784) Most famous for his *Dictionary of the English Language* and his complete edition of Shakespeare, Johnson left Oxford without a degree, and went up to London at age 28. He frequented London's coffeehouses and founded what is still the most famous London eating club. Original members of "The Club" included playwright Oliver Goldsmith, political philosopher Edmund Burke, and painter Joshua Reynolds. Johnson was a master of aphorism, as evidenced by his definition of fishing: "A stick and string with a worm on one end and a fool on the other."

Residence: 17 Gough Square, E.C.4.

Favorite Haunt: The Cheshire Cheese on Little Essex Street, a small passage off Fleet Street.

Accomplishments: The first edition of Johnson's *Dictionary* can be seen in the attic of the Gough Square museum dedicated to him.

**Karl Marx** (1818–1883) After being expelled from Paris, Marx moved to London in 1849. Extremely poor, he lived with his family in 2 small rooms in Soho, often subsisting on potatoes and bread. His studies in the British Museum Reading Room were his primary task, and it was here that he wrote his most famous work, *Das Kapital.* He took part in the first meeting of the International Working Men's Association, held in London's St. Martin's Hall in

**DATELINE**

office buildings erected, including the controversial Centre Point Tower and Barbican Centre.

- **1981** Prince Charles marries Lady Diana Spencer in St. Paul's Cathedral.
- **1982** The Thames Flood Barrier is completed downstream at Woolwich.
- **1990** Margaret Thatcher steps down, ending longest tenure as prime minister in 20th-century Britain.
- **1992** England joins European Common Market (EC).
- **1993** Channel Tunnel scheduled to open, connecting England with France and continental Europe.

September of 1864. Marx is buried in Highgate Cemetery.

Residence: 28 Dean Street, W.1.

**Samuel Pepys** (1633–1703) Most famous for his *Diaries* (1660–1669), in which he meticulously recorded the events of his day, offering a vivid insight into a man's daily life and the lives of those around him. Pepys founded the civil administration of the Royal Navy, converting it from an occasional service to a permanent and efficient military force.

Residence: Site of what is now 12-14 Buckingham Street, W.C.2.

**Henry Purcell** (1659–1695) One of England's finest native composers, the major figure of English baroque music. He was an organist at Westminster Abbey. Composer of the opera *Dido and Aenaes,* he also wrote many odes, of which the most famous is *Sound the Trumpets,* composed for James II's birthday.

Accomplishments: His works are performed in concert halls around the world, including the one named in his honor in London's South Bank Arts Centre.

**Joseph Mallord William Turner** (1775–1851) Son of a London barber, J. M. W. Turner became Britain's greatest landscape painter. A prodigious artist, he entered the Royal Academy at age 14, and went on to paint topographical watercolors, and seascapes in the Dutch tradition. His obsession with the violent moods of nature has been attributed to the affect his mother's madness had on him.

Residence: 23 Queen Anne Street, W.1.

**Virginia Woolf** (1882–1941) There is, perhaps, no other modern figure as intimately connected with London. Whether directly, as in the essay *Street Haunting,* or indirectly—through Mrs. Dalloway—Woolf's excitement about her city appears in almost all of her writings. From about 1906, Woolf joined with a brilliant circle of writers and artists calling themselves the Bloomsbury Group.

Residence: 29 Fitzroy Square, W.1.

Haunts: She loved to "ramble the streets," and regularly walked by Russell Square, Southampton Row, and the Strand.

**Christopher Wren** (1632–1723) Mathematician and astronomer, he became a celebrated architect responsible for many new buildings after the Great Fire of London (1666). He designed 52 churches, including St. Paul's Cathedral, St. Bride's, in Fleet Street, and St. Mary-le-Bow in The City. He was also responsible for the

---

### IMPRESSIONS

*It is my belief, Watson . . . that the lowest and vilest alleys of London do not present a more dreadful record of sin than does the smiling and beautiful countryside.*

—Sir Arthur Conan Doyle, *The Adventures of Sherlock Holmes*

*Hell is a city much like London—a populous and smoky city.*

—Percy Bysshe Shelley, *Peter Bell the Third*

Royal Hospital in Chelsea, and the Royal Navel College, in Greenwich. Wren was knighted for his service, and is buried in St. Paul's Cathedral.

Accomplishments: St. Paul's Cathedral, churches in The City, and municipal buildings all over town.

### History on the Streets

The very layout of London's undisciplined maze of winding streets, alleys, and lanes is a significant testament to the city's history. The structures of the past are long gone, but former times are widely reflected by street names, and can be readily recalled by reading a sign or studying a map. Bucklersbury and Lothbury were named after "burhs," the stone mansions of Norman barons. Ludgate, Aldgate, Cripplegate, and other city streets were named for the gates of The City wall that stood where the streets now run. Barbican derived its name from the watchtower that once stood there. To people in the Middle Ages, "cheaps" were markets: hence modern street names like Eastcheap and Cheapside. Some streets are even named for the products that were sold there. Look for Milk Street, Bread Street, and Friday Street (where fish was sold).

## POLITICS

London is the capital of the Kingdom of Great Britain and Northern Ireland (that's its name), lands encompassing England, Scotland, Wales, and Northern Ireland. The kingdom is a constitutional monarchy, and Queen Elizabeth II is the head of state. She is not the head of the government, however. That dubious honor goes to the prime minister, who is selected by the majority party in Parliament.

Technically, Parliament is comprised of three separate entities: the sovereign, the House of Lords, and the House of Commons. In actuality, however, only the "lower" house, the House of Commons, makes law. Although they do have the power to sway public opinion, the roles of the sovereign and the members of the House of Lords are chiefly ceremonial.

There are currently two major political parties in Britain: Conservative and Labour. The Conservatives, or "Tories," are currently led by John Major, Margaret Thatcher's successor.

Parliamentary debates are usually quite lively, and can be a treat to watch. See Chapter 6, "What to See and Do," for information on how you can attend.

---

## IMPRESSIONS

*London, that great cesspool into which all the loungers of the Empire are irresistibly drained.*

—Sir Arthur Conan Doyle, *A Study in Scarlet*

# ART, ARCHITECTURE & CULTURAL LIFE

Art and architecture in London have evolved through many periods, most characterized by, and named for, the monarch who ruled at the time. Excellent collections of English art are housed in the museums of London.

Many old architectural examples still stand—in ruins or reconstructed—throughout the city. The interested visitor should see Chapter 6, "Special-Interest Sightseeing," for specific information on city buildings.

## ART

Like the early art of most of the Western world, early English art was religious in nature, comprised of intricately wrought crosses, illuminated manuscripts, stained-glass windows, religious statuary, and ecclesiastical paintings. Prehistoric baubles and utensils aside, these religious pieces, and other works associated with abbeys and churches, are the oldest extant art in England.

Grinling Gibbons was perhaps the country's greatest sculptor, carving prolifically in the late 17th and early 18th centuries. Many of his works, including a baptismal font, can be seen in the churches of The City. It was not until the 20th century that English sculpture came into its own, however, produced by artists like Sir Jacob Epstein, Kenneth Armitage, Barbara Hepworth, and Henry Moore, to name a few.

Portraiture was the first style of oil painting to become popular in England, and today the National Portrait Gallery is packed with faces from the Tudor and Stuart periods. Many of the artists commissioned for this work, including Van Dyck and Lely, were not English-born.

For the most part, native English painters didn't flourish until the 18th century, when landscape painting and social satire came into vogue. Constable, Gainsborough, Hogarth, Reynolds, Romny, and Turner are considered the masters. Much of their work hangs in the Tate Gallery, and in private collections and small museums all around the city.

## ARCHITECTURE

Many of London's oldest monuments, built in the centuries after the Norman Conquest (1066), remain potent symbols of the city's economic and military might. Westminster Abbey and the Tower of

---

### IMPRESSIONS

*So poetry, which is in Oxford made*
*An art, in London only is a trade.*
—John Dryden

London are but two extant examples of structures sporting medieval designs. Guildhall, the seat of The City of London's local government, and Southwark Cathedral, founded in 1106, are both widely regarded Gothic masterpieces.

Inigo Jones and Christopher Wren were two of London's most celebrated 17th-century architects. Their work is all over the city, and includes such illustrious buildings as Jones's Banqueting House and St. Paul's Church, and Wren's St. Paul's Cathedral and Chelsea Royal Hospital.

Many of the city's residential neighborhoods were built in the 18th century, and reflect distinct styles of the Georgian period. Look for flat façades and large windows in houses facing squares and crescents.

London's most flamboyant buildings are pure Victoriana. These include such huge masterpieces as St. Pancras Station, the Houses of Parliament, and the Royal Courts of Justice. See Chapter 6 for more information on these and other more modern structures.

## CULTURAL LIFE

One of the greatest advantages of visiting England is that we speak the language, and can easily immerse ourselves into a foreign culture. London is very rich in culture; dozens of playhouses, symphony spaces, jazz halls, and rock music clubs attest to this fact every night of the week.

Several participatory and spectator sports are uniquely British, and interesting for the way their appeal is class-distinctive. In fact, nowhere is the dichotomy between the classes more apparent than with regard to sports.

So-called aristocratic sports include horse racing at Ascot, cricket at Lord's Cricket Ground, and tennis at Wimbledon. Fox hunting and horseback riding (dressage) are also traditional upper-class activities.

In contrast, football (soccer) and rugby grounds have always been bastions of the working class. Fiercely loyal fans often become infamously rowdy crowds. Greyhound dog racing is the working class's race of choice; and snooker, played on a pocketless pool table, conjures up images of dark dens and a misspent youth.

Literature has probably been Britain's most successful cultural export, and the panoply of brilliant British artists is astounding. Shakespeare is, of course, the most famous English bard. But even without him, the list is impressive. From the Old English epic poem, *Beowulf*, to the contemporary fiction writers included each quarter in the British literary magazine *Granta*, there are enough top writers to fill an encyclopedia.

Geoffrey Chaucer's *Canterbury Tales* has traversed centuries to remain the best-known Middle English work. During Tudor and Elizabethan times, Sir Thomas More (*Utopia*), Edmund Spenser (*The Faerie Queen*), and Christopher Marlowe (*The Tragical History of Dr. Faustus*) were the primary stars in the literary sky.

John Milton was the literary giant of the 17th century, penning *Paradise Lost* less than a hundred years after King James I ordered the translation of the Bible, known today as the King James Version.

Daniel Defoe (*Robinson Crusoe*), Henry Fielding (*Tom Jones*), and Alexander Pope (*An Essay of Man*) were just three of the many 18th-century middle-class writers who catapulted onto the literary scene. But none has had more lasting impact than Samuel Johnson, whose *Dictionary of the English Language* made him England's premier lexicographer.

For literature, the 19th century was England's most glorious age. A mere mention of a few famous names should give you a good idea. Blake, Wordsworth, Coleridge, Byron, Keats, Shelley, Austen, the Brontë sisters, Lewis Carroll, George Eliot, Oscar Wilde . . . the list is endless. And don't forget Charles Dickens, the country's most famous Victorian writer.

Many of England's best modern writers have taken on contentious topics, and have been instrumental in changing the way we look at ourselves. Virginia Woolf (*A Room of One's Own*), Aldous Huxley (*Brave New World*), D. H. Lawrence (*Women in Love*), and George Orwell (*1984*) are just a few of the important British writers of this century.

# 2. FOOD & DRINK

British cooking has long been the butt of jokes, and for the most part, this is well deserved. Deep-fried fish and chips is the national dish, and bangers (sausages), fried eggs, and doughy meat pies also enjoy wide popularity. There are, of course, some bright British kitchens that prepare national dishes with top ingredients and a minimum of grease; several are listed in Chapter 5. Understand, however, that this "nouvelle British" cuisine is a result of modern trends, and not reflective of what most people eat.

## MEALS & DINING CUSTOMS

See Chapter 5, "London Dining." If you're coming from another English-speaking country, it's doubtful that you'll see much here in the way of food and dining customs that you haven't seen before. But, I'll fill you in on a few specialties and idiosyncracies of eating in Britain.

## THE CUISINE

Meals often begin with an appetizer, which the British call a "starter." Most menus feature soups, salads, or a specialty like avocado prawns; half an avocado filled with small, sweet shrimp in salad dressing.

Typical main courses, or "main meals," include meat pies, roast beef, and fried fish, all of which are most always served with "mash" (mashed potatoes) or "chips" (french fries).

Steak-and-kidney pie is baked in a deep dish and covered with pastry. Shepherd's pie is made of minced (chopped) meat, onions, and seasonings, and topped with mashed potatoes.

Roasts are usually carved to order and, like most other main meals, are served with potatoes and a choice of two vegetables—often just called "veg." Whether they are carrots, peas, or both, they are invariably boiled lifeless.

In fish-and-chips shops, or "chippies," you usually have a choice of about a half-dozen varieties. Cod, haddock, plaice, and sole are all popular, though beneath the thick, crispy batter it's hard to tell them apart.

A Cornish pasty makes an excellent, and inexpensive, snack or light meal, and is available at most pubs and many restaurants. A pasty is a pastry envelope filled with minced meat, chopped potato, carrot, onion, and seasoning, and it goes especially well with beer.

Ploughman's lunch is served in almost every pub, and is also meant to be washed down with a pint. It usually includes a hunk of cheese, crusty bread, butter, and some pickled onion or chutney. It's filling and cheap, if not too exciting.

Speaking of cheese, it's the one food that the British are renowned for. The French may disagree, but Cheddar, Cheshire, and blue Stilton can hold their own.

Desserts, or "sweets," are often puddings. Usually made from a custard base, puddings usually share the menu with a variety of cakes ("gâteaux") and fruit pies similar to those served in America. If you order cake with milk, specify that you would like the milk served separately in a glass, otherwise you may get a bowl of cake sitting in milk! Similarly, most Britons drink their coffee after they have finished their dessert. If you want drink your coffee and your cake together, tell the waiter.

## DRINKS

Coca-Cola, orange soda, Dr. Pibbs (like Dr. Pepper), and other familiar soft drinks are all popular in England. Bottled water is readily available, too, though the city tap water seems to be relatively safe. When ordering water in a restaurant, specify if you want tap or bottled, and if you want the latter, say if you want it with or without carbonation.

Wine is served in most restaurants, and, like other alcoholic beverages, is sold in corner stores and supermarkets. There is such a thing as English wine, but unless you like it sweet and fruity, do as the locals do and order Italian, German, or French.

## PUBS

The Houses of .Parliament mean government, and Buckingham Palace symbolizes aristocracy, but only the public house is representative of the people.

### IMPRESSIONS

*Would I were in an alehouse in London!*
*I would give all my fame for a pot of ale, and safety.*
—SHAKESPEARE, *Henry V*

Beer is the main drink here, and there are often four or more to choose from. Sold in Imperial half-pints and pints (20% larger than U.S. measures), the primary distinction is between lager and bitter. Lager is what Americans are used to, light, bubbly, and cold; but most British prefer bitter, higher in alcohol, more assertive in taste, less carbonated, and usually served at room temperature.

Many pubs also offer particularly good "real" ales, distinguishable at the bar by hand-pumps that must be "pulled" by the barkeep. Real ales are natural "live" beers, allowed to ferment in the cask.

Cider, most of which comes from nearby Taunton, is a flavorful fermented apple juice that is also available in most pubs. Many people disagree, but I think it's great.

## 3. RECOMMENDED BOOKS & RECORDINGS

Of London, countless pages have been written, and endless hours of recordings made. Below, I list a *few* of the highlights.

### BOOKS

Since we speak English, we can not only read *about* London, we can learn about life in the city through English novels, poems, and histories. Shakespeare and Dickens, Britain's two most popular authors, can give us some notion of what London was like in their eras. In addition, you can get a good idea of what life was like and what people were thinking by reading the works of such notables as William Blake, John Keats, Jane Austen, Emily and Charlotte Brontë, Lewis Carroll, George Eliot, and Oscar Wilde.

Virginia Woolf's *A Room of One's Own,* T.S. Eliot's *Wasteland,* and George Orwell's *Down and Out in Paris and London* are excellent literary windows into London's more recent past. Insight into the London of earlier times comes from *The Survey of London,* by John Story, *The Life of Samuel Johnson,* by James Boswell, and the *Diaries of Samuel Pepys.*

In the category of "good reads" are some of the best mystery and suspense novels to be found. Sir Arthur Conan Doyle's Sherlock Holmes series and Agatha Christie's novels are the most famous, but look to books by Ellis Peters and Dorothy Sayers for other excellent reads in the genre.

Accessible academic works on British social history include *London Life in the Eighteenth Century,* by M. Dorothy George, an enlightened and readable study of life in the Georgian period; *The Making of Modern London,* by Gavin Weightman and Steve Humphries—my pick from the mountain of books on the Victorian development of London; and *The Long Weekend,* by Robert Graves and Alan Hodge, a fascinating and straightforward account of Britain between the wars.

## RECORDINGS

From the time Henry Purcell wrote the first English opera, *Dido and Aeneas,* in 1689, classical music began to gain in popularity in London. In the 18th century, Italian opera became the rage, even as Sir John Gay satirized the genre in *The Beggar's Opera* in 1728. Handel, who became a British subject, composed *Messiah* and other operas and oratorios in England. Gilbert and Sullivan were the most famous English composers of their time, and their operettas livened up an otherwise unremarkable 19th century in English music. For "serious" music, Benjamin Britten and Sir Edward Elgar are the country's most famous 20th-century figures.

But Britain didn't really come into its own musically until the advent of the rock era, the story of which is well known. In the 1960s, the Beatles began a movement that has come to be known as the British Invasion. Continuing with groups like the Who, the Rolling Stones, Pink Floyd, and Led Zeppelin, British rock-and-roll topped music charts in America and around the world. Individual British musicians like David Bowie and Eric Clapton continue to dominate the music scene, along with more contemporary artists such as Sting and Elvis Costello.

# CHAPTER 2

# PLANNING A TRIP TO LONDON



London's abundance of entertainment, shopping, and sightseeing opportunities means you can get here without any prior arrangements and still have full, fun-filled days. You may not get your first pick of accommodations, but there are enough hotels in the city to ensure you won't have to sleep on a park bench. Still, I'm a believer in preparation. This chapter is designed to help you plan your trip, save money and time, and get the most out of your London stay.

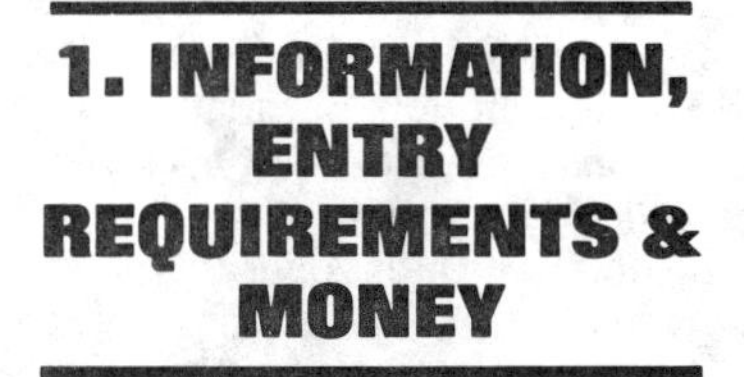

## 1. INFORMATION, ENTRY REQUIREMENTS & MONEY

### SOURCES OF INFORMATION

Information about travel in London and all of Britain can be obtained from a **British Tourist Authority (BTA)** office in your home country. **In the United States,** the main BTA office is 40 W. 57th St., New York, NY 10019 (tel. 212/581-4700). Other U.S. offices include 625 N. Michigan Ave., Suite 1510, Chicago, IL 60611 (tel. 312/787-0490); and World Trade Center, 350 S. Figueroa St., Suite 450, Los Angeles, CA 90071 (tel. 213/628-3525).

**In Australia:** 171 Clarence St., Sydney NSW 2000 (tel. 02/29-8627).

**In Canada:** 94 Cumberland St., Suite 600, Toronto, ON, M5R 3N3 (tel. 416/925-6326).

**In New Zealand:** Norwich Insurance House, 8th floor, Queen and Durham Sts., Auckland 1 (tel. 09/31-446).

In England, visit the main British Tourist Authority office in the British Travel Centre, 4-12 Lower Regent St., London S.W.1 (tel.

071/730-3400). In addition to information on all of Britain, the center has a British Rail ticket office, a travel agency, a theater ticket agency, a hotel-booking service, a bookstore, an American Express office, and a souvenir shop. Hours are 9am to 6:30pm Monday through Friday and 10am to 4pm Saturday and Sunday. Weekend hours are extended from June through September.

See Chapter 3, under "Information" in "Fast Facts: London," for a full list of information sources in London.

## ENTRY REQUIREMENTS

### DOCUMENTS

Citizens of the United States, Canada, Australia, and New Zealand need only a valid passport to enter Great Britain. However, Customs officials tend to ask younger travelers and suspicious-looking others to prove they have enough cash and/or an onward ticket before admitting them into the country. Some streetwise student travelers avoid this hassle at Passport Control by writing the name of an expensive hotel on their landing cards.

### CUSTOMS

Overseas visitors are allowed to import 400 cigarettes and 1 quart of liquor duty free. Film, toiletries, and other items can be imported free of tax, provided they are for your personal use. Live animals, plants, and produce are forbidden. When returning to the United States, citizens are allowed to bring back $400 worth of merchandise duty free. After that amount, you will be charged a flat 10% tax on the next $1,000 worth of goods. If you do shop in London, make sure you retain your receipts to show Customs officials.

## MONEY

### CASH & CURRENCY

The English **pound (£),** a small, thick, round coin, is divided into 100 **pence.** Pence, often called "p," come in 1p, 2p, 5p, 10p, and 50p coins. You may still see some 1- and 2-shilling coins, which are equivalent to 5p and 10p, respectively. Notes are issued in £5, £10, £20, and £50 denominations.

At press time, it costs $1.80 to buy 1 English pound ($1.80 = £1). To make budgeting easier, prices quoted in this book are accompanied by their equivalents in U.S. dollars. Exchange rates are volatile, so remember that these conversions are to be used as a guide only. See Chapter 3, under "Currency Exchange" in "Fast Facts: London," for information on banks and changing money.

### TRAVELER'S CHECKS

Foreign-currency traveler's checks are easily exchanged in London. Banks and traveler's-check companies like American Express and Thomas Cook offer the best rates. As a rule, traveler's checks

## THE POUND & THE DOLLAR

At this writing $1 = approximately 55p (or £1 = $1.80), and this was the rate of exchange used to calculate the dollar values given in this book (rounded to the nearest nickel). This rate fluctuates from time to time and may not be the same when you travel to London. Therefore the following table should be used only as a guide.

| £ | $U.S. | £ | $U.S. |
|---|---|---|---|
| .05 | .09 | 6 | 10.80 |
| .10 | .18 | 7 | 12.60 |
| .25 | .45 | 8 | 14.40 |
| .50 | .90 | 9 | 16.20 |
| .75 | 1.35 | 10 | 18.00 |
| 1 | 1.80 | 15 | 27.00 |
| 2 | 3.60 | 20 | 36.00 |
| 3 | 5.40 | 25 | 45.00 |
| 4 | 7.20 | 30 | 54.00 |
| 5 | 9.00 | 35 | 63.00 |

command a better exchange rate than cash, and are therefore an excellent way to bring money into the country. Some restaurants and hotels—especially the nicer ones—will exchange foreign-currency traveler's checks, but their exchange rates will routinely be lower than in a bank. Chequepoint and other private currency exchange businesses maintain offices throughout the city, especially in the most heavily touristed areas. As a rule, they keep long hours, sometimes all night, but their rates are deceptive. The exchange rate may look lucrative, but commissions at these places are uniformly stiff.

Traveler's checks issued in British pounds are accepted at most shops, restaurants, hotels, theaters, and attractions. For the foreign traveler, however, there are two drawbacks to carrying them. First, you will have to exchange your money into pounds at home, a transaction that usually proves more costly than in London. Second, you will have to re-exchange your unused pounds after your trip, thus incurring a second transaction fee.

### CREDIT CARDS

It is comforting to know that American Express, Diners Club, MasterCard, VISA, and other credit cards are widely accepted in London. Using plastic can be economical—eliminating commissions and being billed later. However, be forewarned that rate of exchange might be unfavorable to you at the time of billing. In England, Access is MasterCard, and Barclaycard is VISA.

| WHAT THINGS COST IN LONDON | U.S. $ |
| --- | --- |
| Taxi from Victoria Station to a Bayswater hotel | 11.70 |
| Underground from Heathrow Airport to central London | 3.80 |
| Local telephone call | .18 |
| Double room at the Dorchester Hotel (deluxe) | 495.00 |
| Double room at the Strand Palace Hotel (moderate) | 180.00 |
| Double room at the Oakley Hotel (budget) | 59.40 |
| Lunch for one at the Hard Rock Café (moderate) | 13.50 |
| Lunch for one at most pubs (budget) | 5.85 |
| Dinner for one, without wine, at Le Gavroche (deluxe) | 99.00 |
| Dinner for one, without wine, at the English House (moderate) | 41.40 |
| Dinner for one, without wine, at Khan's (budget) | 10.80 |
| Pint of beer | 2.35 |
| Coca-Cola in a restaurant | 1.45 |
| Cup of coffee | 1.15 |
| Roll of ASA 100 film, 36 exposures | 7.55 |
| Admission to the British Museum | free |
| Movie ticket | 8.10 |
| Cheapest West End theater ticket | 11.25 |

## 2. WHEN TO GO — CLIMATE, HOLIDAYS & EVENTS

Seasonal spirit is strong in London. Spring is celebrated with festive fairs and a fresh, friendly attitude as locals shed their coats and restaurateurs return their tables to the sidewalks. Summer means open-air theaters, park picnics, and late-night laughter around bustling Leicester Square. In the autumn, London's trees blaze orange and red, and churches are decorated with flowers and fruits of the harvest. And winter is best for culture. The opera and ballet seasons are in full swing, and theaters, museums, restaurants, and all the major sights are mercifully free of crowds.

## CLIMATE

London's infamous pea-soup fog was never fog at all. It was smog, from sooty chimneys and coal-burning power plants. Today, rigidly enforced air-pollution controls make it an offense to use a fireplace for its intended purpose, and "fog" is no longer in the forecast. Rain is, however, and it falls at an average rate throughout the year. A typical weather forecast any time of year predicts "scattered clouds with sunny periods and showers, possibly heavy at times." Temperatures are temperate, and rarely go below freezing in winter, or above 70° Fahrenheit in summer.

### London's Average Daytime Temperature & Rainfall

| | Jan | Feb | Mar | Apr | May | June | July | Aug | Sept | Oct | Nov | Dec |
|---|---|---|---|---|---|---|---|---|---|---|---|---|
| Temp. (°F) | 40 | 40 | 44 | 49 | 55 | 61 | 64 | 64 | 59 | 52 | 46 | 42 |
| Rainfall " | 2.1 | 1.6 | 1.5 | 1.5 | 1.8 | 1.8 | 2.2 | 2.3 | 1.9 | 2.2 | 2.5 | 1.9 |

## HOLIDAYS

Most businesses are closed December 25 and 26, January 1, Good Friday, Easter Monday, and May 1. In addition, many stores close on bank holidays, which are scattered throughout the year. There is no uniform policy for museums, restaurants, and attractions with regard to holidays. To avoid disappointment, always phone before setting out.

## LONDON CALENDAR OF EVENTS

### JANUARY

☐ **Charles I Commemoration.** Banqueting House, Whitehall. Hundreds of cavaliers march through central London in 17th-century dress to mark the anniversary of the 1649 execution of King Charles I.

Last Sunday in January.

### FEBRUARY

☐ **Chinese New Year Parade.** Chinatown, at Gerrard and Lisle streets. Festive crowds line the decorated streets of Soho to watch the famous Lion Dancers.

Late January or early February (based on the lunar calendar).

## MARCH

☐ **The Easter Parade.** Battersea Park. London's largest parade features brightly colored floats and marching bands, kicking off a full day of activities.
Easter morning.

## MAY

✪ ***CHELSEA FLOWER SHOW*** *This international spectacular features the best of British gardening, with displays of plants and flowers of all seasons. The location, on the breathtakingly beautiful grounds of the Chelsea Royal Hospital, helps make this exposition a world-class affair.*
***Where:*** *Chelsea Royal Hospital, Chelsea.* ***When:*** *Late May.* ***How:*** *For ticket information, see "More Attractions: Parks and Gardens," in Chapter 6.*

## JUNE

☐ **Trooping the Colour.** The Mall and Horse Guard's Parade. The Queen's official birthday. Visitors can catch a glimpse of the royal party as it parades down The Mall from Buckingham Palace.
Early June.

---

✪ ***WIMBLEDON LAWN TENNIS CHAMPIONSHIPS*** *The most prestigious event in tennis. Tickets are usually available at the gate for early rounds of play, but to attend later rounds usually requires planning.*
***Where:*** *Wimbledon, London.* ***When:*** *End of June.* ***How:*** *For information on booking seats in the center court, see "Spectator Sports," in Chapter 6.*

## AUGUST

✪ ***THE NOTTING HILL CARNIVAL*** *One of the largest annual street festivals in Europe, this African-Caribbean fair attracts over half a million people during its two days. Live reggae and soul music combine with great Caribbean food, camaraderie, and an unusual air of excitement. Free.*
***Where:*** *Notting Hill, London.* ***When:*** *Late August.* ***How:*** *Just show up.*

## NOVEMBER

☐ **State Opening of Parliament.** Whitehall and Parliament Square. Although the ceremony itself is not open to the public, crowds pack the parade route to see the royal procession.
Late October or early November.

✪ ***FIREWORKS NIGHT*** *Commemorates the anniversary of the "Gunpowder Plot," an attempt to blow up King James I and his parliament. Huge organized bonfires are lit throughout the city and Guy Fawkes, the plot's most famous conspirator, is burned in effigy. Free.*

***Where:*** *Hyde Park, Battersea Park, and other public areas in London.* ***When:*** *Early November.* ***How:*** *Follow the crowds . . . and the smoke.*

☐ **The Lord Mayor's Show.** The City. An elaborate parade celebrating the inauguration of the new chief of The City of London. 2nd week in November.

# 3. HEALTH, INSURANCE & OTHER CONCERNS

Health, safety, loss, and theft are serious issues. Take a little time before your trip to make sure these concerns don't ruin it.

## MEDICAL REQUIREMENTS

Unless you are arriving from an area known to be suffering from an epidemic, no inoculations or vaccinations are required to enter Britain. If you are currently on medication, be sure to carry a doctor's prescription along with any controlled substances you possess.

## INSURANCE

### HEALTH INSURANCE

Citizens of Australia and New Zealand are entitled to free medical treatment and subsidized dental care while in Britain. Americans and other nationals will usually have to pay up-front for services rendered. Doctors and hospitals can be expensive, so although it is not required of travelers, health insurance is highly recommended. Most American travelers are covered by their hometown policies in the event of an accident or sudden illness while away on vacation. Also, some credit card companies offer free, automatic travel-accident insurance, up to $100,000, when you purchase travel tickets on their cards. Before you purchase additional protection, check to see if you are already covered in foreign countries by your health maintenance organization (HMO) or insurance carrier.

### OTHER TRAVEL-RELATED INSURANCE

You can also protect your travel investment by insuring against lost or damaged baggage, and trip cancellation or interruption costs. These coverages are often combined into a single comprehensive plan, and sold through travel agents, credit card companies, and the following firms:

**Tele-Trip (Mutual of Omaha),** 3201 Farnam St., Omaha, NB 68131 (tel. 402/345-2400 or toll free 800/228-9792). In addition to selling all types of travel-related insurance, the company offers out-of-country major medical insurance for $3 per day, with a 10-day minimum.

**Travel Guard International,** 1100 Center Point Dr., Stevens Point, WI 54481 (tel. toll free 800/826-1300, in Wisconsin 800/634-0644). A 7-day comprehensive insurance package costs $52. Some limitations apply.

**Travel Insurance Pak,** Travelers Insurance Co., One Tower Square, 15NB, Hartford, CT 06183-5040 (tel. 203/277-2318 or toll free 800/243-3174). Travel-accident and illness coverage starts at $10 for 6 to 10 days; $500 worth of coverage for lost, damaged, or delayed baggage costs $20 for 6 to 10 days; and trip-cancellation coverage costs $5.50 for $100 worth of coverage (up to $110 for $2,000).

### BACKUP DOCUMENTS

Before you leave home, make two copies of each important document you are carrying—passport (copy the inside page with your photo), airline ticket, driver's license, prescriptions, and the like. Leave one set of copies at home, and put the other in your luggage separate from the originals. Should the documents be lost or stolen, you'll have invaluable backup information to aid you in replacing them.

## 4. WHAT TO PACK

Virtually everything can be purchased in London, so keep the "lug" out of your luggage by eliminating items that you might need "just in case." Still, unless you plan to buy an umbrella abroad, or want to use the rain as yet another excuse to duck into a pub, pack this essential item. In addition, few budget hotels provide hair dryers or electrical current converters. If you bring appliances that need to be plugged in, you will need to convert them. In Britain, electric appliances run on 240 volts and plug into a three-pronged socket different from those used in North America and on the Continent.

Winter temperatures in London rarely drop below freezing, and in summer, 85°F is considered a heat wave. But because of the unpredictability of island weather, you should be prepared for anything. A warm sweater is essential, no matter what time of year, as well as a jacket or coat (preferably waterproof) appropriate to the season.

Like most cities, London is best explored on foot, and most enjoyable in a comfortable and sturdy pair of shoes.

Finally, Londoners are a rather conservative lot when it comes to dress. Even the famous "punks" follow a fairly strict, if unconventional, dress code. Although you will rarely be turned away because of your dress, simple styles and dark colors are best.

## 5. TIPS & DISCOUNT OPPORTUNITIES FOR SPECIAL TRAVELERS

### FOR THE DISABLED

Although it has not always been the case, most of London's major museums and tourist attractions are now fitted with wheelchair ramps to accommodate physically challenged visitors. It is common in London for theaters, nightclubs, and attractions to offer discounts, called "concessions," to people with disabilities. Ask for these before paying full price. ***London Made Easy,*** published by the London Tourist Board, offers specialized information and advice to wheelchair-bound visitors. It costs £2.50 ($4.50), and is available from the British Tourist Authority abroad, and Tourist Information Centres in London (see "Information," earlier in this chapter, and "Orientation: Tourist Information," in Chapter 3). ***Access in London*** costs £4 ($7.20), and is a bit more comprehensive, covering theaters, pubs, shopping, and the like. *Access* is available from larger bookstores in London, or by sending a check in pounds sterling to 39 Bradley Gardens, West Ealing, London W13 8HE, England.

London Regional Transport's **Unit for Disabled Passengers** (tel. 071/227-3312) answers questions on public transportation, and can help you plan a trip using their special facilities.

**Artsline** (tel. 071/388-2227) offers free information on accessibility to theaters, galleries, and events around the city, Monday to Friday from 10am to 5:30pm.

### FOR OLDER TRAVELERS

In Britain, "senior citizen" usually means a woman at least 60 years old and a man at least 65. Seniors often receive the same discounts as students, set forth below under their appropriate headings. Unfortunately for tourists, some discounts are available only to seniors who are also British citizens. More often, however, your passport or other proof of age will also be your passport to cutting costs.

Older travelers are particularly encouraged to purchase travel insurance (see "Health, Insurance & Other Concerns," above), and would be well advised to be very frugal when it comes to packing.

When making airline reservations, ask about a senior discount (usually 10%), but find out if there is a cheaper promotional fare before committing.

Despite the name, London's youth hostels welcome older guests. These are some of the cheapest accommodations in the city, and are listed under a special heading in Chapter 4.

In addition to organizing tours, the **American Association of Retired Persons (AARP) Travel Service,** 100 N. Sepulveda Blvd., Suite 1020, El Segundo, CA 90024, provides a list of travel suppliers who offer discounts to members.

## FOR SINGLE TRAVELERS

When you travel alone, you usually end up spending more for accommodations than tourists traveling in pairs or in groups. Single travelers who want to save should look closely in Chapter 4 for hotels with good rates for single rooms. You might also consider the multishare accommodations listed there under "Super-Budget Choices."

The **Travel Companion Exchange,** P.O. Box 833-F, Amityville, NY 11701 (tel. 516/454-0880), provides listings of people interested in finding partners in travel. Matches are made by a computer, which groups travelers into categories by special interests, education, age, and location. The service costs $36 for six months and boasts over 2,000 active participants.

## FOR FAMILIES

Children add joys and a different level of experience to travel. They help you see things in a different way, and will often draw otherwise reticent local people like a magnet. Taking kids to London also obviously requires more thorough planning. All children, even infants, are required to have a passport. For airline flights, special-order children's meals as far in advance as possible. Most airlines don't carry baby food, but they will be glad to heat up any you've brought with you. Pack first-aid supplies, such as a thermometer, Band-Aids, cough drops, and children's aspirin, and always carry snacks like raisins, crackers, fruit, water, or juice.

London is full of sightseeing opportunities and special activities geared toward children. See "Cool for Kids," Chapter 6, for information and ideas for visiting families.

## FOR STUDENTS

Students in England regularly enjoy discounts on travel, theater, and museum tickets, and in some nightspots; many student specials are listed throughout this chapter under their appropriate headings.

The **International Student Identity Card (ISIC)** is the most readily accepted proof of student status, and is available from most university travel agents, and from the Council on International Educational Exchange, 205 East 42nd St., New York, NY 10017 (tel. 212/661-1414). To be eligible for the card, you must be enrolled in a degree program. The application must include proof of student status via an official letter from the school registrar or high school principal, a $10 registration fee, and one passport-size photo. The card should be purchased before you leave home, but if you've arrived in London without one and are a good enough talker (or just happen to be carrying a validated copy of your current school transcript), you can obtain one for about £5.50 ($9.90) from **S.T.A. Travel,** 74 Old Brompton Road, S.W.7 (tel. 071/937-9962), near the South Kensington tube station. The office is open Monday through Friday from 9am to 6pm, and Saturday from 10am to 4pm.

London's youth hostels are not only some of the cheapest places to stay, they are also great spots to meet other student travelers. You have to be a member of the **International Youth Hostel Federation** to lodge at official youth hostels, but joining is easy, as membership cards are issued at every hostel in London. If you want to take care of these arrangements in advance, apply to American Youth Hostels, Inc., P.O. Box 37613, Washington, DC 20013-7613. Membership costs $25 a year for people 18 to 54; those 17 and younger (and 55 and older) pay just $15.

## FOR EVERYONE

You can start saving money even before you leave home by requesting information from your local British Tourist Authority (BTA). Many of their **tourist publications** that carry a price tag in Britain are distributed free at BTA offices overseas. Ask for a London map as well as a copy of *London Planner,* a monthly magazine listing pageantry and cultural events, sports highlights, sightseeing options, art galleries, museums, theaters, dance and music performances, trade exhibitions, and special events. You can also request any specialized information you might need. See "Information, Entry Requirements & Money," at the beginning of this chapter, for addresses of the BTA's foreign offices.

If you have forgotten your camera, don't despair: Kodak sponsors a **free camera loan service** at the British Travel Centre, 12 Regent Street, just off Piccadilly Circus. The cameras, good-quality 35-mm automatics, require a credit card imprint or a refundable £30 ($54) deposit.

If you want to get a **European haircut** for a fraction of the usual cost, visit one of London's hairdressing schools. The **Vidal Sassoon Training School,** 56 Davies Mews, W.1 (tel. 071/629-4635), at the Bond Street tube, charges a uniform £6 ($10.80) for a cut and dry. Tints and perms are also available at modest charge. Vidal is open Monday through Friday, and an appointment is required.

Keep an eye out for other discounts and money-saving opportunities throughout this book.

## 6. ALTERNATIVE TRAVEL

### EDUCATIONAL TRAVEL

For curious minds of all ages, educational travel provides one of the most invigorating ways to learn, and allows for a nice mix of schooling and vagabonding. The **American Institute for Foreign Study,** 102 Greenwich Ave., Greenwich, CT 06830 (tel. 203/863-6087, or toll free 800/727-2437), offers 3- to 12-week study-travel programs starting at about $2,100, including airfare from New York. Add-ons from other U.S. cities are available.

The **Institute for International Education,** 809 United Nations Plaza, New York, NY 10017 (tel. 212/883-8200), also administers students' applications for study-abroad programs in England and other European countries. Write for their free booklet, "Basic Facts on Study Abroad." You may also wish to purchase their guide, *Study in the United Kingdom and Ireland* ($14.95), or *Teaching Abroad* ($21.95).

The **Council on International Educational Exchange,** 205 E. 42nd St., New York, NY 10017 (tel. 212/661-1414; ask for the Work Abroad Department), publishes a free booklet, "Student Travel Catalog: The Q's and A's of Work, Study and Travel Abroad," as well as a larger book, *Work, Study, Travel Abroad: The Whole World Handbook,* edited by Del Franz (St. Martin's Press, $10.95), updated in even-numbered years. The book lists almost 1,000 study opportunities, including many in Britain.

Those 60 and older, along with their spouses of any age (or a "significant other" 50 or older), can take advantage of an educational program sponsored by **Elderhostel,** 80 Boylston St., Boston, MA 02116 (tel. 617/426-7788). This organization sends almost 16,000 people to school abroad every year. Courses last 2 to 4 weeks, and start at $1,600, including airfare, meals, lodging, daily classroom instruction, and admission fees.

It is also possible to enroll yourself in summer courses at Cambridge or Oxford University. Request the free brochure "Tours and Special Interest Holidays" from the British Tourist Authority, 40 W. 57th St., Suite 320, New York, NY 10019 (tel. 212/581-4700).

### HOME STAYS

The idea of a stay in an English home conjures up romantic images of fireside chats, big family breakfasts, and putting children to bed under overstuffed, cozy comforters. Needless to say, some lucky visitors are treated to wonderfully personal experiences, but the outcome of such a visit will depend entirely on the chemistry between visitor and host. There is sometimes a fine line between a home stay and a stay in a bed-and-breakfast. I have stayed in B&Bs where I felt like part of the family, and with families where I felt like a guest. It is hard to gauge in advance which families are truly interested in meeting other citizens of the world, and which are simply in the business of hostelry. **Servas** (from the Esperanto work meaning "to serve"), represented in the U.S. by the U.S. Servas Committee, 11 John St., Suite 706, New York, NY 10038 (tel. 212/267-0252), seeks to promote friendship and goodwill through two-night home stays. Although it costs $45 per year to join, finding a family through Servas is one of the purest ways to experience local living, because hosts are not paid. Membership requires an interview to make sure of the traveler's seriousness of intent. There is then a refundable $15 deposit for a list which provides information on hosts' location, occupation, age, languages spoken, and interests. The traveler writes the host and sets up the visit. You may stay with several hosts in the same city, and are not required to reciprocate by becoming a host yourself.

Several London-based home stay agencies can also set you up with a local family. Prices range from £25 to £35 ($45 to $63) per night for a double room, most of which are located away from the city's tourist center. **Host and Guest Service,** 592A King's Road, London S.W.3 (tel. 071/731-5340) and **London Homestead Services,** 154 Warwick Rd., London W.14 (tel. 071/371-1411) make all the arrangements and require a 10% to 20% deposit. If you are planning far enough in advance, send a letter to one of these agencies requesting a list of available homes. Include your dates of travel and location preference. You can also phone for availabilities, then forward a deposit by mail.

## HOME EXCHANGES

The **Vacation Exchange Club,** 12006 111th Ave., Unit 12, Youngtown, AZ 85363 (tel. 602/972-2186), can help you set up a home swap—your house or apartment for a residence in London, in England, or in any other country. The cost of a listing in the directory is about $25. If you prefer not to be listed but would like a copy of the listings, it costs about $16.

# 7. GETTING THERE

Go to a travel agent and buy your ticket, right? You can, but it may not be the cheapest nor most interesting way to travel. London is easy to get to, but be warned: Not all transportation options are created equal. There are many exciting travel alternatives, some of which you may not have thought of. Look beyond the obvious choices and explore your options; shopping around will ensure that you get there the right way at the best price.

## BY AIR

Close to 90 scheduled airlines serve London, including almost every major American and international carrier. The city is so well connected that the problem is never getting there, but sorting out the right service and fare. Your air transportation options run the gamut, from courier flights to the Concord (including a courier flight on the Concord). The major American carriers offering regularly scheduled London flights include: **American Airlines** (tel. toll free 800/433-7300), **Continental** (tel. toll free 800/231-0856), **Northwest Airlines** (tel. toll free 800/225-2525), **Pan American** (tel. toll free 800/221-1111), **TWA** (tel. toll free 800/892-4141), and **United Airlines** (tel. toll free 800/241-6522).

**British Airways** (tel. toll free 800/247-9297), the largest British airline, offers a good standard of service from about a dozen U.S. gateways.

## BEST-FOR-THE-BUDGET ALTERNATIVES

Alternatives to the traditional travel agent ticket have their advantages (usually price), and their drawbacks (usually freedom). Here's the lowdown:

### Bucket Shops

By negotiating directly with airlines, consolidators, or "bucket shops," can sell tickets on major scheduled carriers at deeply discounted rates. The resulting fares are now the least expensive means of traveling to Europe, lower in most instances than charter-flight fares. For example, in winter from New York, you can buy bucket-shop tickets to London on well-known international airlines for as little as $200 each way; figure about $330 in summer. Flying to other, more distant European cities is slightly more expensive. There are drawbacks, however. The tickets are restrictive, valid only for a particular date or flight, nontransferable, and nonrefundable except directly from the bucket shop. Also, consolidators usually don't offer travel counseling, and don't book hotels or rental cars. On the plus side, bucket-shop tickets are rarely restricted by advance-purchase requirements; if space is available, you can buy your ticket just days before departure.

The lowest-priced bucket shops are usually local operations with low profiles and overheads. Look for their advertisements in the travel or classified section of your local newspaper. Ads for consolidators are typically small, usually a single column in width and a few lines deep. They contain a list of cities and, opposite it, a list of corresponding prices. Short and to the point.

While prices for flights available through bucket shops are low, at times they may be eclipsed by special offers by the airlines. As usual, compare prices before you buy.

Nationally advertised consolidators are usually not as competitive as the smaller boiler-room operations, but they have toll-free telephone numbers, and are easily accessible. Four leading retailers include **Access International, Inc.,** 101 W. 31st St., Suite 1104, New York, NY 10107 (tel. 212/333-7280, or toll free 800/827-3633); **Maharajah Travels, Inc.,** 518 Fifth Ave., New York, NY

10036 (tel. 212/391-0122, or toll free 800/223-6862); **Sunline Express Holidays, Inc.,** 607 Market St., San Francisco, CA 94105 (tel. 415/541-7800, or toll free 800/877-2111); and **Euro-Asia, Inc.,** 4203 E. Indian School Rd., Suite 210, Phoenix AZ 85018 (tel. 602/955-2742, or toll free 800/525-3876).

## Charters

The second-cheapest way to cross the Atlantic is on a charter flight. Competition from the bucket shops, not to mention fiercely competitive commercial airlines, has pared their number somewhat, but there are still plenty from which to choose. Most charter operators advertise and sell their seats through travel agents, making these local professionals your best source of information for available flights. Two well-known operators that sell tickets directly to passengers include **Travac,** 989 Sixth Ave., New York, NY 10018 (tel. 212/563-3303, or toll free 800/872-8800); and **Council Charters,** 205 E. 42nd St., New York, NY 10017 (tel. 212/661-0311, or toll free 800/223-7402). Look for midwinter fares as low as $450 round-trip from New York and Miami; $650 or so in summer.

Before deciding to take a charter flight, check the restrictions on the ticket. You may be asked to purchase a tour package, pay far in advance of the flight, be amenable if the day of departure or the destination is changed, pay a service charge, fly on an airline with which you are not familiar (this usually is not the case), and pay harsh penalties if you cancel but be understanding if the charter does not fill up and is canceled up to 10 days before departure. Summer charters fill up more quickly than others and are almost sure to fly, but if you decide on a charter flight, seriously consider cancellation and baggage insurance (see "Health, Insurance & Other Concerns," earlier in this chapter).

## Standbys

Standbys provide another inexpensive means of crossing the Atlantic. In order to fill seats that would otherwise go unsold, many of the airlines listed above offer discounted fares to last-minute travelers. Standby service is usually offered from April to November only, and eliminated in winter. London-based **Virgin Atlantic Airways** offers a day-of-departure as well as a day-prior-to-departure fare from New York, Los Angeles, and Miami to London. You can usually save about $50.

There is, of course, a chance that you won't get on a standby flight, but if you are at all flexible and have somewhere to stay should you not be able to board, it's an economical way to go.

## Going as a Courier

Companies transporting time-sensitive materials, such as film, blood, or documents for banks and insurance firms, regularly hire air couriers. Travelers who wear two caps, that of airline passenger and that of courier, stand to save a lot of money crossing the Atlantic. It's not difficult, as the courier company handles the check-in and pickup of packages at each airport. All you have to do is give up your checked-baggage allowance and make do with carry-on. Expect to meet a courier-service representative at the airport before departure to get the manifest of the checked items; upon arrival, you deliver the baggage-claim tag to a waiting courier agent. Flights are often offered at the last minute, and you may have to arrange a pretrip interview to make sure you're right for the job.

One drawback, besides restricted baggage, is that you have to travel alone, since only one person can take advantage of any given flight. If there are two of you, try to arrange your departures on two consecutive days; the first to arrive can secure the hotel room and learn the lay of the land.

Three popular courier services are **Now Voyager, Inc.,** 74 Varick St., Suite 307, New York, NY 10013 (tel. 212/431-1616, 11:30am–6pm); **Halbart Express,** 147-05 176th St., Jamaica, NY 11434 (tel. 718/656-8189, 10am–3pm); and **TNT Skypak,** 845 Cowan Rd., Burlingame, CA 94010 (tel. 415/692-9600, or toll free 800/558-5555), for flights from San Francisco.

Most flights depart from New York, so you may have to tack on the additional cost to get to the gateway city. Prices change all the time, from low to very low. If a company needs emergency courier service and you can fly immediately, you could travel free or for next to nothing—say, $50 round-trip.

Expect spring 1992 fares to be about $425 round-trip from New York to London. Many less popular European destinations can be up to $100 cheaper. Flights are booked on a round-trip basis exclusively, though there is often nothing to carry on the way home.

## Price-Conscious Airlines

An almost equally frugal way to get to London is to fly aboard an airline that is a relative newcomer to a transatlantic route. To attract attention, these carriers drop their fares below those of the more established competition. In most cases, the only thing cheap about these airlines is their price structure, not their service, standards, or safety. **Virgin Atlantic Airways** (tel. toll free 800/862-8621) is an excellent example of the way in which low price does not affect the quality of service. In fact, Virgin has consistently won awards for its unusually high standards, and even in coach class, the airline's seats provide noticeably more leg room than any other major airline. Virgin flies from New York and Newark, N.J., as well as from Boston, Los Angeles, and Miami. When the airline opened its route from John F. Kennedy Airport to London in 1989, it offered as a promotion an incredible $99 round-trip fare (with $23 tax); the offer was not advertised, which goes to show how lucrative it can be to call around.

**Continental Airlines** (tel. toll free 800/231-0856) offered spring 1991 round-trip midweek flights from Newark, N.J., to London starting at $567 for a highly restricted fare. As a rule, the lower the fare, the more restrictions it has placed on it.

## REGULAR AIRFARES

London's popularity means that the city is often at the heart of any "fare war" the airlines might be waging. Even when hostilities have cooled, flights to the city are usually pretty reasonably priced. Check the newspapers for advertisements, and call a few of the major carriers before committing.

### Economy

The cheapest standard economy-class fare usually comes with serious restrictions and steep penalties for altering dates and itineraries. When purchasing these tickets, don't use terms like "APEX," "excursion," or other airline jargon, just ask for the lowest fare. If you are flexible with dates and times, say so. Ask if you can get it cheaper by staying an extra day, flying during the middle of the week, or by purchasing your ticket a certain number of days in advance. Most airlines won't volunteer this information. At the time of this writing, the lowest round-trip summer fare from New York was $709, from Chicago $773, and from Los Angeles $664 (not a misprint). You may even find it cheaper.

### Business Class

Business class-seats can cost more than twice the price of coach. You should know that airlines sometimes offer "free" business-class upgrades to passengers who purchase an unrestricted coach-class ticket. Unrestricted fares are the most expensive, but may still be less than a business-class seat. Ask about this when purchasing your ticket.

### First Class

Predictably expensive, most airlines only offer a handful of first-class seats on their London flights. Before buying, see if your airline offers a first-class upgrade with a full-fare business-class ticket.

### FROMMER'S SMART TRAVELER: AIRFARES

1. Shop all the airlines that fly to your destination.
2. Always ask for the lowest fare, not "discount," "APEX," or "excursion."
3. Keep calling the airline—availability of cheap seats changes daily.
4. Seek out budget alternatives. Phone "bucket shops," charter companies, and discount travel agents.
5. Plan to travel midweek, when rates are usually lower.
6. If you have the option, fly into Heathrow instead of Gatwick; you'll save more than $12 in ground transportation costs.

## BY SHIP

Flying is the cheapest way to London, but travel by ship is not exorbitantly expensive, and makes the journey as memorable as the destination.

Only one cruise ship plies the Atlantic with regularity anymore—the ***Queen Elizabeth 2,*** and it's not cheap. Prices start at about $1,500 for the 5-day crossing, including return airfare. For more information, contact **Cunard,** 555 Fifth Ave., New York, NY 10017 (tel. 212/661-7777, or toll free 800/5-CUNARD outside New York).

Freighters are usually, but not always, less expensive than cruise ships. Most freighters carry no more than 12 passengers (otherwise they'd have to carry a doctor on board), charge less than cruise lines (though more than airlines), and provide unbeatable service. You'll have the run of the ship and form a fast camaraderie with the other passengers and the crew. You may also find yourself at the mercy of erratic sailing schedules.

By freighter tradition, passengers pay for a fixed number of days; if the trip comes in early, they receive a refund; if it takes longer, and it often does, they get the extra days free. Tipping is expected, as it is on cruise ships. On a freighter, you pay about half the daily cost of a passenger liner, or about $100 a day.

Although many freighters dock in northern Europe, most do not go as far north as England. Since schedules change often, you'll have to do some research. Start by talking with your travel agent and studying your librarian's copy of the monthly ***Official Steamship Guide,*** which has a transatlantic section that lists ships and passenger freighters, date of departure, port of embarkation, ports of call, port of debarkation, length of cruise, lowest available price, and telephone number. For more information, contact the *Official Steamship Guide* at 111 Cherry St., Suite 205, New Canaan, CT 06840 (tel. 508/252-9896).

## PACKAGES & TOURS

Tours and packages are offered by tour operators, airlines, hotels, and transportation companies. A tour usually refers to an escorted group, and often includes transportation, touring, meals, and accommodations. The entire group travels together and all share the same preplanned activities. A package, on the other hand, can include any or all of the above components, but travelers are usually unescorted, and free to make their own itinerary. Many travelers who purchase airfare, hotel, and theater tickets from their travel agents may not even be aware of the fact that they are buying a tour operator's package.

Even if you are an independent traveler, don't shy away from a package; it can be a very good value. Packagers buy in bulk, which sometimes allows them to sell their services at a discount.

For the latest in what's available in tours and packages today, check the ads in the travel section of your newspaper. Tours and packages are most often put together by airlines, charter companies, hotels, or tour operators, and sold through travel agents. Before signing up for one, read the fine print carefully and do some homework.

*How reputable is the tour operator?* Ask for references of people who have participated in tours run by the same company. Call travel agents and the local Better Business Bureau, and check with the consumer department of the U.S. Tour Operators Association, 212 E. 51st St., Suite 12B, New York, NY 10022 (tel. 212/944-5727). Be leery of any outfit that does not give you details of the itinerary before demanding payment.

*What is the size of the tour?* Decide whether you can handle an experience shared by 40 other people, or if your limit is 20. A smaller tour is a better-quality tour.

*What kind of hotels will be used and where are they located?* Get the names of the hotels and then look them up in guidebooks, or in your travel agent's hotel guide. If you sense that the hotels provide only minimal essentials, so might the entire tour. If the hotel is not conveniently located, it will be less expensive, but you may feel isolated or unsafe, and you'll spend extra money and time getting to and from attractions and nightspots.

*If meals are included, how elaborate are they?* Is breakfast continental, English, or buffet? Is the menu for the group limited to a few items?

*How extensive is the sightseeing?* You may have the chance to get on and off the bus many times to explore a number of attractions, or you may see them only from the bus window. If you like to explore, pick an attraction you are interested in and ask the operator precisely how much time you can expect to spend there. Find out if all admissions are included in the price of the tour.

*Are the optional activities offered at an additional price?* This is usually the case, so make sure the activities that particularly interest you are included in the tour price.

*What is the refund policy should you cancel?*

*How is the package price paid?* If a charter flight is involved, make sure that you can pay into an escrow account (ask for the name of the bank) to ensure proper use of the funds, or their return in case the operator cancels the trip.

Most of the airlines listed above offer both escorted tours and on-your-own packages. Dozens of other companies also compete for this lucrative business. Top London tour operators include **Globus Gateway Cosmos** (tel. toll free 800/556-5454), **Trafalgar Tours** (tel. toll free 800/854-0103), and **Frames-Rickards** (tel. toll free 800/527-2473). Discuss all your options with a travel agent, and compare package prices to those in this guidebook.

# 8. ENJOYING LONDON ON A BUDGET

## THE $45-A-DAY BUDGET

London on $45 a day means spending $45 on accommodations and meals only. Expect to use about half the sum on accommodations. Obviously, if two of you are traveling it's easier to achieve—$45 for accommodations and $45 for meals. Trim travel costs by taking advantage of the many low alternative airfares to Europe, traveling off-season—January through May and October through December (excluding Christmas and Easter)—and planning a relatively short stay (a week to 10 days, say, instead of a full two weeks).

Prices quoted in this book are obviously subject to change depending on inflation and currency fluctuations. For up-to-date exchange rates, check the business pages of your newspaper, contact the British Tourist Authority (see "Information, Entry Requirements & Money," above, for addresses), or call an office of Deak International (tel. 212/757-6915).

## SAVING MONEY ON ACCOMMODATIONS

Keep prices down by traveling off-season and off the beaten track. Politely negotiate the price of the room, especially if you sense there are plenty of empty ones from which to choose—you might find yourself paying 25% less than you expected. Negotiate a trade-off; a lower price for a smaller room, one without a television, or one on the top floor. Ask if they will offer a better rate if you stay several nights. If you are a student or an older traveler, ask for a special discount. Be pleasant, not pushy. Make it clear you are shopping around and, if the proprietor is not easily persuaded, try elsewhere or hope for better luck next time.

One of the least expensive ways to keep a roof over your head is by taking advantage of youth hostels. There are four International Youth Hostel Association (IYHA) hostels in central London, all welcoming travelers of all ages (see "Super-Budget Choices," in Chapter 4). Other creative travel alternatives include bedding in multishare accommodations, and staying in university accommodations. See Chapter 4 for details on these accommodations and other money-saving tips.

## SAVING MONEY ON MEALS

Most hotels in London include breakfast in their room rates. Check to see if the breakfast offered is continental or English-style; the former consists of coffee or tea and a roll or danish, while the latter is a banquet of eggs, toast, cereal, and coffee or tea.

If you love fine food, but not necessarily by candlelight, consider having your big meal of the day at lunch. Outstanding restaurants may serve the same or similar meals for lunch and dinner, but the fixed-price lunch is likely to be half as expensive. Lunch reservations are easier to come by, as well. Indulge in afternoon tea; it's not cheap, but will cut your appetite for a huge meal later in the evening. In fish-and-chips shops, eat standing, since sitting will increase the price of your meal significantly. Wherever you eat, be sure to check the menu to see if a service charge has been added; don't tip twice by accident.

Never skip a meal just to save money. You might end up sick or run-down, and that's the one thing you can't afford during your trip.

See Chapter 5 for more specific information on how to save money on meals in London.

## SAVING MONEY ON SIGHTSEEING

It's been said that the best things in life are free. In London, the best things in sightseeing are, too. Open-air entertainment at Covent Garden is free, as is the Changing of the Guards ceremony at Buckingham Palace. Most of the city's major museums are free, including the British Museum and the Tate Gallery, as are the city's streets, parks, and churches. Visit a London Tourist Board office upon your arrival for free event information (see "Orientation: Tourist Information," in Chapter 3), and use this guidebook well, checking for free attractions, free museum days, and special rate reductions.

## SAVING MONEY ON SHOPPING

London has many bargains, if you know where to look for them. Good deals are often found in markets, at auctions, and during department-store sales. Look in craft and specialty shops to get an idea of what unique merchandise is available. Check advertisements in local newspapers and compare prices in several shops before you buy. In general, prices in London are fixed, and not subject to negotiation. Goods sold at certain outdoor markets are an exception to this rule; vendors may lower a price here, or throw in an additional item there.

Duty-free shopping is available in airports, on cruise ships, and in some downtown stores. Most of us take advantage of tax-free savings by dashing into airport duty-free shops to get rid of leftover foreign currency. The only way to actually save money through duty-free shopping, however, is to know the going prices on the same merchandise at home to be able to compare. Once you're in an airport duty-free shop, you're on your way out of the country so you can't run back to town to buy for less. If you're only saving a couple of bucks, it's hardly worth it to lug the stuff home.

The limit on duty-free items Americans can bring back into the U.S. is $400, including 1 liter of alcohol. Beyond the allotted exemption, the next $1,000 worth of goods is taxed at a flat rate of 10%.

The British government encourages tourists to part with their pounds by offering to refund the Value-Added Tax (VAT). Not all retailers participate in the refund program, and those that do require a minimum purchase, usually £50 ($90). The reclamation procedure is cumbersome: To reclaim VAT, show the sales clerk your passport and fill out a special form at each shop you visit. Then present the forms and the goods to a Customs officer upon departing Great Britain. After the official validates your VAT forms, mail them back to the stores where you made your purchases. Several months later you will receive your refund—in pounds sterling and minus a small commission charge. You can avoid the bank charges usually encountered when cashing foreign-currency checks by using your credit cards for the purchases and requesting that your VAT refund be credited to your account.

See Chapter 8 for details on London shopping and specialty stores.

## SAVING MONEY ON TRANSPORTATION

### BY AIR

For the most part, air transport within Europe remains in the realm of the business traveler and not the budget tourist. The cost is usually so prohibitively high that budget travelers consider it only as a splurge or when they are in a pinch for time. Some airlines offer **special promotions** as well as 7- and 14-day advance-purchase fares. For instance, British Airways has a $114 fare from London to Dublin with 14-day advance purchase.

Lower-priced airfares are available throughout Europe on **charter flights** rather than on regularly scheduled ones. Look in local newspapers, or visit a European travel agent to find out about them. The charter arm of British Airways is Caledonian Airways, serving the Mediterranean and booked through the Thompson or Red Wing travel agencies.

European skies are changing. With the economic unification of the European Community (EC) in 1992, there will be an official relaxation of airline restrictions. The changes will not be so drastic as those that came after airline deregulation in the U.S., but they will be noticeable and will result in lower airfares, perhaps a few fare wars, and special deals and discounts for the air traveler. As this occurs, charter travel may diminish and regularly scheduled carriers may take over a larger chunk of the leisure travel market.

### BY TRAIN

British trains are less expensive than those in the United States and far more genteel. Within the British Isles, it often takes less time to travel from one city center to another by train than by plane.

The cost of a train ride from London to Edinburgh on BritRail is $129 in first class, or $87 in second class. The difference between the classes is relatively small, a matter of one or two inches of padding on the seats, and slightly more leg room.

If you plan to travel around Britain by train, you can usually save money by investing in a train pass. A first-class BritRail Pass costs $285 for 8 days, $409 for 15 days, $499 for 22 days, and $589 for 1 month. A second-class pass costs $189, $285, $351, and $415, respectively, for the same time periods. Children under 16 ride for half fare.

The BritRail Flexipass can save you even more money, as it does not require you to travel on consecutive days. The first-class pass costs $229 for any 4 days of travel within 8 days, $329 for any 8 days of travel within 15 days, and $479 for any 15 days of travel within 1 month. Second-class passes cost $159, $229, and $329, respectively, for the same time periods.

All passes must be purchased outside Britain, but ask about the BritRail/Drive, Senior Citizen, and Youth passes before buying. The U.S. BritRail office is located at 1500 Broadway, New York, NY 10036; in Canada, write to 94 Cumberland St., Toronto M5R 1A3, ON; or 409 Granville St., Vancouver V6C 1T2, BC.

## BY CAR

Budget travel and rental cars do not usually go hand in hand, and you definitely do not need to rent a car in London. But if you are traveling in a group of four and want to get out into the countryside, driving will be cheaper than traveling by train. In addition, your own car will give you added mobility to find a budget hotel or a comfortable spot to camp. And you can carry more bags more easily.

Not only are rental cars pricey in Britain, but gasoline (petrol) costs much more than in America—about $3.50 per imperial gallon (1.2 U.S. gallons). Resign yourself to allocating a chunk of your travel budget to gasoline if you drive. On the brighter side, European cars generally use gas more efficiently than American models.

Expect to be given a standard-shift vehicle unless you specifically ask for an automatic. Find out all the charges you are likely to incur from the car-rental company; besides the daily or weekly rental charge, determine the mileage charge, the cost of insurance and fuel, and the tax on the total rental bill (15% in Great Britain). In addition, you will be paying for parking and tolls along the way. If you already have collision coverage on your own automobile insurance, you're most likely covered when you are behind the wheel of a rental car; check with your insurance carrier. If you decide on European insurance, be sure it doesn't come with a $1,000 deductible.

A collision-damage waiver costs a hefty $7 to $13 per day, and can jack the price of a rental car up incredibly. The good news is that some credit-card companies (American Express is one) automatically insure their cardholders against collision damage at no additional charge when they rent a car using the card as payment. Also, Travel Guard International (see "Health, Insurance & Other Concerns," above) sells low-cost auto insurance at rates that are more attractive than those offered by car-rental firms.

Car rates can be negotiable. Try to get the best possible deal with the rental company by asking about special discounts. Special rates are sometimes offered for keeping the car longer, or sometimes you can get a rate that includes unlimited mileage (or at least some miles thrown in free), or a bigger car for the price of a compact. You can often get discounts as a member of a union or association. Check before you leave home and take a member identification card with you.

To begin the shopping-around process, contact some of the American car-rental companies with international branches: **Avis** (tel. toll free 800/331-1084); **Budget** (tel. toll free 800/527-0700); **Dollar Rent-a-Car,** called **InterRent** in Europe (tel. toll free 800/421-6878); **Hertz** (tel. toll free 800/654-3001); or **National,** called **Europcar** in Europe (tel. toll free 800/227-3876).

U.S.-based companies specializing in European car rentals include: **Auto-Europe** (tel. toll free 800/223-5555), **Cortell International** (tel. toll free 800/228-2535), **Europe by Car** (tel. toll free 800/223-1516), and **Kemwel** (tel. toll free 800/678-0678).

See "Getting Around," in Chapter 3, for information on inexpensive local London car-rental firms.

Some distances between London and major cities in England and Scotland are: Aberdeen 558 miles; Cambridge 121 miles; Edinburgh 491 miles; Glasgow 416 miles; Oxford 59 miles.

## SAVING MONEY ON SERVICES

### TIPPING

Rules for tipping are not as strict in England as they are in the U.S., but when you are presented with good service, 10% to 15% is customary.

Tour guides should be tipped, along with any guides at a church or historic site. Washroom and cloakroom attendants usually receive something, and porters in airports and rail stations usually receive about 50p per bag. Taxi drivers in London expect 15%, and if no service charge has been added to your hotel bill, you might want to leave 50p per day. The owners of bed-and-breakfast establishments generally are not tipped. Check restaurant menus to see if service is included before leaving an additional tip.

For more information on tipping, see "Fast Facts: London," in Chapter 3.

### LONG-DISTANCE TELEPHONE CALLS

Phone charges are higher in England than they are in the United States. In addition, hotels usually add their own surcharge, sometimes as much as 100% to 200%, which you may be unaware of until you are presented with the bill.

Whether or not you are calling person-to-person, collect calls are charged at the same high rate, making them pricey, too. Charging a long-distance call to your credit card is often the most economical way to phone home.

The fastest, most convenient way to call the U.S. from Europe is through **USA Direct.** This service bypasses the foreign operator and automatically links you to an AT&T operator in America. The access number in Great Britain is 0800-89-0011. When calling from a pay phone, you must first insert 10p, or a phonecard. See "Fast Facts: London," in Chapter 3, for more information on phoning from British telephones.

# CHAPTER 3

# GETTING TO KNOW LONDON



By any estimate, London is a grand city. Close to 7 million people, spread out over 600-plus square miles, perpetuate a dynamic urban growth that has been intensifying for centuries.

Today, the metropolis boasts thousands of restaurants, hundreds of hotels, dozens of important historical sites, and a half dozen world-class museums. Without a doubt, London is also one of the best shopping cities in the world, and is justly famous for its theater and nightlife.

Despite it's size, however, London is surprisingly user-friendly. The city's intricate public transportation network (one of the world's largest) seems tailor-made for tourists, from the clean Undergrounds and the fun double-decker buses to the famous big black taxis. In addition, visitor information services and tourist resources abound, helping to make your stay less complicated and more enjoyable.

London is big, but not overwhelming. Take a little time to brush up on the basic ins and outs of the city, and learn about the many services London can offer you. Time and again, experience has proved that a little preparation goes a long way to making travels more enjoyable. This chapter is designed to help you toward that end, to ease your way into one of the greatest cities of all.

## 1. ORIENTATION

### ARRIVING

#### BY PLANE

London is served by two major airports: Heathrow and Gatwick; both have good public transport links to central London.

The cheapest route from **Heathrow Airport** is by Underground ("the tube"). The 15-mile journey takes approximately 45 minutes and costs £2.10 ($3.80) to any downtown station (see "Getting Around," below, for information on transportation discounts). Service is convenient, as the Underground platforms are directly below the airport's four terminals. Most transatlantic flights arrive (and depart) from Terminals 1 and 2. Terminal 3 is home to the bulk of intra-European flights, while Terminal 4 is the long-haul hub for British Airways exclusively. Heathrow is big, so even those with light luggage would be well advised to use one of the free baggage carts for the long walk to the Underground. Trains depart every 4 to 10 minutes from 6am to midnight.

There are two ways of making the 25-mile trek from **Gatwick Airport** to the city center. The first, and more popular, is by express train, which takes 30 minutes to reach Victoria Station. Unfortunately, it costs a hefty £6.30 ($11.35) each way. The station is just below the airport, and trains depart every 15 minutes from 6am to 10pm (hourly, on the hour, at other times). You can also take the Flightline 777 bus operated by Green Line (tel. 081/668-7261). The 70-minute journey costs £6 ($10.80) one way, or £8 ($14.40) round-trip. Buses destined for Victoria Coach Station depart from Gatwick's North Terminal hourly, at different times throughout the day.

If you are flying to London on a smaller European commuter plane, you may land at **London City Airport,** located about 6 miles east of The City of London. There are no direct rail links to this airport, so you can either taxi the entire way, and expect to pay around £13 ($23.40), or take the Underground to Plaistow (the closest tube station) and taxi from there. The taxi/tube option should set you back about £7 ($12.60).

## BY TRAIN

Trains from Paris arrive at Victoria Station (tel. 071/928-5100, daily 24 hours), visitors from Amsterdam are deposited at Liverpool Street Station (tel. 071/928-5100, daily 24 hours), and arrivals from Edinburgh pull into King's Cross Station (tel. 071/278-2477, daily 7am–11pm). All three are well connected to the city's extensive bus and Underground network. The stations all contain London Transport Information Centres, luggage lockers, telephones, restaurants, and, of course, pubs!

Seats can be purchased up until the moment of departure, but reservations are recommended, especially for weekend and summer travel. Rail Travel Centres, located in all the major stations, provide information and sell tickets.

Britain is said to be a country made for the train, and the BritRail network is one of the most extensive in the world. It seems as though almost every little hamlet is interconnected, and it may be so. More than 15,000 trains each day depart for over 2,400 destinations. Eurailpasses are not valid in Great Britain. BritRail sells its own passes, available for varying periods of time, in either first or standard class. An 8-day first-class pass, good for unlimited travel, costs about $300; a standard-class pass costs about $200. A 15-day first-class pass costs about $425, while a standard-class pass for the same length of time costs about $300.

BritRail also offers a host of other passes, each good for varying lengths of time. None are available for purchase in Britain; they must be secured before you leave home. For more information on passes and prices, contact your local travel agent or **BritRail Travel International,** 1500 Broadway, New York, NY 10036. In Canada, contact BritRail at 94 Cumberland St., Toronto M5R 1A3, ON.

See Chapter 10, "Easy Excursions From London," for more information on getting around Britain.

### BY BUS

Buses usually meet European ferries and hovercrafts arriving in Dover and other British ports. Whether you're coming from the Continent or from another part of England, London-bound buses almost always go to (and leave from) **Victoria Coach Station,** Buckingham Palace Rd. (tel. 071/730-0202), located 1 block from Victoria Railway Station.

Buses in Britain typically cost half the price of trains, and reservations should be made as far in advance as possible. The **Credit Card Sales Department** (tel. 071/730-3499) of Victoria Coach Station can make reservations and sell tickets on any domestic bus service.

The **Britexpress Card** costs just £10 ($18), and is good for one third off all adult **National Express** bus tickets. National Express is the country's primary coach carrier, servicing close to 1,500 destinations throughout the British Isles.

The **Tourist Trail Card** costs £50 ($90), and is good for 5 days of unlimited bus travel throughout Britain. Both cards can be purchased in London at the British Travel Centre, 12 Regent St., W.1 (tel. 071/730-3400), just steps from Piccadilly Circus.

See Chapter 10, "Easy Excursions From London," for more information on these and other transportation options.

### BY CAR

Like spokes on a wheel, highways radiate from London in all directions. Thus, from all points in England, it seems as though all roads lead to the capital.

Major roads are named with numbers, each of which start with the letter "M," "A," or "B." "M-roads" are expressways or "motorways," connecting London with cities to the north, east, south and west. "A-roads" and "B-roads" are, respectively, smaller and slower, though usually prettier.

The M25 "ring road" circles Greater London, and connects with the M1 to Birmingham, the M40 to Oxford, the M4 to Bristol, the M3 to Southampton, the M20 to Dover, and the M11 to Cambridge.

## TOURIST INFORMATION

The **London Tourist Board (LTB)** maintains several Information Centres throughout the capital. They distribute city maps, answer questions, and, in a pinch, can help you find accommodations. When

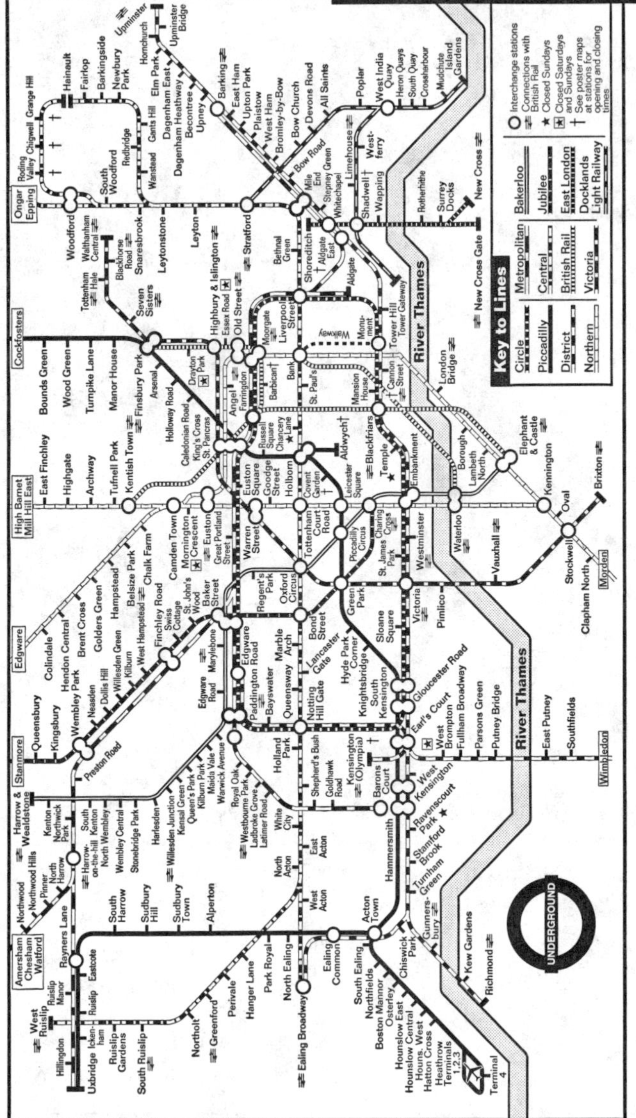


entering England via Heathrow, visit the LTB in the arrival terminal before making your journey into the city; it's open daily from 9am to 6pm. Those arriving via Gatwick, or by train from Paris, can visit the well-staffed office in Victoria Station's forecourt. The office is open daily from 9am to 8pm Easter to October; the rest of the year, Monday through Saturday from 9am to 7pm and on Sunday from 9am to 5pm. Other LTB Information Centres are located in Harrods

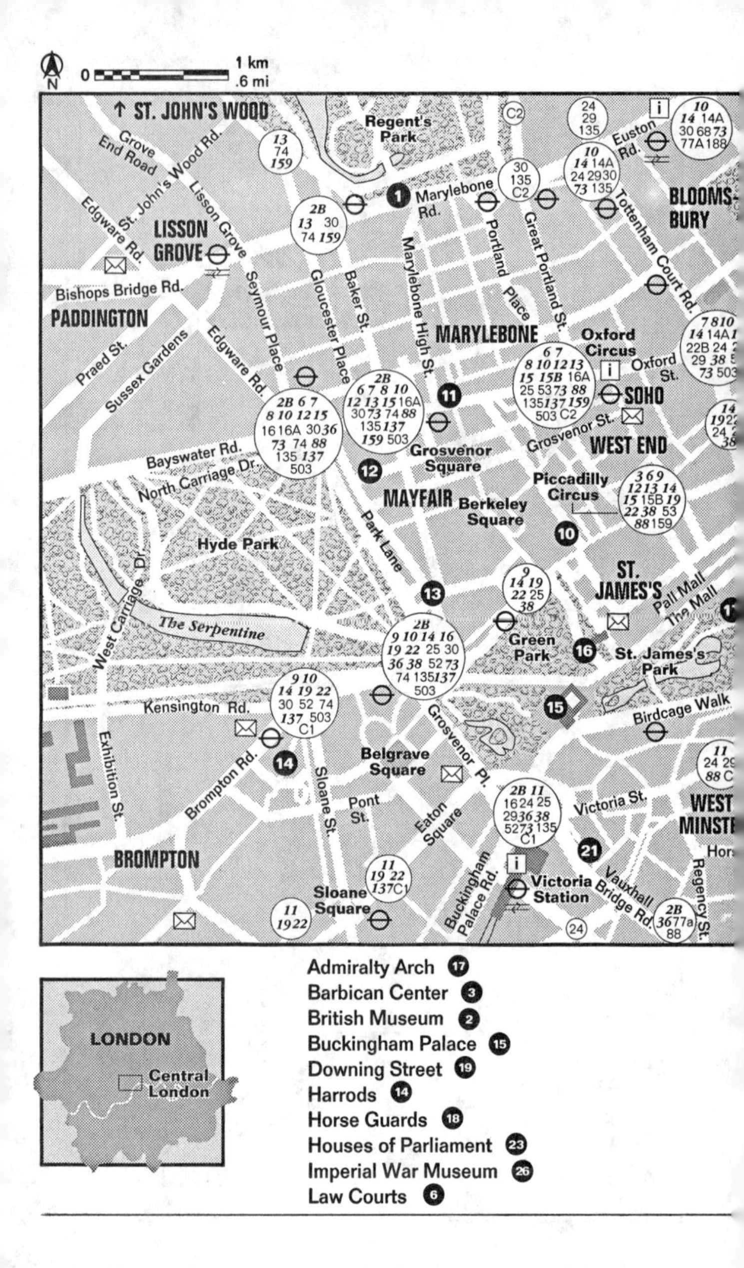


and Selfridges department stores, both open year round during store hours (see Chapter 8, "Shopping A to Z"), and at the Tower of London, open from 10am to 6pm daily, Easter to October only. For information by phone, call the **British Tourist Authority** (tel. 071/730-3488) weekdays between 9am and 6pm.

The **British Travel Centre,** 12 Regent St., W.1 (tel. 071/730-3400), is just steps from Piccadilly Circus and provides information

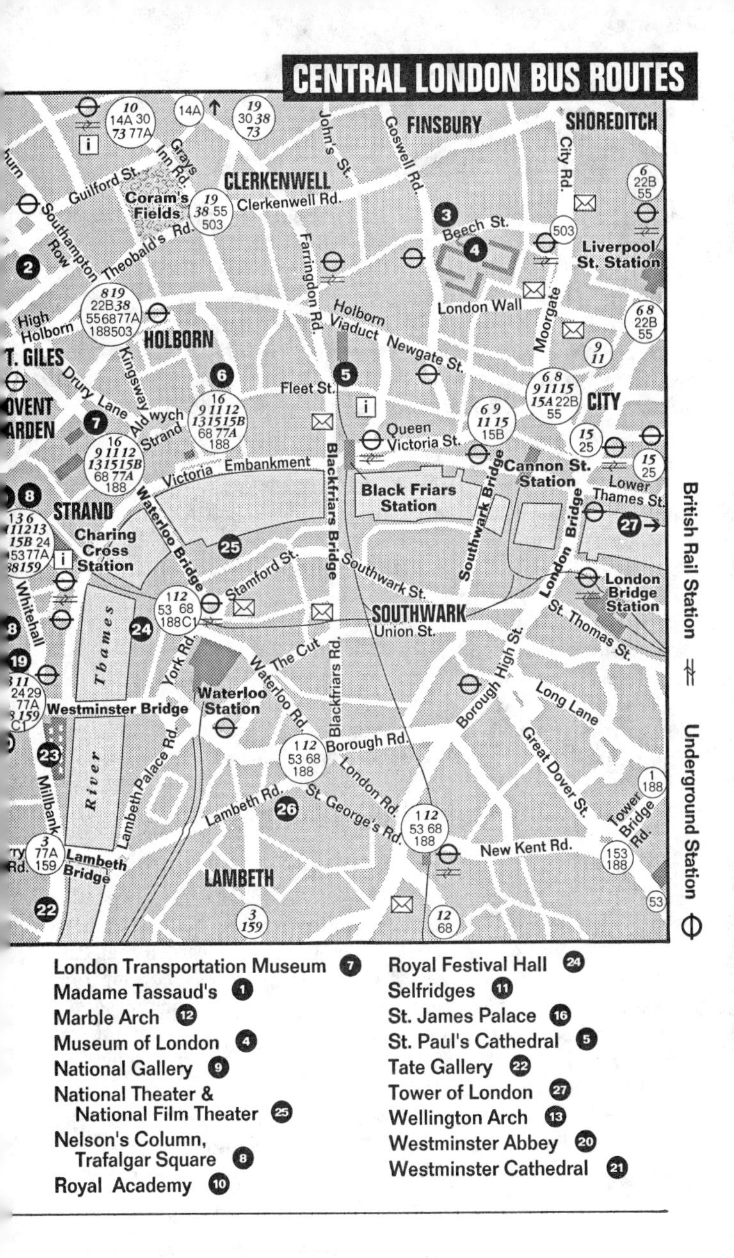


on all of Britain. It's open from 9am to 6:30pm Monday through Friday, 9am to 5pm on Saturday, and 10am to 4pm on Sunday. Hours are usually slightly reduced in winter.

For information about travel by bus, tube, or British Rail, visit a **London Transport Information Centre** in any of the major train stations, or call the **London Regional Transport Travel Information Service** (tel. 071/222-1234), open 24 hours daily.

# CITY LAYOUT

## MAIN ARTERIES AND STREETS

Marked by an infestation of pigeons and a tall, statue-topped column, **Trafalgar Square** is the hub of central London. On the north side of the square is the National Gallery, England's most important repository for fine art through the ages. Beyond the museum lies cinema-wrapped **Leicester Square,** restaurant-packed **Soho,** and London's **theater district. Bloomsbury** is farther north still, anchored by the massive British Museum and dotted with a good number of moderately priced hotels.

**The Strand** branches out east from Trafalgar Square, and connects the **West End** with **The City.** A stroll down this street will reveal an eclectic mix of hotels, restaurants, shops, and office buildings. **Covent Garden Market,** a landmark for tourists and shoppers alike, is located just a few blocks north of The Strand.

South of Trafalgar Square is **Whitehall,** the address of many of Great Britain's most important government buildings. No. 10 Downing Street, the official residence of the prime minister, is just off Whitehall, and Big Ben, Westminster Abbey, and Parliament Square are all located at the bottom of the street.

**The Mall** is a long, pretty road that runs west to Buckingham Palace from Trafalgar Square. **Hyde Park** is farther west still, as are the fashionable districts of **South Kensington** and **Chelsea.**

## FINDING AN ADDRESS

You will get lost in London. To the chagrin of tourists and postal workers alike, the city's tangle of streets follows no discernable pattern whatsoever. Furthermore, there seems to be no rhyme or reason to street naming or house numbering. Be warned that Park Walk is not necessarily near Park Crescent, to say nothing of a similarly named street, road, mews, and close. Sometimes odd-numbered houses are on one side of a street, while even-numbered homes are on the other. Other times, numbers will run straight up one side of a street, then down the other.

There are a couple of consoling factors, however. One is the well-placed, legible street signs, found either on street corners or posted on the sides of building. The other is extraordinarily helpful locals who will always stop to give a visitor a hand.

# NEIGHBORHOODS IN BRIEF

**The City** London is often referred to as a "city of villages" that have sprung up around the square mile of the original walled Roman city. Although most of the walls have long since disappeared, the political autonomy of The City of London still separates it from the surrounding areas. The City has always been London's financial center, and it is crammed with tiny streets and a sense of history befitting its ancient beginnings. The boroughs of Greater London, which flank The City, encompass over 600 square miles, though mercifully, the main tourist attractions are fairly close together.

**The West End** West of The City, to Hyde Park, lies the West End. You will get to know this area well. The Houses of Parliament, Buckingham Palace, and the nation's densest cluster of shops, restaurants, and theaters all make their homes here. Oxford Street, which runs the length of the West End, challenges nearby Covent Garden and Soho for the attention of shoppers and tourists.

**South Kensington and Chelsea** Beyond the West End, south of Hyde Park, are the fashionable residential areas of South Kensington and Chelsea. Take a close look at these neighborhoods—you've probably never seen so many beautiful city buildings that you'd like to own.

**The East End** Hugging The City's eastern side is one of London's poorest areas. Traditionally, the East End was undesirable because both the prevailing winds and the west-to-east flow of the River Thames could bring disease to its inhabitants. Today the East End is still home to poorer immigrants as well as to the capital's famous Cockneys.

**Southwark** The borough of Southwark lies across the river from The City, on the south bank of the Thames. Now under heavy reconstruction, Southwark became famous as London's entertainment quarter during the Elizabethan era, when theaters and brothels were banned from The City.

**Street Maps** A London street map is essential, even if you are staying on the beaten track. Bookstores, food markets, souvenir shops, and most sidewalk newsagents sell local maps. Expect to pay 60p to £1 ($1.10–$1.80).

For an in-depth look at London's web of streets, buy the map book *London A to Z* (pronounced "A to Zed"), or one of the many comprehensive oversized London survey maps. These and other maps are available at the **London Tourist Board Bookshop,** in the Tourist Information Centre, Victoria Station Forecourt (tel. 071/730-3488). It's open Easter to October daily from 9am to 8pm; the rest of the year Monday to Saturday 9am to 6:30pm, Sunday 9am to 5pm.

# 2. GETTING AROUND

## BY PUBLIC TRANSPORTATION

Commuters constantly complain about it, but to tourists, London's public transportation network is both vast and efficient. In central London, Underground stations abound. Above ground, the city's famous red double-decker buses traverse the city in all directions.

Both the Underground and buses are operated by London Regional Transport (LRT), which maintains fares based on a zone system: You pay for each zone you cross. For most tube trips you will be traveling within the same zone and the fare will be 70p ($1.25).

London Regional Transport Travel Information Centres can be found in most of the major Underground stations, including Heathrow Central, King's Cross, Oxford Circus, Piccadilly Circus, and Victoria. Off-hour times vary, but all provide service weekdays from 9am to 5pm. LRT also maintains a 24-hour telephone information service (tel. 071/222-1234).

## SAVING MONEY

You can save money by purchasing one of three Travelcards. A central London **1-day Travelcard** is good for unlimited transportation within 3 zones on the bus and tube after 9:30am Monday through Friday and anytime during weekends and public holidays. The card costs £2.30 ($4.15) for adults, and 90p ($1.60) for children aged 5 to 15. Children 4 and under always ride free. **Weekly Travelcards** valid within the Central London Zone cost £7.10 ($12.80) for adults, and £2.80 ($5.05) for children. **Monthly Travelcards** cost £27.30 ($49.15) for adults, and £20.20 ($38.15) for children. You will need to present a passport-size photo to buy the weekly ticket; photo booths are located in tube stations—four photographs cost £2 ($3.60).

## BY UNDERGROUND

Except for Christmas Day, when the tube is closed, trains run every few minutes from about 5:30am Monday through Saturday and from 7am or so on Sunday. Closing times vary with each station, but the last trains always leave between 11:30pm and 1am. Last train times are posted at the entrance of each station. Tickets can be purchased at the station ticket window or from an adjacent coin-operated machine. An alphabetized fare chart is posted next to most ticket machines. For travel within central London, most places you will visit will cost a uniform 70p ($1.25). Hold on to your ticket throughout your ride; you'll need it to exit. Pick up a handy tube map, distributed free at station ticket windows.

## BY BUS

It looks as though the red open-back platform buses will one day be a thing of the past, replaced by the more economical driver-only type. But for now, you can still make a flying leap onto a departing vehicle. Take a seat, either upstairs or down, and wait for the conductor to collect your fare. On the newer buses, pay the driver as you enter, and exit through the rear doors. Bus fare within Central London Zone 1 is 70p ($1.25); short hops (two or three stops) cost 50p ($.90).

Many tourist shy away from riding the buses because their routes can be confusing. Get a free bus map from the tourist office, or just ask any conductor about the route, and take advantage of a "top deck" sightseeing adventure.

Regular bus service stops after midnight. Night buses have different routes and different numbers from their daytime counterparts, and service is not as frequent; most routes are serviced only once per hour. Unlike weekly and monthly Travelcards, one-day passes are not valid on night buses. If you've just missed your night bus, expect a long wait for the next one or hunt down a minicab (see below). The central London night-bus terminus is Trafalgar Square.

## BY TAXI

For three or four people traveling a short distance, cabs can almost be economically viable. The city's big black cabs now come in other colors (primarily maroon), but the ride remains as fun as ever. A taxi is available when the yellow sign on its roof is illuminated. Hail a cab by raising your arm. The driver will lower the window when he pulls to the curb so you can state your destination before climbing in. You can hail a cab on the street or in front of train stations, large hotels, and popular tourist attractions. If you know in advance you'll be needing a cab, you can order one by calling 071/253-5000 or 071/286-0286.

The meter begins at £1 ($1.80), then climbs at a fast clip. There is an additional charge of 20p ($.35) per person, 10p ($.20) per large piece of luggage, and 60p ($1.10) on weekends and after midnight. But the thrill of viewing London's famous monuments from the roomy back seat of a black taxi is almost enough fun to get your eye off the meter.

Minicabs are meterless cars driven by any entrepreneur with a license. Technically, these taxis are not allowed to cruise for fares, but must operate from sidewalk offices—many of which are centered around Leicester Square. Minicabs are handy after the tube shuts down for the night and black cabs become suddenly scarce. Minicabs are often cheaper than black cabs, are available around the clock, and can be ordered in advance by calling 071/602-1234. Always negotiate the fare beforehand, and if you're approached by a driver (away from the sidewalk offices), hard bargaining is in order.

## BY CAR

### RENTAL

It's not smart to keep a car in the city, but for excursions a rental is well worth looking into. The big American car-rental firms are expensive, but most offer reduced rates for advance booking from the U.S. During summer, with a 2-day advance booking, **Avis** (tel. toll free 800/331-1084) charges £98.70 ($177.66) per week for their cheapest tin can, exclusive of damage waiver. The lowest summer rate at **Hertz** (tel. toll free 800/654-3001), guaranteed in U.S. dollars, is $322, with a 21-day advance purchase.

If you wait until you reach London and rent from a local firm, expect to pay £80 to £100 ($144–$180) per week, depending on the season. The least expensive rentals I have found are from **Practical Used Car Rental,** 111 Bartholomew Rd., N.W.5 (tel. 071/284-0199); and **Supercars,** 16 Warner St., E.C.1 (tel. 071/278-6001). Look in the phone book under "Car Hire" for alternatives, and use the big American chains as a last resort. Make sure the rate you pay includes unlimited mileage, all taxes, and the collision damage waiver, as these extras can send prices into the stratosphere.

### GASOLINE

**Dorset House Service Station,** 170 Marylebone Rd. (tel. 071/486-6389), accepts all major credit cards, and is one of the few city gas stations open 24 hours. Gasoline (petrol) costs about £1.85 ($3.35) per Imperial gallon (1.2 U.S. gallons).

### PARKING

Finding a parking spot can sometimes prove more of a challenge than driving in this maze of a city. Most parking meters are enforced from 6am to 6:30pm, but read the signs on the meters to be sure. Blue signs point the way to **National Car Parks (NCP),** which are located throughout the city. To find the closest, call NCP (tel. 071/499-7050).

Fines for illegal parking can be stiff, but worse are the wheel clamps which immobilize violators until the ticket is paid. If you find your car clamped, take the ticket and attached penalty notice to the nearest car pound (the address is on the ticket), or call 071/252-2222.

### DRIVING RULES

In Britain, wearing a seat belt is the law. You may not turn right on a red light, and automobiles must stop whenever a pedestrian steps into a crosswalk. Many crosswalks are located in the middle of the block, not at the corner. They are usually marked by white stripes on the pavement (zebra striping), and flashing orange lights on either sidewalk.

## BY BICYCLE

Bike lanes are unheard of and cars are unyielding—still, some people do ride. If you want to rent a bike, try **On Your Bike,** 22 Duke St. Hill, S.E.1 (tel. 071/407-1309). A 10-speed bike rents for a steep £10

($18) per day and £30 ($54) per week, plus a £40 ($72) deposit. The shop is open Monday through Friday from 9am to 6pm, and Saturday from 9:30am to 5:30pm.

Serious pedalers should check out the **London Cycling Campaign,** Tress House, 3 Stamford St., S.E.1 (tel. 071/928-7220), for information and advice on biking in the city. Be sure to pick up a copy of *On Your Bike,* a booklet of maps and information for city cyclers. The publication, which costs £2.50 ($4.50), is also available at London's bigger bookshops.

## ON FOOT

London can be a difficult city to negotiate. It seems as though no two streets run parallel, and even locals regularly consult maps. Construction sites further challenge walkers, but in the winding streets of The City and in the tourist area of the West End, there is no better way to go. Don't forget that cars drive on the left, and look both ways before stepping off the curb. Also, cars have the right-of-way over pedestrians; take care even when the light seems to be in your favor.

**Airports** For flight information, phone **Heathrow Airport** (tel. 081/759-4321), **Gatwick Airport** (tel. 0293/31299), or **London City Airport** (tel. 071/474-5555). Alternatively, phone your airline directly. See "Orientation: Arriving," earlier in this chapter, for information on transportation to and from the airports.

**American Express** has almost a dozen city offices, including 6 Haymarket, S.W.1 (tel. 071/930-8422), and The British Travel Center, 4 Lower Regent St., S.W.1 (tel. 071/839-2682). Most are open Mon–Fri 9am–6pm, Sat 9am–noon. To report lost or stolen cards, call 071/222-9633, 24 hours.

**Area Code** The area code is 071 in central London, 081 in outer London. Area codes are necessary when dialing from outside the code. From the U.S. dial 71 and 81, respectively.

**Auto Rental** See "Getting Around," above.

**Baby-sitters** Ask for a recommendation at your hotel, or call **Babysitters Unlimited,** 271 King St., W.6 (tel. 081/741-5566). This 20-year-old company provides sitters for about £3.50 ($6.30) per hour. Reservations are accepted Mon–Fri 10am–5:30pm, Sat 9:30am–1pm.

**Bookstores** Dillons the Bookstore, 82 Gower St., W.C.1 (tel. 071/636-1577), is one of the biggest and best chain bookshops in town. Open Mon and Wed–Fri 9am–7pm, Tues 9:30am–7pm, Sat 9:30am–5:30pm. Hatchards, 187 Piccadilly, W.1 (tel. 071/437-3924), is known as an upscale bookshop, and is another good choice for popular books. Open Mon–Fri 9am–6pm, Sat 9am–5pm. See Chapter 8, "Shopping A to Z," for more bookstore information.

**Business Hours** Most **banks** are open Mon–Fri 9:30am–3:30pm. Some are also open Saturday 9:30am–noon. **Offices** are generally open Mon–Fri from 8:30 or 9am until 5 or 5:30pm. By law, **pubs** can open Mon–Sat 11am–11pm, and Sun 11am–3pm and 6–11pm. Note, however, that some pubs begin serving later than others, and many keep Sunday hours throughout the week. **Restaurants** usually open for lunch at 11am, and stay open until 11pm or midnight. A very few stay open later (see Chapter 5, "London Dining"). **Stores** are usually open Mon–Sat 10am–6pm, but most stay open at least one extra hour one night during the week. Some shops around touristy Covent Garden stay open until 7 or 8pm nightly. By law, most stores are closed Sunday.

**Climate** See "When to Go," Chapter 2.

**Currency** See "Information, Entry Requirements & Money," Chapter 2.

**Currency Exchange** As a rule, you will get a better rate for traveler's checks than you will for cash. Banks generally offer the best exchange rates, but American Express and Thomas Cook are competitive and do not charge commission for cashing traveler's checks no matter the brand. I haven't been afraid to use my credit cards; I have found that bank card exchange rates not only are favorable but are regularly to my advantage when conversion costs are figured in. However, be advised that rates can change and your bill, a month later, can be a surprise. **American Express** maintains several offices throughout the city (see above). A conveniently located **Thomas Cook** office is at 1 Marble Arch, W.1 (tel. 071/837-5275); open Mon–Fri 9am–5pm, Sat 9am–noon.

Places with the longest hours (sometimes open all night) also offer the worst rates. Beware of **Chequepoint** and other high-commission bureaux de change.

**Doctors and Dentists** If you need a physician or dentist, and your condition is not life-threatening, call the operator (100) and ask for the local police. They will put you in touch with a specialist. You can also visit **Medical Express,** Chapel Place, W.1 (tel. 071/499-1991), a private walk-in clinic open Mon–Fri 9am–7pm, Sat 10am–5pm. Consultations begin at £50 ($90). **Emergency Dental Service** (tel. 071/752-0133) matches dental emergencies with local specialists. The service is available 24 hours a day.

Citizens of Australia and New Zealand are entitled to free medical treatment and subsidized dental care while in Britain.

**Driving Rules** See "Getting Around," above.

**Drugstores** **Bliss Chemist,** 5 Marble Arch, W.1 (tel. 071/723-6116), is open daily 9am–midnight year round. Call the operator (100) and ask for the police for the opening hours and addresses of other late-opening "chemists."

**Electricity** English appliances operate on 220 volts, and plug into 3-pronged outlets that differ from those in America and on the Continent. Hair dryers, irons, shavers, and other electric goods designed for the American market must be equipped with an adapter and a transformer. Do not attempt to plug an American appliance into a European electrical outlet without a transformer; you will ruin your appliance and possibly start a fire.

**Embassies** The **U.S. Embassy,** 24 Grosvenor Square, W.1 (tel. 071/499-9000), does not accept visitors—all inquiries must be made by mail or phone. The **Canadian High Commission,** Macdonald House, 1 Grosvenor Square, W.1 (tel. 071/629-9492), is open Mon–Fri 9am–5pm. The **Australian High Commission** is in Australia House on The Strand, W.C.2 (tel. 071/379-4334), and is open Mon–Fri 9am–1pm. The **New Zealand High Commission** is in New Zealand House, Haymarket, S.W.1 (tel. 071/930-8422), open Mon–Fri 9am–5pm.

**Emergencies** Police, fire, and ambulance can be reached by dialing **999** from any phone. No money is required.

**Eyeglasses** A number of spectacle shops line Oxford Street, King's Road, and other major shopping streets. The department stores Harrods and Selfridges (see Chapter 8, "Shopping A to Z") also have a good selection of frames, and opticians on duty. The **Contact Lens Centre,** 32 Camden High St., N.W.1 (tel. 071/383-3838), is one of the cheapest shops for contacts as well as glasses. Even if you forgot to bring your prescription with you, chances are you can get an exam and new glasses in the same day. Open Mon–Fri 9am–7pm, Sat 9am–5pm. No credit cards.

**Hairdressers/Barbers** **Jingles,** 125 Wilton Rd., S.W.1 (tel. 071/834-0032), one of London's most respected salons, also offers one of the best-priced cuts in the West End. Prices average £14 ($25.20) for men and £16 ($28.80) for women. Open Mon–Fri 8:30am–8:30pm, Sat 8am–5pm. The **Long Hair Clinic,** fifth floor, Harrods Department Store, Knightsbridge S.W.1 (tel. 071/584-8881), is an innovative specialty salon for both men and women. Cuts cost from about £16 ($28.80). Open Mon–Tues, Thurs–Sat 9am–6pm; Wed 9:30am–7pm.

**Holidays** See "When to Go," Chapter 2.

**Hospitals** In an emergency, dial 999 from any phone; no money is needed. **University College Hospital,** Gower St., W.1 (tel. 081/387-9300), is one of the most centrally located. A dozen other city hospitals also offer 24-hour walk-in emergency care. Dial 100 and ask the operator to connect you with the police. They will tell you which is closest.

**Hotlines** The **Restaurant Switchboard** (tel. 081/888-8080) makes restaurant recommendations and reservations free of charge. It's open Mon–Sat 9am–8pm; **Events of the Day** (tel. 071/246-8041) plays an up-to-date recorded message about goings-on around town; and at **Capital Helpline** (tel. 071/388-7575), a live human being will answer any legitimate question about London, the universe, or anything. The Helpline is open Mon–Wed and Fri 9:30am–5:30pm; Thurs 9:30am–9pm.

**Information** See "Orientation: Tourist Information," above.

**Laundry/Dry Cleaning** Laundries abound. Most are open every day. Near Russell Square, try **Red and White Laundries,** 78 Marchmont St., open daily 8am–10pm; a wash costs £2

($3.60), and dryers and soap are 50p (90¢). **Ashbourne Laundry,** 93 Pimlico Rd., is similarly priced and convenient to Victoria Station hotels. **Launderette House,** 18 London St., is open 8am–8pm daily, and is a good pick in the Bayswater area.

**Dry cleaning** is very expensive in London. Expect to pay about £1.50 ($2.70) per shirt, and £3 ($5.40) for a pair of pants. With over 40 branches, **Sketchley,** 49 Maddox St., W.1 (tel. 071/629-1292), is one of the city's largest cleaning chains. Check the telephone directory for other locations.

**Libraries** The British Library, Great Russell St., W.C.1 (tel. 071/636-1544) is one of the largest in the world, holding at least one copy of every book published in Britain. The library's immense size makes it a bit unwieldy for the casual reader, and the helpful staff may direct you to one of the city's more accessible local or specialized libraries. **Westminster Central Reference Library,** St. Martin's St., W.C.2 (tel. 071/798-2034) has the city's best collection of reference materials and periodicals. It is open to the public Mon–Fri 10am–7pm, Sat 10am–5pm.

**Liquor Laws** Under British law, no one under 18 years of age may legally purchase or consume alcohol. Beer and wine are sold by supermarkets, liquor stores (called "bottle shops"), and food shops advertising "off-license" sales. Some supermarkets also sell stronger spirits, at some of the best prices in town. Admission-charging nightclubs are allowed to serve alcohol to patrons until 3am or so. By law, hotel bars may serve drinks to registered guests only after 11pm. See "Business Hours," above, for pub hours.

**Lost Property** If you lose something on the bus or tube, allow two days before contacting London Regional Transport, 200 Baker St., N.W.1 (tel. 071/486-2496), open Mon–Fri 9:30am–2pm. The **Taxi Lost Property Office,** 15 Penton St., N.1 (tel. 071/833-0996), is open Mon–Fri 9am–4pm. Lost-property offices are also located in all the major British Rail stations.

**To report a loss or theft,** call the operator (100) and ask for the police.

**Luggage Storage/Lockers** The **Gatwick Airport Left Luggage Office** (tel. 081/668-4211) never closes, and charges £1.25 ($2.25) per item for the first 24 hours, then £2.50 ($4.50) for each additional day. The **Heathrow Airport Left Luggage Offices** (tel. 081/759-4321), at Terminals 1, 3, and 4, are open daily from about 6am to 10:30pm. They charge £1.60 ($2.90) per item for the first day, £2.25 ($4.05) for each additional 24-hour period. The **London City Airport Left Luggage Office** (tel. 071/474-5555) is situated at the information desk, and open daily from 6am to 10pm. Luggage lockers are available at **Victoria** (tel. 071/928-5151, ext. 27514), **King's Cross** (tel. 071/922-9081), and other major British Rail stations. Lockers cost £2 to £4 ($3.60–$7.20) per day, depending on size. Finally, you don't need to tell the bellhop of a fancy, well-located hotel that you are not one of their guests. At an economical average of £1 ($1.80) per item, your bags can stay at the Ritz, even if you can't.

**Mail** Post offices are plentiful and are normally open Mon–Fri 9am–5pm, Sat 9am–noon. The **Main Post Office,** St. Martin's Place, Trafalgar Square, W.C.2 (tel. 071/930-9580), is open Mon–Sat 8am–8pm. Mailboxes, which are round and red, are well distributed throughout the city. Airmail letters weighing up to 10 grams cost 37p (65¢), and postcards require a 31p (55¢) stamp to all destinations outside Europe. If you ask for special-issue stamps, you will probably get something pretty. Budget travelers can get more post for the pound by purchasing aerograms for 32p (60¢) each. The deal is even sweeter at £1.80 ($3.25) per half dozen.

You can receive mail in London, marked "Poste Restante," and addressed to you, care of the London Chief Post Office, King Edward St., London EC1A 1AA, England. The office is located near St. Paul's Cathedral and is open Mon–Fri 8:30am–6:30pm. You will need to show identification to collect your mail. If you have an American Express card, or are carrying traveler's checks issued by that company, you can receive mail care of American Express, 6 Haymarket, London S.W.1., England.

**Newspapers/Magazines** The extraordinarily large number of local newspapers in London are generally divided into two categories—broadsheets and tabloids. In general, tabloids like *The Sun, Today,* and the *Daily Mirror* sensationalize news more than the larger-format papers. *The Times* is the grandaddy of London's opinionated papers, and features a particularly hefty Sunday edition. The *Guardian* is the city's largest left-of-center paper, with in-depth investigative stories, and good local reporting. The *Daily Telegraph,* known in some circles as the "Torygraph," leans right politically, and is particularly strong in foreign coverage. The *Independent,* one of London's newest newspapers, is trying to make inroads with solid middle-of-the-road reporting. This paper features Britain's best arts section every Sunday.

The weekly listings magazines *Time Out* and *City Limits* are indispensable for comprehensive coverage of what's happening in the city. Newsstands are located outside most tube stations, and good-sized, international-magazine shops are in major hotels and on most busy shopping streets.

**Photographic Needs** Photo processing in London is more expensive than similar services Stateside. **Dixons,** 88 Oxford St., W.1 (tel. 071/636-8511), with over 80 branches in London, is the best source for most photographic needs.

**Police** In an emergency, dial 999 from any phone; no money is needed. At other times, dial the operator (100) and ask to be connected with the police.

**Radio** Recent deregulation is improving London radio with an expanding number of stations, but variety is still limited. The dozen or so sanctioned stations—heavy on new pop, talk, and news—are supplemented by a handful of adventurous "pirate" broadcasters. The legal FM stations include: BBC1 (104.8), featuring a Top 40 format; BBC2 (89.1), a middle-of-the-road music station; BBC3 (between 90 and 92), Britain's best classical; BBC4 (95), talk, humor, and call-in shows; BBC Greater London Radio (94.9), album-oriented rock; LBC Crown FM (97.3), news, call-in shows, and updates on city arts happenings; Capital FM (95.8), American-format pop rock; Choice FM (96.9), jazz, reggae, and Latin music; Jazz FM (102.2), Blues, R&B, big band, and the like; and Kiss FM (100), dance music for young hipsters.

**Religious Services** It sometimes seems that the only things in London more ubiquitous than pubs are churches. **Protestant** houses of worship are on almost every street in The City, and you are welcome to attend Sunday services in any one of them. The London Tourist Board can provide you with a complete list. For a special treat, think about spending Sunday morning in St. Paul's Cathedral (tel. 071/248-2705) or Westminster Abbey (tel. 071/222-5152). Services are held at the Abbey at 8am, 10am, 11:15am, 3pm, 5:45pm, and 6:30pm. Times vary at St. Paul's; call for information. Westminster Cathedral, Ashley Place, S.W.1 (tel. 071/834-7452), is England's **Roman Catholic** headquarters, and a spectacular sightseeing destination in its own right (see "Special-Interest Sightseeing," in Chapter 6). Services are held at 7am, 8am, 9am, 10:30am, noon, 5:30pm, and 7pm. The **Liberal Jewish Synagogue,** 152 Loudoun Rd., N.W.8 (tel. 071/722-8872), holds services Friday at 8pm, and Saturday at 11am. **The Buddhist Society,** 58 Eccleston Square, S.W.1 (tel. 071/834-5858), holds regular lectures and meditations. Call Mon–Sat 2–5pm for information.

**Rest Rooms** Even if you don't drink, you'll find London's many pubs handy for their facilities. My first pick for rest rooms, however, is the lobby-level lavatories in the city's better-known hotels. Lately automatic toilets have been popping up on sidewalks throughout the city. These beige-and-silver lifesavers are automatically sterilized top to bottom after each use. They are well-lit, include piped-in music, and cost just 10p (20¢).

**Safety** Whenever you're traveling in an unfamiliar city or country, stay alert. Be aware of your immediate surroundings. Wear a moneybelt and keep a close eye on your possessions. Be particularly careful with cameras, purses, and wallets, all favorite targets for thieves and pickpockets. Take particular caution when exploring the East End, Brixton, and Notting Hill, London's poorest areas.

**Shoe Repair** Most of the major tube stations have "heel bars" that can make quick repairs. More extensive work can be performed in any of the major department stores (see Chapter 8, "Shopping A to Z"), or at **Jeeves Snob Shop,** 10 Pont St., S.W.1 (tel. 071/235-1101). It's open Mon–Fri 8:30am–5:30pm, Sat 8:30am–1pm.

**Taxes** Unlike in the United States, where tax is tacked on at the register, in England a 15% Value-Added Tax (VAT) is already figured into the ticket price of most items. Restaurants usually include VAT in menu prices, but sometimes it is added to the bill, along with a service charge. The policy is usually written on the menu. There is no additional airport tax upon departure, and tax is included in all hotel rates quoted in this book. Foreign tourists can reclaim the VAT for major purchases. See "Enjoying London on a Budget," in Chapter 2, for details.

**Taxis** London's famous cabs can be hailed in the street; an illuminated yellow roof light means they are available. If you will need a taxi from your hotel early in the morning, it is advisable to make a reservation the night before. Try **Computer-cab** (tel. 071/286-0286) or **Radio Taxicabs** (tel. 071/272-0272). For more information on taxis, see "Getting Around," above.

**Telephone & Fax** London now has two **area codes:** 071 (for central London) and 081 (for outer London). Use these codes only when calling from one area to another. When you're calling from the U.S., the area codes are 71 and 81, respectively.

Two kinds of pay phones are regularly used. One accepts coins and the other uses a Phonecard, available from newsagents in £1, £2, £4, £10, and £20 denominations. The minimum cost of a local call is 10p (18¢) for the first two minutes (during peak hours). You can deposit up to four coins at a time, but telephones don't make change, so unless you are calling long distance, use 10p coins exclusively. Phonecard telephones automatically deduct the price of your call from the card. Cards are especially handy if you want to call abroad, as you don't have to continuously pop in the pounds. Some large hotels and touristy streetcorners also have credit-card telephones that accept major credit cards. Lift the handle and follow the instructions on the screen.

To reach the **local operator,** dial 100. The **international operator** is 155. **London phone information** (called "directory inquiries") can be reached by dialing 142 and is free of charge.

If you need to communicate by fax and your hotel is not equipped, contact **Chesham Executive Centre,** 150 Regent St., W.1 (tel. 071/439-6288). They charge about £5.50 ($9.90) per page and are open Mon–Fri 9am–6pm, Sat 9am–noon.

**Television** The BBC produces some great television programs, but they're few and far between. There are only four local TV stations, so you can quickly flip through the channels before deciding there's nothing on. Many hotels now offer stations from the European Cable Network. These include Eurosport, a sports channel; Sky News, a 24-hour news channel; and MTV, a clone of the American version.

**Time** Since London is located just 6 miles west of the Prime Meridian in Greenwich, its clocks are set on Greenwich mean time, 5 hours ahead of U.S. eastern standard time. Clocks here spring forward and fall back for daylight savings time, but the semiannual ritual commences on a slightly different schedule than in the States. To find out the exact time by phone, dial **Timeline** (tel. 123).

**Tipping** Most **restaurants** automatically add a service charge. The restaurant's policy will be written on the menu. When a service charge is not included, a 10% to 15% tip is customary. **Taxi drivers** expect 10% to 15% of the fare. Note that tipping is rare in both pubs and theaters.

**Transit Information** The **London Regional Transport**

**(LRT) Travel Information Service** (tel. 071/222-1234) offers schedule and fare information for bus, Underground, and British Rail service within Greater London. Open 24 hours.

**Water** There's plenty of it here and, compared to many capital cities, it's relatively safe to drink. Designer waters like Perrier are popular at restaurants; specify tap water if that's what you want.

**Weather** **Weathercall** (tel. 0898/500401) keeps tabs on the temperature and readies you for the next rainfall.

# 3. NETWORKS & RESOURCES

## FOR STUDENTS

The **University of London** is the largest school in the city. Although many of its associated colleges are spread throughout London, the areas just north and east of Russell Square in Bloomsbury contain most of the university's main buildings. Like many urban schools, this university does not really have a campus, but the pubs and inexpensive restaurants of the neighborhood serve as frequent student hangouts. Since the University of London is largely a commuter school, Bloomsbury unfortunately lacks the verve and bustle of a college community. Students who plan on attending school in London should invest £1.75 ($3.15) or so in the well-written and informative *Time Out London Student Guide,* published at the beginning of each school year and available from most large newsagents.

The **University of London Student Union (ULU),** Malet St., W.C.1 (tel. 071/580-9551), caters to over 55,000 students and may be the largest of its kind in the world. In addition to a gym and fitness center, the Malet Street building houses several shops, two restaurants, a health club, two banks, a ticket booking agency, and an STA travel office. Concerts and dances are also regularly scheduled here. Stop by or phone for information on university activities. The student union building is open Monday through Saturday from 9:30am to 11pm; Sunday from 9:30am to noon, and from 12:30 to 10pm. Tube: Goodge Street.

**Student Nightline** (tel. 071/581-2468) is a help and information service run by and for students. It deals primarily with emotional difficulties, but can help with a myriad of other problems as well.

If you want to perform on the street for money, you can set up legally either in Carnaby Street, W.1, or at either end of Covent Garden Market, W.C.2. Despite the proliferation of songsters, performing is illegal in Underground stations, and on most of London's streets. Fines can reach £100 ($180), though few are prosecuted.

## FOR GAY MEN & LESBIANS

Although anti-gay legislation abounds, homophobic hostility is rare. There is a large gay community in London, supported by a plethora of publications, shops, pubs, nightclubs, cafés, and special services. *Capital Gay* is the city's premiere alternative paper. Written by and for gay men and women, this free weekly features previews, reviews, news, and events. *The Pink Paper* is nationally distributed, and is also free. Both publications are available at gay bars, bookstores, and cafés. At least 2 monthlies are regularly available at newsstands around town: *Gay Times* is oriented toward men and is known for both news and features; *HIM* supplements it's high-quality reporting with glossy beefcake photos. The city's popular listings magazines, *Time Out* and *City Limits,* also provide excellent coverage. Several locally produced guidebooks, written for local and visiting gays and lesbians, are available from several dealers, including the **London Tourist Board Bookshop,** in the Tourist Information Centre, Victoria Station Forecourt, S.W.1 (tel. 071/730-3488). Open from Easter to October daily 9am to 8pm, and November to Easter Monday through Saturday 9am to 6:30pm, Sunday 9am to 5pm. The **Lesbian and Gay Switchboard** (tel. 071/837-7324) offers information, advice, and counseling, as well as a free accommodations agency. The line is open 24 hours, and is almost always busy. The **Lesbian Line** (tel. 071/251-6911) offers similar services to women only. It's open Monday through Thursday 7 to 10pm, Friday 2 to 10pm.

**THE LONDON LESBIAN & GAY CENTRE, 67–69 Cowcross St., E.C.1. Tel. 071/608-1471.**

London's most popular center for gays and lesbians encompasses 5 floors, and includes a theater, disco, two bars, a café, a bookshop, and a women-only floor. This is a great place to get information on the local scene.

**Admission:** 40p ($1).

**Open:** Mon 5:30–11pm, Tues–Thurs noon–11pm, Fri–Sat noon–2am (admission until midnight), Sun noon–midnight. **Tube:** Farringdon.

**GAY'S THE WORD BOOKSHOP, 66 Marchmont St., W.C.1. Tel. 071/278-7654.**

In addition to the largest selection of gay and lesbian biographies, novels, and "how-to" books around, this store stocks calendars, kitsch clothing, jewelry, and associated paraphernalia, and holds regular readings.

**Open:** Mon–Sat 11am–7pm, Sun 2–6pm. **Tube:** Russell Square.

**THE ZIPPER STORE, 283 Camden High St., N.W.1. Tel. 071/267-7665.**

Leisure wear, leather wear, and a large assortment of "novelties" can be purchased here at London's only licensed gay sex store.

**Open:** Mon–Thurs and Sat 10:30am–6:30pm, Fri 10:30am–7pm. **Tube:** Camden Town.

**FIRST OUT COFFEE SHOP, 52 St. Giles High St., W.C.2. Tel. 071/240-8042.**

Breakfast, lunch, and light snacks all day complement the espresso in this good-looking Parisian-style café. Good music, a comfortable atmosphere, and a bulletin board advertising local happenings has made First Out a natural meeting house.

**Open:** Mon–Sat 11am–midnight, Sun 1–8pm. **Tube:** Tottenham Court Road.

## FOR WOMEN

London is safer than many other large cities, but women are advised to take special precautions. Use your common sense. Try not to walk alone at night, especially on small, deserted streets. Always carry some emergency money, and don't hesitate to spend it on a taxi if you feel the least bit uneasy. The **London Rape Crisis Centre** (tel. 071/837-1600) offers immediate help, advice, and counseling to victims.

*Spare Rib,* a widely distributed monthly magazine, features news and commentary on feminist issues. It is available at larger newsstands around the city. **Silver Moon Women's Bookshop,** 68 Charing Cross Rd., W.C.2 (tel. 071/836-7906), is Soho's only dedicated feminist bookseller. Located in the heart of London's book district, Silver Moon boasts a huge selection of fiction and nonfiction titles by and for women, as well as nonsexist children's books. It's open Monday through Saturday from 10:30am to 6:30pm. Tube: Leicester Square.

Women-only dance events occur almost every night in London at nightspots all around the city. These clubs are designed for both straights and lesbians who are not looking to attract the attention of men. Call **London Friend** (tel. 071/837-7324) or check the listings magazines for upcoming events.

# CHAPTER 4

# LONDON ACCOMMODATIONS



The bed-and-breakfast is one of England's greatest traditions. Morning-meal menus differ, but most hotels serve up a whopper that usually includes cold cereal, eggs, bacon or sausage, toast, and all the coffee or tea you can drink. It's hearty, and just might last you through the day. The bad news is that, in general, London's budget hotels are not as nice or as cheap as those on the Continent. Rooms are uniformly small and worn. But British hoteliers are famous for their good-humored hospitality, the huge free breakfast means you can stay on budget in London even if you have to pay a little more for a room here than on the Continent.

Summer is a seller's market. Hordes of tourists jousting for coveted hotel rooms keep rates high, and fairly rigid. But there are ebbs in the tide, and if you sense that rooms are going unoccupied, questioning the rate is definitely in order. In the off-season, prices tumble—sometimes by as much as 30%—and there is often room for further negotiation. Never accept a room until you are sure you've secured the lowest price. Remember that hotel rooms are a perishable commodity; unoccupied, they are worthless to their owners. Upon hearing an American accent, hoteliers will usually offer their best room at their highest rate. Make it clear that you are a budget traveler, and be willing to lower your standards. If you are shopping around, make this fact clear. Always ask if they have anything cheaper, and note that many hotels will offer a discount for a stay of a week or more. Everyone, especially single travelers, should ask to see their room before renting it. Most hotels will accommodate a single person in a larger room if one is available, and asking to view the room beforehand will encourage this.

Here are a few things to keep in mind when renting a room in London: Although beds are made up daily, sheets are usually not changed during a stay of less than a week. If you need new bedding, request it. Remember that even local telephone calls made from your room can be deathly expensive. Inquire about the rate before dialing. And finally, a personal observation: While a television in the room may be a nice benefit, it's unfortunate when it is installed there instead of in a public lounge area. The guest lounge is the hearth of a hotel—it's a place where travelers can meet, exchange ideas, and make new friends. Unfortunately, these public areas are quickly fading from budget hotels to make way for an additional money-making bedroom. If you are lucky enough to stay in a hotel with a comfortable lounge area, don't ignore it.

*Note:* Rates quoted below include Value-Added Tax, and are accurate for the summer of 1992. Expect reductions before and after the season.

## ABOUT RESERVATIONS

Although most hotels rarely fill to capacity, occupancy rates are higher in budget-priced hotels. When traveling during the low seasons, don't worry about booking in advance unless you are set on one particular hotel, or are arriving very late in the day. In summer, a confirmed reservation will save you time and anxiety, as many hotels fill up early in the day.

Except where noted, hotels listed below all accept advance reservations. Rooms are typically held with a nonrefundable deposit (preferably in pounds) equaling the cost of one night's stay. When sending a deposit, ask for a confirmation so there is no mistake as to when you are arriving. You may also wish to follow up your reservation request with a telephone call to the hotel. **And if you call from the U.S., remember to drop the zeros from the London area codes: dial 71, not 071.**

If you arrive in London without a reservation, check availability by phone before setting out. Most hotels will hold a room for you for an hour or so.

## HOTEL-BOOKING SERVICES

If, after inquiring about room availability at the hotels listed in this chapter, you still come up empty-handed (an extremely unlikely prospect), you can always book a room through one of the city's many hotel-booking agencies.

**Victoria Station Hotel Reservation Service** (tel. 071/828-4646) books B&Bs and hotels in all price categories. The company works with many budget-priced properties, but their best rates are for London's fancier rooms. By negotiating with some of the city's best hotels, this service can offer cut-price rooms to same-day arrivals—savings of up to 50% during the off-season. There is a £3 ($5.40) booking fee. The reservation service window is open daily from 7am to 11pm, and is located across from the ticket office, by the entrance to platform 9. A second office is located in King's Cross Rail Station (tel. 071/837-5682), next to the Pullman Lounge, at the head of platform 8.

**London Tourist Board Information Centre Hotel-Booking Service** (tel. 071/730-3488) offers similar services inside their many city offices. A small booking fee must be paid, along with a deposit which is applied to the price of the room. Offices and hours include: Victoria Station Forecourt, open from Easter through October daily from 9am to 8pm, and the rest of the year Monday through Saturday 9am to 7pm, Sunday 9am to 5pm; Heathrow Airport, open daily 8am to 6:30pm; Tower of London, West Gate, open daily from April through October 10am to 6pm; Harrods Department Store, open Monday, Tuesday, and Thursday through Saturday 9am to 6pm, Wednesday 9:30am to 7pm; and Selfridges Department Store, open Monday through Wednesday and Friday and Saturday 9am to 6pm, Thursday 9am to 8pm.

## 1. DOUBLES FOR LESS THAN £35.50 [$63.90]

### BAYSWATER & PADDINGTON

The unofficial district of Bayswater runs along the northern edge of Hyde Park and encompasses Paddington Station, one of the city's major gateways to the north. It is a densely packed residential community, populated by a large number of Indians and Pakistanis. It is also jammed with budget hotels. The area's proximity to the park, good restaurants (especially along Queensway and Westbourne Grove), and transportation links to the West End, make Bayswater a desirable location for budget travelers. The Central and District Underground lines run to Bayswater and Paddington stations, while buses 12, 88, and 289 travel the length of Bayswater Road.

**CENTRE FRANÇAIS, 61–69 Chepstow Place, London W.2. Tel. 071/221-8134.** 200 beds (none with bath). **Tube:** Notting Hill Gate.

**$ Rates** (including continental breakfast): £20 ($36) single; £35 ($63) twin. V.

Welcoming visitors with a particular interest in French culture, Centre Français is an exceptionally friendly place with the look and feel of a college dormitory. Ample-size rectangular rooms are equipped with a desk and chair, and open onto corridors where French is as likely to be heard as English. The center is predominantly occupied by students in the 16- to 35-year-old range, but the warden, Mrs. Lynch, is quick to point out that older visitors are also welcome, especially if they are in the teaching profession. A three-course dinner is available in the hotel restaurant for £4.45 ($8).

From the Notting Hill Gate station, cross the street to Pembridge

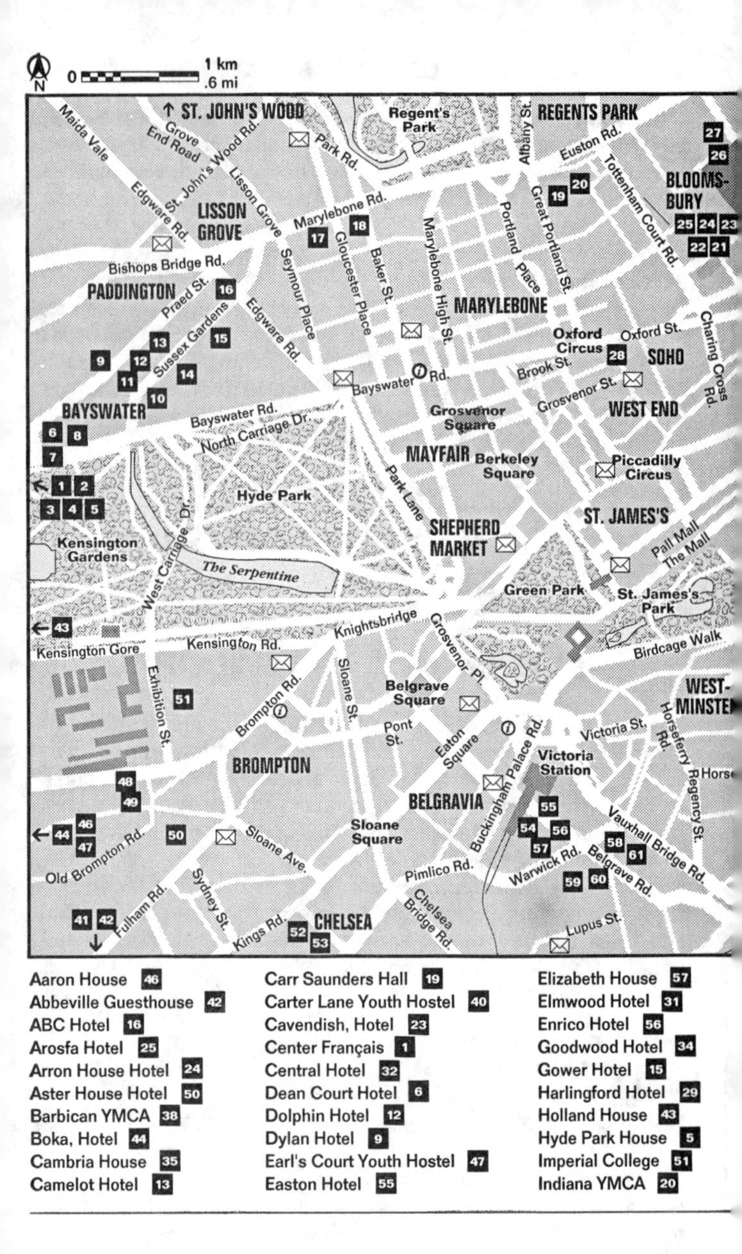


Gardens. Turn right on Pembridge Square, then left onto Chepstow Place. It's a 5-minute walk in all.

**HYDE PARK HOUSE, 48 St. Petersburgh Place, London W.2. Tel. 071/229-1687.** 18 rms (none with bath). TV **Tube:** Bayswater.

**$ Rates** (including continental breakfast): £20 ($36) single without

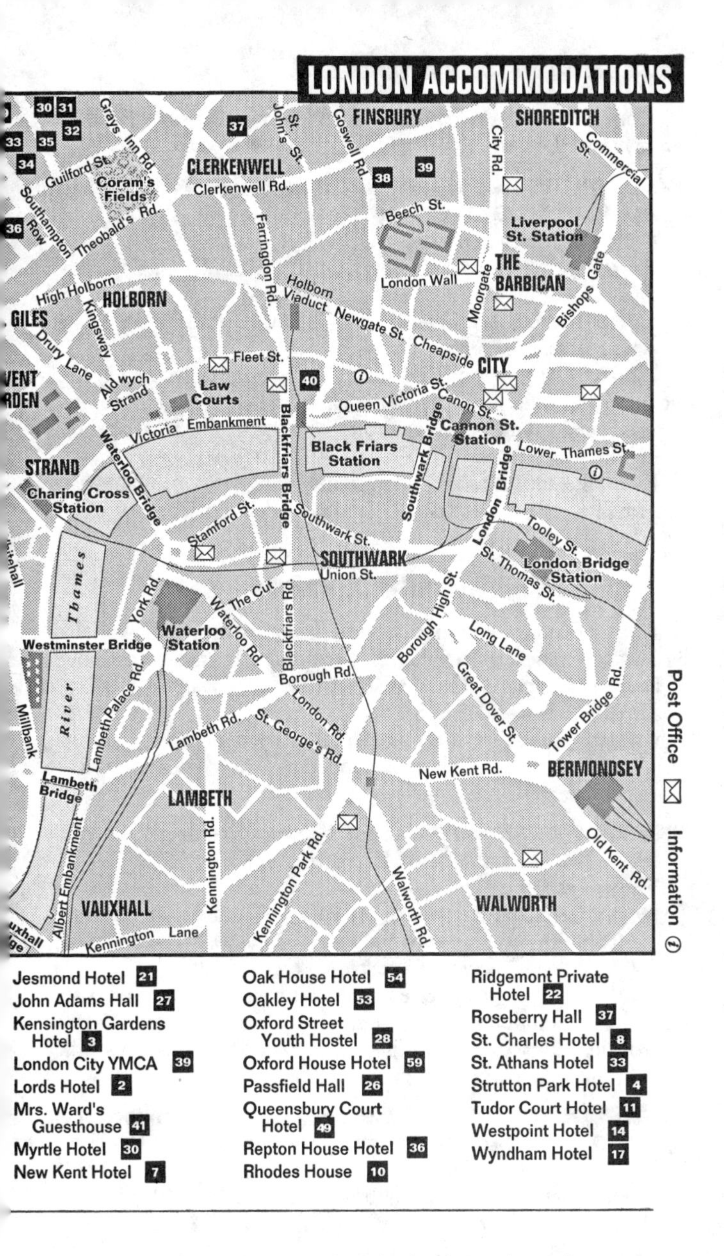


bath; £32 ($57.60) twin without bath. No credit cards.

"Charming" sounds corny, but no other word accurately describes this top pick for good, clean, quiet accommodations. Announced by a small awning in the middle of a block of rowhouses, this family-run B&B puts a quilt on every bed and a refrigerator in every room. Prices include free use of the kitchen, and unlimited attention from the family's friendly small dogs.

From Bayswater Underground, turn left onto Moscow Road and left again at the church.

**ST. CHARLES HOTEL, 66 Queensborough Terrace, London W.2. Tel. 071/221-0022.** 16 rms (all with shower; 4 with toilet). **Tube:** Queensway.

**$ Rates** (including English breakfast): £22 ($39.60) single without toilet, £27 ($48.60) with toilet; £35 ($63) twin without toilet, £37 ($66.66) with toilet. There's a £2 ($3.60) surcharge for 1-night stays. No credit cards.

Mr. and Mrs. Wildrige are the hotel's caring proprietors, and indeed, the interior is beautifully kept. Opulent wood paneling and carefully restored ceilings suggest a high tariff, but a few of the bathless rooms are within our budget.

From the Queensway Underground, turn left onto Bayswater Road and after two blocks, take another left onto Queensborough Terrace.

## SUSSEX GARDENS

Despite its quiet-sounding name, Sussex Gardens is one of Bayswater's busiest thoroughfares. Beginning as a traffic circle south of Paddington Station, the long street runs straight up to Edgeware Road. Along both sides of Sussex Gardens there is hardly a house that doesn't announce itself as a hotel. Accommodations are uniformly nondescript, but rates are good, and fierce competition in the off-season means everything's negotiable.

**RHODES HOUSE HOTEL, 195 Sussex Gardens, London W.2. Tel. 071/262-0537.** 16 rms (12 with bath). TV TEL **Tube:** Paddington.

**$ Rates** (including continental breakfast): £23 ($41.40) basic single, £35 ($63) with shower and toilet; £33 ($59.40) basic double, £40 ($72) with shower and toilet. No credit cards.

Most of the rooms here are equipped with private bath, but a few basic singles and doubles are within our budget. If Rhodes House is full, owner Chris Crias will direct you to Argos House, his other hotel around the corner.

**WESTPOINT HOTEL, 170 Sussex Gardens, London W.2. Tel. 071/402-0281.** 66 rms (most with bath). TV **Tube:** Paddington.

**$ Rates** (including continental breakfast): £28 ($50.40) basic single, £34 ($61.20) with shower and toilet; £32 ($57.60) basic twin, £44 ($79.20) with shower and toilet. AE, MC, V.

Farther along the street from Rhodes House, this hotel is slightly larger than most. It's somewhat plain, but clean and thoroughly recommendable.

**GOWER HOTEL, 129 Sussex Gardens, London W.2. Tel. 071/262-2262.** 22 rms (20 with bath). TV TEL **Tube:** Paddington.

**$ Rates** (including English breakfast): £23 ($41.40) basic single, £31 ($55.80) with shower and toilet; £35 ($63) basic double, £41 ($73.80) with shower and toilet. MC, V.

There are only two bathless rooms here, both on the top floor. Although they are small, due to the slant in the roof, good, clean facilities make it worth the climb.

**ABC HOTEL, 121 Sussex Gardens, London W.2. Tel. 071/723-3945.** 16 rms (none with bath). TV TEL **Tube:** Paddington.

**$ Rates** (including English breakfast): £21 ($37.80) single; £33 ($59.40) twin. MC, V.

In addition to reasonable accommodations, rates include a good breakfast and free use of the kitchen.

## VICTORIA

The rebuilding of Buckingham House into Buckingham Palace in the 1820s helped transform Victoria into a fashionable neighborhood. Bustling Victoria Station bisects the area, separating pricey Belgravia on its northwest from more accessible Pimlico to the southeast. Much of the area was destroyed during World War II when houses took the near misses of bombs directed at Victoria Station. Happily, most of the rebuilding has been faithful to the original Greco-Roman style. If you are shopping around, note that although there are hundreds of hotels here, the majority are not up to standard. Victoria is not known for its sights, shopping, or entertainment. But its proximity to Victoria Station, London's transportation hub, makes getting around relatively easy.

**MELBOURNE HOUSE, 79 Belgrave Rd., London S.W.1. Tel. 071/828-3516.** 15 rms (none with bath). **Tube:** Victoria.

**$ Rates** (including English breakfast): £23 ($41.40) single; £32 ($57.60) double. No credit cards.

The list of hotels to avoid on B&B-packed Belgrave Road far exceed the recommendable choices. Melbourne House, far and away the best on the block, is the only one to earn a listing here. The crumbling front belies a clean, though plain, interior. And the airy rooms here are something of a novelty.

**MELITA HOUSE HOTEL, 33-35 Charlwood St., London S.W.1. Tel. 071/828-0471.** 18 rms (6 with bath). TV **Tube:** Victoria.

**$ Rates** (including continental breakfast): £24 ($43.20) basic single, £35 ($63) with shower and toilet; £33 ($59.40) basic double, £40 ($72) with shower and toilet. No credit cards.

An excellent example of the way quality rises and prices fall just off Belgrave Road. In this spotless and charming hotel, located on a quiet side street, breakfast is served in a ground-floor dining room, a refreshing change from the basements of most hotels.

To reach Charlwood Street, turn right off Belgrave Road, south of Warwick Way.

**THE OAK HOUSE, 29 Hugh St., London S.W.1. Tel. 071/834-7151.** 6 rms (none with bath). **Tube:** Victoria.

**$ Rates:** £26 ($46.80) twin. No credit cards.

One of my favorite hotels in this area is also one of the closest to Victoria Station, between Eccleston and Elizabeth bridges. Like the hotel itself, the sign hanging outside stands out from the other B&Bs on the block. It doesn't take a genius to figure out that the resident proprietors, Mr. and Mrs. Symington, are Scottish. The tartan carpeting used throughout the hotel complements the couple's charming accents. There are only six rooms here, all twins, and all very small. But the conscientious owners have fitted each room with orthopedic mattresses, built-in hairdryers, electric-shaver outlets, tea/coffeemaking facilities, a cutting board, a knife, and even a bottle opener. No advance reservations are accepted, so when you get to the station just cross your fingers and call.

### WARWICK WAY

Warwick Way is another hotel-lined thoroughfare, for the most part as undesirable as Belgrave Road. Out of dozens, only two hotels are recommendable, and then only when your other options in the area have been exhausted.

**ENRICO HOTEL, 77-79 Warwick Way, London S.W.1. Tel. 071/834-9538.** 26 rms (none with bath). **Tube:** Victoria.

**$ Rates** (including English breakfast): £24 ($43.20) single; £30 ($54) double. Prices increase by £2 ($3.60) if you stay only one night. No credit cards.

Enrico gets marks for its comfortable beds and cheery breakfast room. Period.

**ELIZABETH HOUSE, 118 Warwick Way, London S.W.1. Tel. 071/630-0741.** 27 rms (9 with bath). **Tube:** Victoria.

**$ Rates** (including continental breakfast): £22 ($39.60) single without bath; £35 ($63) double without bath; £37 ($66.60) basic twin, £39 ($70.20) with shower and toilet. No credit cards.

This is a YWCA guesthouse that accommodates men as well as women. The atmosphere is friendly, the house is clean, and the sparsely furnished rooms will please minimalists.

## NORTHERN BLOOMSBURY

At Bloomsbury's northern edge, opposite King's Cross and St. Pancras stations, are several hotel-packed streets, including Birkenhead, Crestfield, Argyle, and Argyle Square. The area is somewhat shabby and cannot compare with the attractiveness of the more expensive Russell Square area or with the bustle of Bayswater. But the many decrepit, several decent, and even some desirable hotels here are relatively unknown to American tourists, and are very competitively priced (read: cheap).

**MYRTLE HOTEL, 20 Argyle Square, London W.C.1. Tel. 071/837-5759.** 14 rms (none with bath). TV **Tube:** King's Cross.

**$ Rates** (including English breakfast): £20 ($36) single; £26 ($46.80) double. No credit cards.

Typical of the area with regard to comfort, services, and price, the Myrtle, like most hotels here, is centrally heated, and there are TVs and hot and cold running water in the bathless rooms. Accommodations are sparse but clean.

**CENTRAL HOTEL, 16–18 Argyle St., London W.C.1. Tel. 071/837-9008.** 31 rms (none with bath). TV **Tube:** King's Cross.

**$ Rates** (including English breakfast): £25 ($45) single; £30 ($54) double; £35 ($63) triple. MC, V.

One of the four Caruana brothers, the hotel's proprietors, will happily show you to a simple, reasonably sized room. If the Central is full, the staff will show you to their other hotel, the Fairway, across the street. It's not quite as nice; if you can, be choosy.

**ELMWOOD HOTEL, 19 Argyle Square, London W.C.1. Tel. 071/837-9361.** 11 rms (none with bath). TV **Tube:** King's Cross.

 **Rates** (including English breakfast): £18 ($32.40) single; £28 ($50.40) double. No credit cards.

An orange-and-white sign announces this nice B&B, which has been owned by the same resident proprietors for over 15 years. The wooden front door admits you to a hotel of a higher standard than most in the area.

## HUNTER STREET

On Hunter Street, equidistant from the Russell Square and King's Cross Underground stations, you'll find one budget establishment.

**CAMBRIA HOUSE, 37 Hunter St., London W.C.1. Tel. 071/837-1654.** 39 rms (none with bath). **Tube:** Russell Square.

**$ Rates** (including English breakfast): £22 ($39.60) single; £30 ($54) twin. Weekly discounts available. No credit cards.

Located at the corner of Tavistock Place, south of Cartwright Gardens, Cambria House is a Salvation Army establishment in a large red-brick building. Simple rooms and fairly strict rules are balanced by low rates. No alcohol is allowed and the house closes at 11pm, but there is a pub around the corner and late-night keys are available for a £2 ($3.60) deposit. As with most places run by religious groups, the decorator is obviously an ascetic.

## CHELSEA & SOUTH KENSINGTON

The expensive residential areas of Chelsea and South Kensington offer little in the way of accommodations for budget travelers. With few notable exceptions, the cost of lodging here reflects location rather than quality. Chelsea gained fame in the 19th century as London's Bohemia, a place for writers and artists. Thomas Carlyle, George Eliot, Oscar Wilde, Henry James . . . the list of famous former residents is seemingly endless. A room in adjacent South Kensington is only steps away from more than half a dozen top museums and the ritzy boutiques of Knightsbridge. It's unlikely that South Kensington or Chelsea will ever again be home to impoverished artists, as these posh areas are now two of the swankiest neighborhoods in London.

In addition to the establishments recommended below, a couple more Chelsea and South Kensington hotels appear in the next price category.

**OAKLEY HOTEL, 73 Oakley St., London S.W.3. Tel. 071/ 352-5599.** 11 rms (none with bath). **Tube:** Sloane Square.

**$ Rates** (including English breakfast): £19 ($34.20) single; £33 ($59.40) double, £35 ($63) twin; £10 ($18) per person in larger rooms. No credit cards.

Well-decorated rooms and a fun, friendly atmosphere make this economical hotel a welcome oasis in tab-happy Chelsea. The local council of this chic neighborhood forbids a "hotel" sign, but a knock on the green door will be answered by a friendly Australian. Aside from singles and twins, the hotel has several multishare rooms at great rates. All prices include a large breakfast and free use of the kitchen.

From the Sloane Square Underground, take a long walk, or the no. 11 or no. 22 bus down Kings Road to Oakley Street.

**MORE HOUSE, 53 Cromwell Rd., London S.W.7. Tel. 071/ 584-2040.** 55 rms (none with bath). **Tube:** Gloucester Road.

**$ Rates** (including English breakfast): £21 ($37.80) single; £34 ($61.20) twin; £44 ($79.20) triple. 10% discount for stays of one week or more. No credit cards. **Open:** June–Sept.

This Catholic-run dormitory with an institutional feel is home to foreign students during the school year, but singles and twins are rented to visitors of all faiths from June to September. The house is well located across from the Science Museum, and extremely functional. There is a refrigerator on every floor, microwave ovens for guests' use, laundry facilities, and a licensed bar.

Turn right from Gloucester Road Underground and walk 5 short blocks along Cromwell Road.

## EARL'S COURT

Although it is located just west of exclusive Chelsea and Knightsbridge, Earl's Court has been slow to achieve the classy status of its neighbors. There are dozens of hotels here; many are hostel-type multishare accommodations, and quality is often suspect. Earl's Court is well-located, however, and the many ultrabudget accommodations means inexpensive restaurants, pubs, and services are also nearby. Earl's Court tube station is located in the middle of Earl's Court Road, which, along with Old Brompton Road to the south, is the area's chief shopping strip. The main road also contains the world's greatest concentration of "bucket shops" (see "Getting There," in Chapter 2, for bucket-shop information), a must if you're in need of an onward airplane ticket. Affectionately dubbed "Kangaroo Court," Earl's Court is the unofficial headquarters of England's large, ever-changing Australian community.

**THE MANOR HOTEL, 23 Nevern Pl., London S.W.5. Tel. 071/370-6018.** 27 rms (12 with bath). **Tube:** Earl's Court Road.

**$ Rates** (including continental breakfast): £20 ($36) basic single, £24 ($43.20) with shower and toilet; £30 ($54) basic double, £35 ($63) with shower and toilet; £40 ($72) basic triple, £45 ($81) with shower and toilet. Discount for stays of one week or more. No credit cards.

Despite threadbare carpets and some peeling wallpaper, the Manor is light and airy, and happily devoid of the dark Dickensian feel that plagues most of the area's hotels.

The hotel is located 2 blocks north of the Underground station, at the corner of Templeton Place.

**HOTEL BOKA, 33–35 Eardley Crescent, London S.W.5. Tel. 071/370-1388.** 52 rms (23 with shower). **Tube:** Earl's Court Road.

**$ Rates** (including English breakfast): £25 ($45) basic single, £29 ($52.20) with shower; £35 ($63) basic double, £38 ($68.40) with shower; £38 ($68.40) basic twin, £40 ($72) with shower; £16 ($28.80) per person in a multishare. V.

Boka's bright blue-tiled columns stand out in the middle of a pretty Victorian crescent. Inside, expect a friendly staff, unusually high ceilings, and attractive antique bureaus and dressers, some with wood inlay.

From Earl's Court Underground, take the Warwick Road exit, cross the street, and turn left to Eardley Crescent.

**AARON HOUSE, 17 Courtfield Gardens, London S.W.5.**

**Tel. 071/370-3991.** 22 rms (10 with bath). **Tube:** Earl's Court Road.

**$ Rates** (including continental breakfast): £20 ($36) basic single, £25 ($45) with shower and toilet; £32 ($57.60) basic double, £36 ($64.80) with shower and toilet; £43 ($77.40) basic triple. No credit cards.

Announced only by a small gold sign, to the left of the hotel's front door, Aaron House is perhaps the nicest budget hotel in Earl's Court. Beveled glass and beautiful moldings and cornices are the trademarks of this understated B&B. The front rooms, all with bath, are particularly large and overlook a peaceful Victorian square. Televisions are rented for £1 ($1.80) per day.

The hotel is about 3 blocks east of Earl's Court Underground, on the west side of Courtfield Gardens.

## ELSEWHERE AROUND TOWN

**WYNDHAM HOTEL, 30 Wyndham St., London W.1. Tel. 071/723-7204.** 11 rms (all with shower). TV **Tube:** Baker Street.

**$ Rates** (including continental breakfast): £20 ($36) single; £31 ($55.80) twin, £36 ($64.80) triple. *These rates are for Frommer readers only.* No credit cards.

Tucked away on a quiet Marylebone street, this hotel stands apart from others both physically and for value. All 11 rooms have a shower, TV, and coffee/teamaking facilities. Owner Geoffrey Lowe has promised special low rates to bearers of this book, a deep discount off his regular prices.

From the Baker Street Underground, cross Marylebone Road and turn right. Wyndham Street is the fifth on your left.

**ABBEVILLE GUESTHOUSE, 89 Abbeville Rd., London S.W.4. Tel. 071/622-5360.** 7 rms (none with bath). TV **Tube:** Clapham Common.

**$ Rates** (including continental breakfast): £15 ($27) single; £29 ($52.20) twin. Discounts offered for stays of 3 nights or more. No credit cards.

In up-and-coming Clapham Common, south of the River Thames, this quiet home offers good accommodations at reasonable rates. Mr. and Mrs. Coleman have been welcoming guests into their home for about three decades, and they know how to please picky people.

Take the Underground to Clapham Common, leave at the south exit, and walk along Southside Street (with the park on your right) for about 100 yards. Turn left onto Crescent Lane (not Grove), which after 300 more yards crosses Abbeville Road.

**MRS. WARD'S GUESTHOUSE, 98 Hambalt Rd., London S.W.4. Tel. 071/673-1077.** 5 rms (none with bath). **Tube:** Clapham Common.

**$ Rates** (including English breakfast): £10 ($18) per person. No credit cards.

Mrs. Ward's unbelievably low rates include a hearty breakfast cooked by the affable owner. This is one of the best budget deals in London, but the house has only four double rooms (and a tiny single), making it essential that you call in advance.

From Crescent Lane (see Abbeville Guesthouse, above), turn right on Abbeville Road, and left on Hambalt where the shops begin. A 10-minute walk from Clapham Common tube station.

## 2. DOUBLES FOR LESS THAN £38.50 ($69.30)

### BAYSWATER

**LORDS HOTEL, 20-22 Leinster Square, London W.2. Tel. 071/229-8877,** fax 071/229-8377. 42 rms (12 with shower). **Tube:** Bayswater.

**$ Rates** (including continental breakfast): £25 ($45) basic single, £32 ($57.60) with shower, £43 ($77.40) with shower and toilet; £37 ($66.60) basic twin, £44 ($79.20) with shower, £55 ($99) with shower and toilet; £48 ($86.40) basic triple, £63 ($113.40) with shower, £73 ($131.40) with shower and toilet. AE, DC, MC, V.

This well-run budget establishment offers basic rooms that are both

### FROMMER'S SMART TRAVELER: HOTELS

VALUE-CONSCIOUS TRAVELERS SHOULD TAKE ADVANTAGE OF THE FOLLOWING:

1. Travel in the off-season. Room rates tumble—sometimes by as much as 30%—and often there is room for further negotiation.
2. Long-term stays. Many hotels will offer discounts to guests staying a week or more.

QUESTIONS TO ASK IF YOU'RE ON A BUDGET

1. Do you have anything cheaper? You may be surprised how quickly rates can drop when you make it clear you're shopping around.
2. Can I see the room first? Hoteliers are more likely to offer their nicest rooms to travelers who look before they buy.

clean and neat. Some rooms are equipped with televisions and radios, and a few have balconies—all at no extra charge. The hotel caters to people of all ages, though the basement bar (which stays open late) often gets quite lively and crowded with young people.

From the Bayswater Underground, turn left onto Moscow Road, then right at the Russian Orthodox church (Ilchester Gardens); Lords is 2 blocks up on your left.

**STRUTTON PARK HOTEL, 45 Palace Court, London W.2. Tel. 071/727-5074).** 28 rms (all with shower). TV TEL **Tube:** Bayswater.

**$ Rates** (including English breakfast): £37–£42 ($66.60–$75.60) twin. AE, DC, MC, V.

This small and pretty hotel offers twin rooms only, all with shower (no private toilets). There is an elevator to take guests up to their rooms—all equipped with television sets and telephones—and down to a full breakfast.

From the Bayswater Underground, turn left onto Moscow Road and walk about 6 blocks to Palace Court.

**DYLAN HOTEL, 14 Devonshire Terrace, London W.2. Tel. 071/723-3280.** 20 rms (11 with bath). **Tube:** Paddington.

**$ Rates** (including English breakfast): £28 ($50.40) basic single; £36 ($64.80) basic double, £42 ($75.60) with shower and toilet. AE, DC, MC, V.

The proprietors want travelers to think of this establishment as a "home away from home," and you probably will. Mr. and Mrs. Griffiths live here themselves and they take pride in offering their budget-oriented guests the comforts of home. Little touches like coffee/teamaking facilities in the bedrooms, cloth tablecloths, and a cup-and-saucer collection in the breakfast room add to this hotel's charm.

From Paddington Station, follow Craven Road 6 blocks; Devonshire Terrace is on your right.

## NORFOLK SQUARE

Norfolk Square is a budget hotel–packed horseshoe ringing a green just steps south of Paddington Station. There are too many hotels with too few distinguishing marks to mention them all here, but a close inspection has revealed two of the best.

**TUDOR COURT & GALLENCO HOTEL, 10–12 Norfolk Square, London W.2. Tel. 071/723-6553,** fax 071/723-0727. 35 rms (6 with shower and toilet). TV **Tube:** Paddington.

**$ Rates** (including English breakfast): £25 ($45) basic single; £37 ($66.60) basic double, £45 ($81) with shower and toilet; £48 ($86.40) basic triple, £55 ($99) with shower and toilet. AE, DC, MC, V.

This B&B is managed by outgoing owner Dave Gupta. Unlike the singles, which tend to be on the small side, doubles here are well-proportioned, and all rooms are neat and clean.

**DOLPHIN HOTEL, 34 Norfolk Square, London W.2. Tel. 071/402-4943.** 18 rms (7 with bath). TV **Tube:** Paddington.

**$ Rates** (including continental breakfast): £27 ($48.60) basic single; £37 ($66.60) basic double, £45 ($81) with shower and toilet; £43 ($77.40) basic triple. No credit cards.

In-room refrigerators, coffeemakers, and (sometimes) telephones help this hotel stand out from its neighbors. Otherwise, its recently redecorated rooms are typical of the square and a good bet. There is a £3 ($5.40) supplement for an English breakfast, which, like the standard continental, is served in your room.

## VICTORIA

**EASTON HOTEL, 36–40 Belgrave Rd., London S.W.1. Tel. 071/834-5938.** 55 rms (11 with bath). **Tube:** Victoria.

**$ Rates** (including English breakfast): £28 ($50.40) basic single, £37 ($66.60) with shower and toilet; £36 ($64.80) basic double, £46 ($82.80) with shower and toilet. AC, MC, V.

Rooms here are small but adequate, and some on the ground floor let you avoid stairs. An attractive licensed bar almost makes up for the distracting wood paneling on the floor of the breakfast room. The hotel is located on a major thoroughfare just behind Victoria Station.

**LUNA HOUSE, 47–49 Belgrave Rd., London S.W.1. Tel. 071/834-5897.** 18 rms (10 with bath). **Tube:** Victoria.

**$ Rates** (including English breakfast): £19 ($34.20) basic single; £37 ($66.60) basic twin, £45 ($81) with shower and toilet. No credit cards.

Farther along the street is this friendly, family-run hotel recognizable by the bright orange lettering on the columns out front. A hearty breakfast is served in twin dining rooms, which are separated into smoking and no-smoking sections. TVs are in most rooms.

**OXFORD HOUSE HOTEL, 92–94 Cambridge St., London S.W.1. Tel. 071/834-6467.** 17 rms (none with bath). **Tube:** Victoria.

**$ Rates** (including English breakfast): £26 ($46.80) single; £36 ($64.80) double, £46 ($82.80) triple. Prices increase by £2 ($3.60) if you stay only one night. No credit cards.

This hotel is owned by an interior designer, Yanus Kader, and his wife, Terri. Rooms are comfortable and pretty, featuring floral motifs and coordinated curtains. The beautiful dining area, with its open kitchen, will remind every traveler of home. In the backyard, visit Hannibal, the couple's large and friendly rabbit.

The hotel is south of Belgrave Road near Gloucester Street.

## BLOOMSBURY

Bloomsbury's proximity to the West End in general, and to Soho in particular, has long made it a desirable area for tourists. It's also the location for the University of London and the British Museum. From about 1906, a brilliant circle of writers and artists, including Virginia Woolf and E. M. Forster, lived in the neighborhood and called themselves the "Bloomsbury Group," further validating the neighborhood's intellectual and artistic claims. Although heavy demand is often reflected in high prices, there are still some good bargains to be found.

## GOWER STREET

Gower Street's budget hotels are some of the city's most popular. Most of the B&Bs that line this street are so similar to one another that only their addresses distinguish them. Stairs are steep, rooms are basic (almost none with bath), and prices are fairly uniform. Special touches and extra-friendly management do set a few apart from the rest. They are listed here geographically, away from Russell Square. Incidentally, the best way to reach the Gower Street hotels is from the Goodge Street Underground. Cross into Chenies Street and turn left onto Gower.

**JESMOND HOTEL, 63 Gower St., London W.C.1. Tel. 071/636-3199.** 15 rms (none with bath). **Tube:** Goodge Street.

**$ Rates** (including English breakfast): £25 ($45) single; £37 ($66.60) twin. No credit cards.

The hotel's proprietors, Mr. and Mrs. Beynon, have been to the United States many times and are acutely aware of American habits and desires. All rooms have coffee/teamaking facilities.

**THE RIDGEMONT PRIVATE HOTEL, 65 Gower St., London W.C.1. Tel. 071/636-1141.** 15 rms (none with bath). **Tube:** Goodge Street.

**$ Rates** (including English breakfast): £23 ($41.40) single; £36 ($64.80) double. No credit cards.

The Ridgemont's friendly atmosphere and warm-hearted Welsh proprietors, Royden and Gwen Rees, make it another good choice along the strip.

**HOTEL CAVENDISH, 75 Gower St., London W.C.1. Tel. 071/636-9079.** 20 rms (none with bath). **Tube:** Goodge Street.

**$ Rates** (including English breakfast): £27 ($48.60) single; £37 ($66.60) twin. No credit cards.

This is a nicely furnished, clean, and cozy home run by Mrs. Phillips.

**ARRAN HOUSE HOTEL, 77 Gower St., London W.C.1. Tel. 071/636-2186,** fax 071/436-5328. 26 rms (4 with bath). **Tube:** Goodge Street.

**$ Rates** (including English breakfast): £25 ($45) basic single; £36 ($64.80) basic double, £55 ($99) with shower and toilet. MC, V.

Arran House stands out on the block because of its exceptionally kind resident proprietor, Maj. W. J. Richards. He has ensured that even guests in the front rooms get a quiet night's sleep by soundproofing all the windows, a modification that I can assure you really works! In addition to laundry and coffee/teamaking facilities, the hotel offers light meals, prepared by the owner's son, a professional caterer.

**AROSFA HOTEL, 83 Gower St., London W.C.1. Tel. 071/636-2115.** 13 rms (none with bath). **Tube:** Goodge Street.

**$ Rates** (including breakfast): £23 ($41.40) single; £33 ($59.40) double. No credit cards.

This very austere hotel is also the least expensive on the block, and represents very good value. Located at the corner of Torrington Place across from Dillons bookstore, it is the farthest north of the Gower Street B&Bs. Prices here include a breakfast of eggs, toast, and coffee or tea.

## TAVISTOCK PLACE

From the Russell Square Underground, walk straight across to Marchmont Street, and continue straight for two blocks. A left turn here, just before Cartwright Gardens, will put you on Tavistock Place.

**ST. ATHANS HOTEL, 20 Tavistock Place, London W.C.1. Tel. 071/837-9140.** 80 rms (3 with bath). **Tube:** Russell Square.

**$ Rates** (including English breakfast): £28 ($50.40) basic single, £35 ($63) with shower and toilet; £38 ($68.40) basic twin, £48 ($86.40) with shower and toilet. *These rates are for Frommer readers only.* AE, DC, MC, V.

Owner Hans Geyer has guaranteed very special rates to guests who can show him the entire current edition of this book. Room rates in this well-decorated and ideally located hotel include a huge breakfast often cooked by Hans himself.

**GOODWOOD HOTEL, 38-40 Tavistock Place, London W.C.1. Tel. 071/837-0855.** 18 rms (none with bath). TV **Tube:** Russell Square.

**$ Rates** (including continental breakfast): £26 ($46.80) single; £38 ($68.40) double. AE, DC, MC, V.

A few doors down from the St. Athans, the rates here prove a very good value.

## BEDFORD PLACE

Just south of Russell Square, right in the heart of Bloomsbury is Bedford Place, another hotel-lined block. Almost every hotel here charges a uniform £45 ($81) for a double, and if you can afford it, this street is well worth checking out.

**REPTON HOUSE HOTEL, 31 Bedford Place, London W.C.2. Tel. 071/636-7045.** 38 rms (16 with bath). **Tube:** Russell Square.

**$ Rates** (including continental breakfast): £25 ($45) basic single;

£36 ($64.80) basic double, £45 ($81) with shower and toilet; £16 ($28.80) per bed in multishare. No credit cards. **Open:** Apr–Sept.

The last hotel on the block within our budget is open to tourists during summer months only and definitely worth a stay. The owner stresses cleanliness rather than fanciness, and the sparse but spotless rooms bear this out.

Take the tube to Russell Square, turn left, and walk to the square's south side.

## CHELSEA & SOUTH KENSINGTON

**MAGNOLIA HOTEL, 104-105 Oakley St., London S.W.3. Tel. 071/352-0187.** 21 rms (7 with bath). TV **Tube:** Sloane Square.

**$ Rates** (including continental breakfast with boiled egg): £27 ($48.60) basic single; £37 ($66.60) basic double, £43 ($77.40) with shower and toilet; £47 ($84.60) basic triple. AE, MC, V.

Located just off King's Road in Chelsea, this is an extraordinarily well kept bed-and-breakfast with contemporary decor. The smart, clean rooms have recently been recarpeted and painted by the Magnolia's new Yugoslavian owners.

From the Sloane Square Underground Station, take a long walk or bus no. 11 or no. 22 down King's Road.

**THE QUEENSBURY COURT HOTEL, 7-11 Queensbury Place., London S.W.7. Tel. 071/589-3693.** 35 rms (15 with bath). **Tube:** Gloucester Road.

**$ Rates** (including continental breakfast): £27 ($48.60) basic single, £32 ($57.60) with shower and toilet; £38 ($68.40) basic twin, £42 ($75.60) with shower and toilet. No credit cards.

Home to visiting students, this hotel is also open to tourists year-round. This small, pretty hotel offers clean, simple rooms and a great location. Not recommended for conservative adults, as students are prone to partying.

To reach the hotel, turn right from Gloucester Road Underground, and walk 5 short blocks along Cromwell Road, then turn right just past More House.

# 3. SUPER-BUDGET CHOICES

## PRIVATE HOSTELS

Many hotels offer dormitory accommodations (often called "multishares") where single visitors share a room with other travelers. If you are traveling with a backpack and arrive at one of London's major railroad stations, you may be handed advertisements for these "unofficial" hostels. These are no doubt legitimate, but investigate the location before you commit. In addition to Hotel Boka in Earl's

## FROMMER'S COOL FOR KIDS

### Hotels

**Oakely Hotel** (*see p. 74*) Families will appreciate the Oakley's well-decorated rooms and friendly atmosphere. A good pick in an otherwise pricey area.

**Oxford House Hotel** (*see p. 79*) In addition to comfortable and pretty rooms, rates include breakfast in the Kader family's beautiful open kitchen. In the backyard, kids will love Hannibal, the couple's large and friendly rabbit.

**Carr Saunders Hall** (*see p. 86*) Although it is open to tourists only during summer months, the self-contained apartments offered by this student dormitory are some of the best priced in London. Located near the West End, each has a private bath and kitchen. Write for reservations as far in advance as possible.

**Camelot Hotel** (*see p. 88*) Near Bayswater's Paddington Station, the Camelot is the best choice for families amidst the "splurge" hotels. Rooms are on the smallish side, but in London, that's par for the course. All are equipped with color TV (with free in-house movies), and include an all-you-can-eat breakfast.

Court, the Oakley Hotel in Chelsea, and the Repton House Hotel in Bloomsbury, the following hotels offer multishare accommodations along with private rooms.

**KENSINGTON GARDENS HOTEL, 84 Kensington Gardens, London W.2. Tel. 071/229-2913.** 19 rms (7 are multishares; none with bath). **Tube:** Bayswater.

**$ Rates** (including English breakfast): £9.50 ($17.10) per person per night, £51.50 ($92.70) per week, in a multishare. No credit cards.

This Bayswater hotel is known for its friendly Australian management and party atmosphere. It is well located, near the late-night budget eateries along Queensway, and it is well served by transportation links to the West End. Prices include a large breakfast and free use of kitchen facilities.

From Bayswater Underground, turn left onto Queensway; make another left at Whiteley's Shopping Center and Kensington Gardens is just up on your right.

**DEAN COURT HOTEL, 57 Inverness Terrace, London W.2. Tel. 071/229-2961.** 16 rms (25 multishare beds; none with bath). **Tube:** Bayswater.

**$ Rates** (including continental breakfast): £9.50 ($17.10) per person per night, £51.50 ($92.70) per week, in a multishare; £28 ($50.40) per night twin. No credit cards.

This hotel overlooks a quiet Bayswater street, just 50 yards from bustling Queensway. Recently renovated rooms, a large breakfast, and capable management are all hallmarks of this top budget hotel. There are rarely, if ever, more than four people sharing a room, but if you require more privacy, ask for one of the well-furnished twins.

**NEW KENT HOTEL, 55 Inverness Terrace, London W.2. Tel. 071/229-9982.** 16 rms (25 multishare beds; none with bath). **Tube:** Bayswater.

**$ Rates** (including English breakfast): £9.50 ($17.10) per person per night, £51.50 ($92.70) per week, in a multishare; £28 ($50.40) per night twin. No credit cards.

With the same owner and same integrity as the adjacent Dean Court, this hotel is clean, friendly, and recently redecorated.

From Bayswater Underground, cross Queensway onto Inverness Place. Inverness Terrace is just one block away.

## IYHF HOSTELS

The International Youth Hostel Federation (IYHF) has four establishments in central London, all of which are very crowded during the summer. You have to have a membership card to stay at one of the organization's hostels, available for £8 ($14.40) at the YHA Shop, 14 Southampton St., W.C.2 (tel. 071/836-8541). The shop is open Monday, Wednesday, Friday, and Saturday from 9:30am to 6pm; Tuesday 10am to 6pm; Thursday 9:30am to 7pm. Like all of London's hostels, the YHA Shop accepts MasterCard and VISA.

The hostels are clean, but sterile in atmosphere, and breakfast is additional. All hostels accept MasterCard and VISA, and you can save around £2 ($3.60) by using your own sheets.

**HOLLAND HOUSE, Holland Park, London W.8. Tel. 071/937-0748.** 190 beds. **Tube:** Holland Park.

**$ Rates:** £9 ($16.20) per person per night for travelers over 21 years if you bring your own sheets; £11.50 ($20.70) with sheets. MC, V.

This hostel enjoys the most beautiful setting of all London's IYHF hostels. It's located right in the middle of Kensington's green Holland Park.

**EARL'S COURT YOUTH HOSTEL, 38 Bolton Gardens, London S.W.5. Tel. 071/373-7083.** 100 beds. **Tube:** Earl's Court.

**$ Rates:** £11 ($19.80) per person per night for travelers over 21 years if you bring your own sheets; £13.50 ($24.30) with sheets and continental breakfast. MC, V.

Located near Holland House, in well-positioned, but slightly seedy Earl's Court. It's lively, and stores in the area tend to stay open late.

Exit Earl's Court Underground and turn right. Bolton Gardens is the fifth street on your left.

**CARTER LANE YOUTH HOSTEL, 36 Carter Lane, London E.C.4. Tel. 071/236-4965.** 280 beds. **Tube:** St. Paul's.

**$ Rates:** £7.50 ($13.50) per person per night for travelers over 21 years (bring your own sheets). MC, V.

After more than a year's worth of renovations, Carter Lane reopened in the summer of 1991 with new walls, beds, and appliances. The hostel is situated smack-dab in the heart of The City of London on a small back street near St. Paul's Cathedral; a location good for sightseeing, but poor for restaurants and nightlife, as everything in The City closes when the bankers go home.

From St. Paul's Underground, turn right and make your way toward the front steps of the cathedral; follow Dean's Court, a small street, to the corner of Carter Lane.

**OXFORD STREET YOUTH HOSTEL, 14–18 Noel St., W.1. Tel. 071/734-1618.** 87 beds. **Tube:** Oxford Circus.

**$ Rates:** £13.50 ($24.30) per person per night including sheets. MC, V.

London's newest "official" hostel is also the smallest and most centrally located. Not surprisingly, it costs more but, if you can get a reservation, it's well worth it.

## Ys

Several YMCAs and YWCAs offer reliable accommodations at great prices, and most include dinner daily. Some encourage long-term stays with cheap weekly rates, which seems to work because most are filled with long-timers throughout the year. Although they are not all well located, there are over a dozen Y hotels in the city. In a pinch, phone the **National Council of YMCAs** (tel. 081/520-5599) for a list of members with available rooms.

**BARBICAN YMCA, 2 Fann St., London E.C.2. Tel. 071/628-0697.** 196 rms (none with bath). **Tube:** Barbican.

**$ Rates** (including English breakfast): £17.50 ($31.50) per person per day without dinner, £95 ($171) per week including dinner. Reserve at least 2 months ahead. No credit cards.

The good news is that this well-located hotel can accommodate almost 250 people. The bad news is that it often does. Make reservations as early as possible.

**LONDON CITY YMCA, 8 Errol St., London E.C.1. Tel. 071/628-8832.** 111 rms (none with bath). TV **Tube:** Barbican or Moorgate.

**$ Rates** (including English breakfast and dinner): £22 ($39.60) per person per night, £100 ($180) per week. No credit cards.

Located near the Barbican Y, this hotel offers a similar standard of accommodations, all in single rooms. Although this place is generally booked with students during the school term, you can probably find space here during the summer.

**INDIAN YMCA, 41 Fitzroy Square, London W.1. Tel. 071/387-0411.** 100 rms (4 with bath). **Tube:** Warren Street.

**$ Rates** (including English breakfast and dinner): £25 ($45) single with or without bath. Discount for stays of one week or more. No credit cards.

Although preference is given to Indian citizens and long-term stays, the hotel does maintain a few beds for tourists of other nationalities. Singles only.

## UNIVERSITY ACCOMMODATIONS

From early July to late September (and sometimes during Christmas and Easter), dozens of dormitories open their doors to tourists. Bedrooms are almost all uniformly sparse, and some residence halls only offer singles, but they are relatively inexpensive and centrally located. Try to reserve months in advance as the rooms are often packed solid. Even if you don't have reservations, though, it can't hurt to call and see if they have a cancellation or a "no-show."

**CARR SAUNDERS HALL, 18–24 Fitzroy St., London W.1. Tel. 071/580-6338.** 223 rms (3 with bath; 78 self-contained apts). **Tube:** Warren Street.

**$ Rates** (including English breakfast): £20 ($36) single with or without bath; £259 ($466.20) per week for an apartment. No credit cards. **Open:** Early July–late Sept.

The best thing about this hall is its location, near inexpensive restaurants and the West End. There are only single rooms here, and all are small and basic. But there is a communal kitchen and laundry facilities. Couples may be interested in renting one of the hall's apartments, which feature private bath and kitchen.

**IMPERIAL COLLEGE, 15 Princes Gardens, London S.W.7. Tel. 071/589-5111, ext. 3600.** 400 rms (none with bath). **Tube:** South Kensington.

**$ Rates:** £22 ($39.60) single, including breakfast; £69 ($124.20) per week in shared rooms, without breakfast. No credit cards. **Open:** Early July–late Sept.

This South Kensington dormitory offers luxurious accommodations beside Hyde Park and Royal Albert Hall. The minimum stay in a multishare is 1 week, but if you're going to be in town that long, you won't mind locating here. Singles are more expensive, though still reasonable by London standards. When phoning, note that the reception is open from 10am to 1pm and again from 2 to 5pm.

**JOHN ADAMS HALL, 15–23 Endsleigh St., London W.C.1. Tel. 071/387-4796.** 146 rms (none with bath). **Tube:** Euston Square.

**$ Rates** (including English breakfast): £20 ($36) single; £40 ($72) twin. MC, V. **Open:** Early July–late Sept, and Easter holidays.

These simple accommodations are typically Georgian, with high ceilings and large windows.

**PASSFIELD HALL, 1 Endsleigh Place, London W.C.1. Tel. 071/387-3584.** 198 beds. **Tube:** Euston Square.

**$ Rates** (including English breakfast): £20 ($36) single; £16 ($28.80) per person in a multishare. No credit cards. **Open:** Early July–late Sept, and Easter and Christmas holidays.

Somewhat cheaper and much more basic than nearby John Adams Hall, the facilities here are good, and include a games room, as well as cooking and laundry facilities.

**ROSEBERY HALL, 90 Rosebery Ave., London E.C.1. Tel. 071/278-3251.** 170 rms (none with bath). **Tube:** Angel.

**$ Rates** (including English breakfast): £22 ($39.60) single. No credit cards. **Open:** Early July–late Sept.

This may be the fanciest hotel of the lot, complete with well-furnished modern single rooms, a bar, and a nice breakfast room. Owned by the London School of Economics, the hall is well located near the Camden Passage antiques market.

## CAMPING

The Queen's constables are touchy about people sleeping in London's Royal Parks, and for safety's sake, it's probably not a good idea anyway. Here are two listings.

**TENT CITY, Old Oak Common Lane, London W.3. Tel. 081/743-5708.** 450 beds; 130 sites. **Tube:** East Acton.

**$ Rates:** £5.50 ($9.90) per person under the field tent; £7 ($12.60) per space when you bring your own roof. No credit cards. **Open:** Late May–early Oct.

There is something of a party atmosphere here when hundreds of summer tourists descend on Tent City's grounds. You don't need to bring your own roof, as there are dormitory-style accommodations under about a dozen large field tents. The campground is a short 10-minute walk from East Acton Underground on the Central Line.

**HACKNEY CAMPING, Millfields Rd., London E.5. Tel. 081/985-7656.** 200 sites. **Directions:** see below.

**$ Rates:** £2.50 ($4.50) per person. **Open:** Mid-June to late Aug.

This large, traditional site takes up part of an East End park beside a canal 4 miles from central London. The campground offers toilets, showers, baggage storage, and a shop.

From Victoria Station take bus 38 to Clapton Pond, then walk down Mullfields Road to Mandeville Street and over the bridge to the site.

## RVs

If you're traveling around Britain by recreational vehicle, the London Tourist Board can supply you with a free brochure listing the many sites in and around London that offer full hookup facilities.

## 4. LONG-TERM STAYS

When staying for a month or more, it's economical to rent an apartment (called a "flat") or a bed-sitting room ("bed-sit")—usually a room in a house, often with cooking facilities. Landlords usually require a security deposit, equal to 1 month's rent, returnable when you vacate the space in good condition. The magazines *Loot,* the *London Weekly Advertiser,* and *Daltons Weekly* are all issued on Thursday and contain good listings. The free, alternative weekly *Capital Gay* also has listings. Every Tuesday at 11am, *Capital Radio* distributes a free list of available flat shares in the lobby of their Euston Tower building at Euston Road, N.W.1 (tube: Warren Street).

Another good place to look for apartments and flat shares is on **bulletin boards** in the area where you're interested in living. The largest and most famous of these is at 214 Earl's Court Rd., next to the Earl's Court Underground.

Finally, there are a number of accommodation agencies that will do the footwork for you. **Jenny Jones Agency,** 40 South Molton St., London W.1 (tel. 493-4801), specializes in low-cost rentals of three months or more, and charges no fees to renters. The office is open Monday through Thursday from 9:30am to 2pm, Friday from 9:30am to 5:30pm. Contact the London Tourist Board for a list of all of London's rental agencies.

## 5. WORTH THE EXTRA BUCKS

Hundreds of hotels fall just slightly beyond our budget, but the following have been selected for their particularly good value.

**MERRYFIELD HOUSE, 42 York St., London W.1. Tel. 071/935-8326.** 7 rms (all with bath). TV **Tube:** Baker Street.

**$ Rates** (including English breakfast): £35 ($63) single; £45 ($81) double. Add £2 ($3.60) per room per night for stays under 4 nights. No credit cards.

This exceedingly friendly hotel is in the Marylebone section of London, just south of Regent's Park, 3 blocks from the Baker Street Underground. Seven compact doubles all have private facilities, a color TV, a hairdryer, and a clock-radio. Owner Anthony Tyler-Smith and his cat, Mimi, live on the premises, and if you are lucky enough to get a room in this hotel, you will enjoy their warm hospitality and a hot breakfast served each morning in your room. York Street is 2 blocks south of Marylebone Road, just off Baker Street.

**CAMELOT HOTEL, 45 Norfolk Square, London W.2. Tel. 071/262-1980.** 44 rms (30 with bath). TV **Tube:** Paddington.

**$ Rates** (including English breakfast): £38 ($68.40) basic single,

£45 ($81) with shower, £55 ($99) with shower and toilet; £74 ($133.20) double with shower and toilet; £85 ($153) triple with shower and toilet. MC, V.

Any way you look at it, this artfully decorated hotel is one of the best-value splurges in London. The ultramodern interior, painted in tasteful pastels, combines the looks and services of a top hotel with the charm and prices of something more modest. All rooms have color TV (with free in-house movies), radio, and tea/coffeemaking facilities. A cooked breakfast with unlimited helpings is also included. Norfolk Square is in Bayswater, one block south of Paddington Station off London Street.

**HARLINGFORD HOTEL, 61–63 Cartwright Gardens, London W.C.1. Tel. 071/387-1551.** 44 rms (30 with bath). TV TEL **Tube:** Russell Square.

**$ Rates** (including English breakfast): £35 ($63) basic single, £45 ($81) with shower and toilet; £49 ($88.20) basic double, £56 ($100.80) with shower and toilet. MC, V.

The Harlingford is the nicest hotel on Bloomsbury's well-located Georgian crescent. You'll be particularly pleased by the bright ground-floor dining room where a hearty breakfast is served every morning. Rooms are equipped with coffee/teamaking facilities, as well as televisions, but let the well-furnished, cozy communal lounge entice you away from the box. A coffee machine on the landing sits next to a free ice dispenser for chilling your bubbly. Cartwright Gardens is located 3 blocks north of the Russell Square Underground.

**ASTER HOUSE HOTEL, 3 Sumner Place, London S.W.7. Tel. 071/581-5888.** 12 rms (all with bath). TV TEL **Tube:** South Kensington.

**$ Rates** (including breakfast): £55 ($99) single; £77 ($138.60) double. AE, MC, V.

Aster House is the most beautiful of a number of small bed-and-breakfasts on this quiet South Kensington street. The pride with which owners Rachel and Peter Carapiet run this hotel is evident the moment you step into the plushly carpeted interior. All rooms have private facilities featuring amenities usually found in more expensive hotels. Take special note of the award-winning garden in the rear. The enormous breakfast buffet includes the usual eggs and sausages, as well as fresh fruits, cold meats, cheeses, yogurt, and meusli. The meal is served in L'Orangerie, the beautiful glass-covered pièce de résistance of this special hotel.

From the South Kensington Station, walk 3 blocks down Old Brompton Road to Sumner Place on your left.

# CHAPTER 5

# LONDON DINING



It's not that England lacks a national cuisine; it's just that the country's national cuisine is lacking! Deep-fried fish and chips is the national dish, and bangers (sausages), fried eggs, and doughy meat pies also enjoy wide popularity. It's all pretty caloric and none too healthy, but it is hearty and filling. Portions are usually large, and often tasty. It's doubtful if you'll see much here that you haven't seen before. Meals often begin with an appetizer (called a "starter"), and conclude with coffee and dessert. Vegetables (often just called "veg") are usually served with the main course, and whether they are carrots, peas, or both, they are invariably boiled lifeless.

London's ethnic restaurants are some of the city's best, and several interesting selections are listed below. Indian is probably the most popular foreign food, and it is usually modified to suit the Western palate.

## TIPS, TAXES & SERVICE CHARGES

Many restaurants automatically add a 12½% tip to the bill, a policy which will be noted on the menu. When it's not, most waiters expect a tip equaling 10% to 15% of the bill. When paying by credit card, note whether a tip has already been figured into the total. Too many restaurants leave the tip space blank, fooling customers into tipping twice.

Without exception, tax is always included in the menu price. Although it is less frequent in the budget category, some restaurants add a small service charge (in lieu of a tip)—50p to £1.50 ($.90 to $2.70) per person—to each bill. The restaurant's policy will be printed on the menu.

## DINING HOURS & RESERVATIONS

Breakfast, which is included in the cost of most hotel rooms, is usually served from about 7 to 9am (later on weekends). Whether you eat in a pub or restaurant, lunch is most often served between noon and 3pm, while dinner is eaten anywhere between 5:30 and 10pm. Unlike most of continental Europe, Britons dine early; don't expect much choice after 10:30pm.

Although few are listed in this budget guide, most of the city's fancier restaurants accept reservations. Reservations are essential on weekends, and recommended throughout the week for trendy or touristy eateries. When reservations are accepted, the policy is noted in the listings below.

**Restaurant Switchboard** (tel. 071/888-8080) is a free referral and reservation service with information and listings on hundreds of centrally located eateries. Tell them what you are looking for in terms of cuisine, location, and price, and they will make suggestions. The switchboard is open Monday through Saturday from 9am to 8pm.

## 1. MEALS FOR LESS THAN £5 ($9)

### IN & AROUND SOHO

**POLLO, 20 Old Compton St., W.1. Tel. 071/734-5917.**
**Cuisine:** ITALIAN. **Tube:** Leicester Square.
**$ Prices:** £4–£6 ($7.20–$10.80). No credit cards.
**Open:** Mon–Sat 11:30am–11:30pm.

This is an authentic Italian restaurant, located right in the heart of the hustle. Although there are lots of tables, this place is so popular that a line of waiting diners regularly stretches out the door. It's packed because the atmosphere is good, the food is great, and the prices are almost embarrassingly low. There must be 150 menu items, and few top £4 ($7.20). Even chicken cacciatore or principessa style (with asparagus) is under £3.25 ($5.85). And pastas of every shape and size are served with so many different kinds of sauces that even a native Italian couldn't keep up. Carbonara, fiorentina, romana, slavia, Alfredo—you name it, they serve it—and the helpful staff is happy to explain it all in plain English. The list of Italian desserts is impressive, too. The restaurant is near Frith Street, a few doors down from the Prince Edward Theater.

**THE STAR CAFE, 22b Great Chapel St., W.1. Tel. 071/437-8778.**
**Cuisine:** ENGLISH. **Tube:** Tottenham Court Road.
**$ Prices:** £2.50–£4.50 ($4.50–$8.10). No credit cards.
**Open:** Mon–Fri 7am–5pm.

A greasy spoon on a tiny side street just off Oxford Street near Tottenham Court Road Underground. It's a favorite of film-industry types who work in the immediate vicinity. Interesting daily specials like Irish stew, beef casserole, and steak-and-kidney pie sell for about £3.75 ($6.75), though it's even cheaper for such English standbys as sausage, beans, and chips. A mannequin in chef's clothes will greet you at the door, and the tables draped in checkered plastic will tell you there are no pretensions here.

**THE THREE LANTERNS RESTAURANT, 5 Panton St., W.1. Tel. 071/839-5031.**
**Cuisine:** ENGLISH. **Tube:** Piccadilly Circus.
**$ Prices:** £3–£4.50 ($5.40–$8.10). No credit cards.

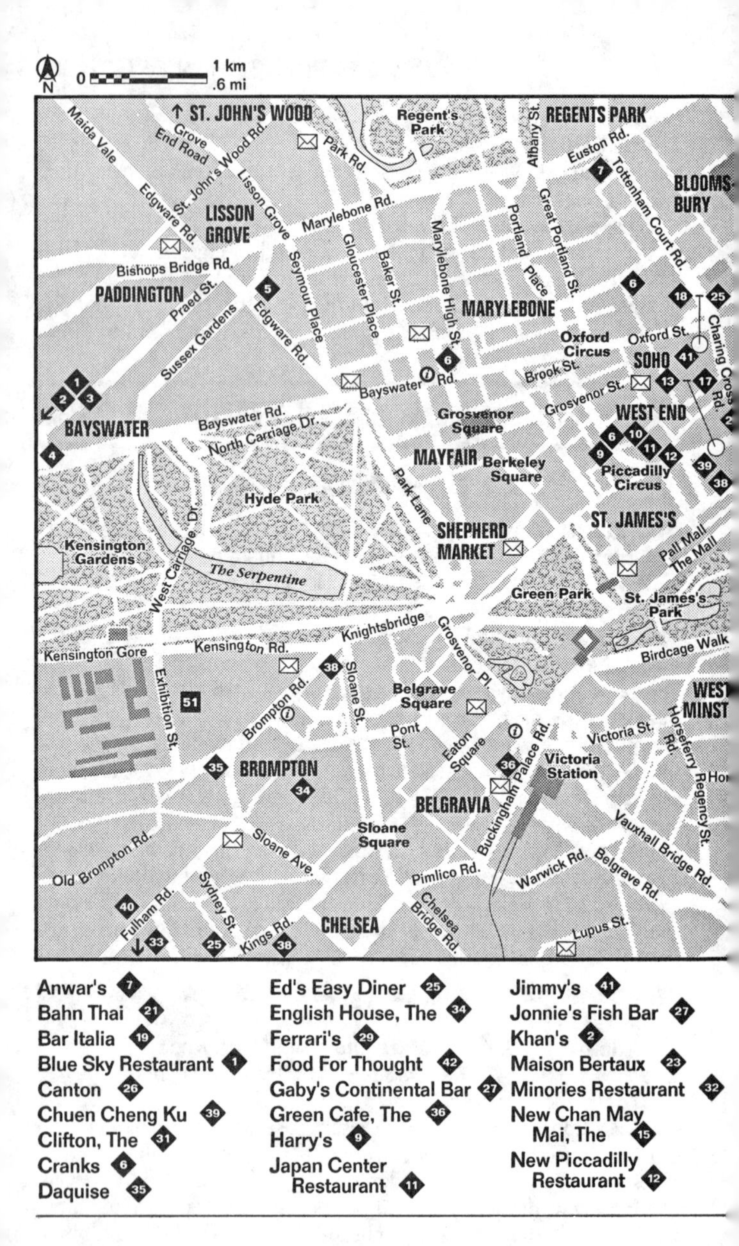


**Open:** Mon–Sat 11:30am–11pm, Sun 11:30am–8pm.
This restaurant is well priced and well located, between Leicester Square and Piccadilly Circus. Wooden booths in an old-world interior are offset by a modern English menu with a continental influence. Most of main courses, such as chicken-mushroom fricassee and moussaka, cost just £3.25 ($5.85) each, including vegetables. Soup is £1 ($1.80), as are most of the desserts, bringing the grand

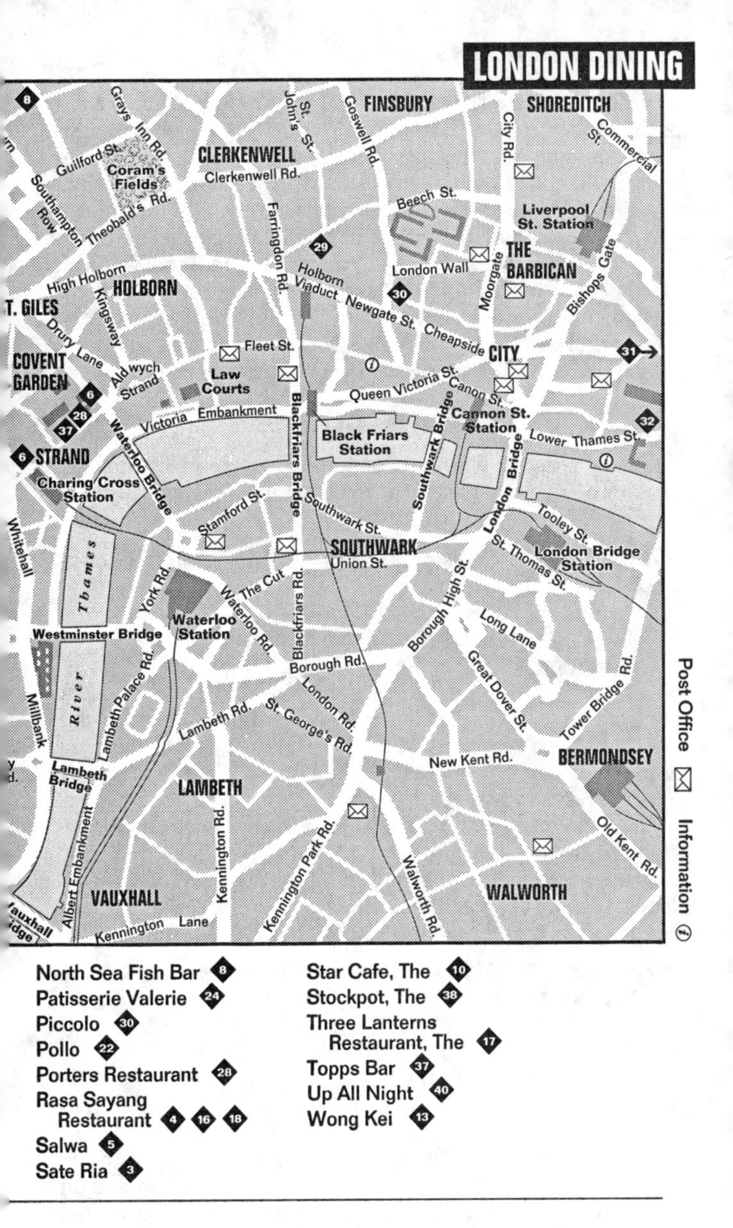


total of a three-course meal to just £5.25 ($9.45). The owner, Mr. Anastasi, is usually on hand to offer an extra-warm welcome.

**WONG KEI, 41–43 Wardour St., W.1. Tel. 071/437-8408.**
**Cuisine:** CHINESE. **Tube:** Leicester Square or Piccadilly Circus.
**$ Prices:** £4–£7 ($7.20–$12.60). No credit cards.
**Open:** Daily noon–11:30pm.

Chinese restaurants first opened in Soho during World War II, answering the demands of British soldiers, who had acquired a taste for the food overseas. Today there are many good and inexpensive Chinese restaurants here, most serving traditional Cantonese fare. Sitting at the end of Chinatown's Gerrard and Lisle streets, Wong Kei is one of the most inexpensive restaurants in the area, featuring an extensive menu. At least a dozen popular dishes, including chicken with garlic sauce and beef with vegetables, cost under £3.50 ($6.30). As is the rule at most Chinese restaurants in London, if you want rice, you have to order it separately, for 70p ($1.25). Tea is free, and hearty eaters can take advantage of a set meal including three dishes plus rice for only £4.90 ($8.80) per person (two-person minimum).

## THE CITY

Almost everyone in the square mile of The City of London goes home by 6pm, and restaurant workers are no exception. Below are some good lunch selections.

**FERRARI'S, 8 West Smithfield, E.C.1. Tel. 071/236-7545.**

**Cuisine:** ENGLISH. **Tube:** St. Paul's.
**$ Prices:** £2–£4 ($3.60–$7.20). No credit cards.
**Open:** Mon–Fri 5:15am–4pm.

For a somewhat nicer meal in the same area as Piccolo (see below), turn left at the Museum of London, and then right onto Little Britain Street, until you reach the Smithfield Market, London's wholesale meat center (about 6 blocks from St. Paul's Underground). The restaurant is just across the square. Although small and plain, Ferrari's is famous for its very unusual sandwich menu that includes selections like Norwegian prawn and farmhouse pâté. The shop's cakes are irresistible, too. Ferrari's is located in London's financial district, but don't expect to hear the latest share prices here. Most of the customers are meat porters from across the street.

**MINORIES RESTAURANT, 105a The Minories, E.C.3. Tel. 071/480-6822.**

**Cuisine:** ENGLISH. **Tube:** Tower Hill.
**$ Prices:** £3–£6 ($5.40–$10.80). No credit cards.
**Open:** Mon–Fri 8:30am–3pm.

Positioned just about 150 yards north of the Tower of London, under a railway bridge, this restaurant may have the most unusual location in London—arched ceiling and all. But it's also one of the few good-quality budget choices close to one of London's biggest tourist attractions. The small menu features roast beef with chips and peas, spaghetti Bolognese, and other home-cooked British standards. The cheerful owner, Mr. Novani, will personally make you feel at home.

**PICCOLO, 7 Gresham St., E.C.2. Tel. 071/606-1492.**

**Cuisine:** ENGLISH. **Tube:** St. Paul's.
**$ Prices:** £1.50–£2.50 ($2.70–$4.50). No credit cards.
**Open:** Mon–Sat 6am–6pm, Sun 6am–2pm.

This is just a sandwich bar with fewer than a dozen stools all facing the street. But it's perfect for a quick bite when visiting St. Paul's Cathedral, and offers quite simply the widest range of sandwiches you're ever likely to come across. Bacon and turkey, roast chicken, and all the standards are priced well below £2 ($3.60). The shop is just off Martin's Le Grand Street, between St. Paul's Underground and the Museum of London.

## COVENT GARDEN & THE STRAND

**FOOD FOR THOUGHT, 31 Neal St., W.C.2. Tel. 071/836-0239.**

**Cuisine:** VEGETARIAN. **Tube:** Covent Garden.

$ **Prices:** £3–£5 ($5.40–$9). No credit cards.

**Open:** Winter, Mon–Sat noon–8pm; summer, Mon–Sat 8:30am–8pm.

This most unusual restaurant makes vegetarian food accessible to all palates and pocketbooks. Delicious choices, such as leek quiche and lasagne, are usually priced around £2.25 ($4.05), and served downstairs in a small, smoke-free environment. Tasty soups and salads are also available, as well as a good selection of healthful desserts. Neal Street is across from the Covent Garden Underground.

**TOPPS BAR, 49 Bedford St., W.C.2.** No telephone.

**Cuisine:** ENGLISH. **Tube:** Covent Garden.

$ **Prices:** £2–£3.50 ($3.60–$6.30). No credit cards.

**Open:** Mon–Fri 8am–6pm.

Located on the south side of Covent Garden Market, just off the Strand, this is a good place for an inexpensive lunch in a very touristy area. The restaurant offers roast lamb, fish and chips, steak pie with vegetables, and other matter-of-fact English staples. Main courses are displayed cafeteria-style, and rarely top £2.50 ($3.40).

## PADDINGTON & BAYSWATER

**BLUE SKY RESTAURANT, 106 Westbourne Grove, W.2. Tel. 071/229-0777.**

**Cuisine:** ENGLISH. **Tube:** Bayswater.

$ **Prices:** £2–£4.50 ($3.60–$8.10). No credit cards.

**Open:** Mon–Sat 7am–10pm.

The Blue Sky looks like an American diner. Sit at a booth and open the menu to find a host of sandwiches for about £1.10 ($2), meat pies for £3 ($5.40), and ice cream for 70p ($1.25). The only things missing are the jukebox selectors mounted above each table. The restaurant is close to Chepstow Road.

**KHAN'S 13–15 Westbourne Grove, W.2. Tel. 071/727-5420.**

**Cuisine:** INDIAN. **Tube:** Bayswater.

$ **Prices:** £4–£7 ($7.20–$12.60). AE, DC, MC, V.

**Open:** Daily noon–3pm for lunch, 6pm–midnight for dinner.

Khan's is famous in these parts for the best Indian food in Bayswater. An airy, cloudlike mural covers the walls, as if to create the feeling of a magic-carpet ride. The menu, which includes chicken jalfrezi and beef curry, assures that only "halal" meat is used, conforming to the Muslim dietary code. Curry dishes cost about £3 ($5.40), while a whole tandoori chicken is under £4.50 ($8.10), and probably enough for two. Turn left onto Westbourne Grove from Queensway.

**SALWA, 4 Crawford Place, W.1. Tel. 071/262-3356.**
**Cuisine:** INDIAN. **Tube:** Edgeware Road.
$ **Prices:** £3–£5 ($5.40–$9). No credit cards.
**Open:** Daily 11:30am–1am.

Where can you get the most authentic Indian food in London? Competition is tough, but Salwa may take the prize. Don't expect the Taj Mahal—this is a small take-out place that's almost literally a hole-in-the-wall. There are three small tables behind an open kitchen, and although few tourists have been here, the staff is more than happy to serve them. Don't be shy. You can see what's cooking and choose by sight. Try the chicken curry, £3.20 ($5.75), add a plate of pillau rice for £1.10 ($2) and a paratha (traditional Indian bread) for 65p ($1.15), and you will walk out full and smiling.

The restaurant is just east of Edgeware Road, about 7 blocks north of Oxford Street.

**SATE RIA, 19 Westbourne Grove, W.2. Tel. 071/229-4841.**
**Cuisine:** MALAYSIAN. **Tube:** Bayswater.
$ **Prices:** £4–£6 ($7.20–$10.80). No credit cards.
**Open:** Daily noon–11pm.

Chicken, beef, lamb, and seafood, grilled on bamboo skewers, is served with the tangy variety of sauces that have made Malaysian chefs famous. Copper fans, ferns, and dark bamboo chairs create a comfortably modern atmosphere behind the homey red storefront. Meals are served with salad, and few dishes top £5 ($9).

Sate Ria is located a few doors down from Khan's (see above).

## BLOOMSBURY

**ANWAR'S, 64 Grafton Way, W.1. Tel. 071/387-6664.**
**Cuisine:** INDIAN. **Tube:** Warren Street.
$ **Prices:** £3–£5 ($5.40–$9). No credit cards.
**Open:** Daily 10am–10pm.

Anwar's not only maintains a very high standard of quality, but it is also one of the cheapest Indian restaurants in London. Few dishes top £4 ($7.20), and most cost just £3 ($5.40). There is a wide choice of homemade meat and vegetable curries and other Indian specialties, including tandoori chicken for £2.95 ($5.30). Service at Anwar's is cafeteria-style; help yourself and bring your meal to a basic Formica-covered table. Despite this "canteen" approach, the food is really top-notch.

## AROUND VICTORIA

**THE GREEN CAFE, 16 Eccleston St., S.W.1. No telephone.**

**Cuisine:** ENGLISH. **Tube:** Victoria.
$ **Prices:** £2.50–£3.50 ($4.50–$6.30). No credit cards.
**Open:** Mon–Fri 9am–6pm.
This is still one of the best value-for-your-money choices near Victoria Station. Located between Buckingham Palace Road and Ebury Street, this café, with only seven tables, really is green, both inside and out, and it offers hearty daily specials for about £2.50 ($4.50). The main course, which might feature roast lamb, or steak-and-kidney pie, is usually preceded by soup. A la carte selections are also available, and you won't have to choose carefully to keep the tab under £3 ($5.40).

## A CHAIN

**THE STOCKPOT**
**Cuisine:** ENGLISH.
$ **Prices:** £3–£5 ($5.40–$9). No credit cards.
**Open:** Daily 9am–11pm (sometimes varies by location).
The restaurants of the Stockpot chain share contemporary decor and a generous, budget-minded philosophy. Menus change daily, and regularly include two homemade soups for 80p ($1.45) each, a dozen selections such as lasagne, roast lamb, and fish and chips for £2 to £2.50 ($3.60 to $4.50), and an excellent selection of cakes for under £1.50 ($2.70). The food is good and the prices make all the 'Pots popular.

Central London locations include: 273 Kings Rd., S.W.3 (tel. 071/823-3175), in Chelsea, a few blocks past the fire station; 6 Basil St., S.W.3 (tel. 071/589-8627), in ultrafashionable Knightsbridge between Harrods and Sloane Street; and 40 Panton St., S.W.1 (tel. 071/839-5142), just off Haymarket, one block south of Piccadilly Circus.

# 2. MEALS FOR LESS THAN £7 ($12.60)

## IN & AROUND SOHO

**GABY'S CONTINENTAL BAR, 30 Charing Cross Rd., W.C.2. Tel. 071/836-4233.**
**Cuisine:** CONTINENTAL. **Tube:** Leicester Square.
$ **Prices:** £3–£6 ($5.40–$10.80). No credit cards.
**Open:** Mon–Sat 8am–midnight, Sun noon–10pm.
This restaurant, just off Leicester Square, is one of the best in London for quality and value. A wonderful assortment of home-cooked specialties like stuffed eggplant, rolled cabbage, and chicken satay are displayed in the window, and will make your mouth water even

before you walk through the door. Most dishes are under £4.50 ($8.10), and are usually served with salad or rice. There is no guarantee that a particular dish will be on the menu the day you visit, because everything is made fresh daily according to the chef's mood, but there is always a wide selection of delicious and reasonably priced meals available. The restaurant is also known for its sandwiches, especially salt beef (England's approximation of corned beef), cheapest when you buy it to take away for about £3 ($5.40). Gaby's is fully licensed.

**THE JAPAN CENTER RESTAURANT, 66–68 Brewer St., W.1. Tel. 071/439-8035.**
**Cuisine:** JAPANESE. **Tube:** Piccadilly Circus.
**$ Prices:** £4–£7 ($7.20–$12.60). No credit cards.
**Open:** Mon–Fri 10am–7:30pm, Sat 11am–6pm.

Located in the basement of the Japan Center, a bookstore and clearinghouse for Japanese culture, the small restaurant serves a good variety of Japanese staples. Most of the seating is around the sushi bar, where a lunch-size portion can be had for about £6.50 ($11.70). Other dishes include chicken katsu (fried chicken cutlet served over rice), and various Japanese-style curries.

**JIMMY'S, 23 Frith St., W.1. Tel. 071/437-9521.**
**Cuisine:** GREEK/CYPRIOT. **Tube:** Leicester Square.
**$ Prices:** £4–£7 ($7.20–$12.60). No credit cards.
**Open:** Lunch Mon–Sat 12:30–3pm; dinner 5:30–11pm.

Across from Ronnie Scott's jazz club (see Chapter 9), Jimmy's is a popular basement bistro with good-quality Greek-Cypriot food. Kleftico (baked lamb), moussaka, and other distinctive Mediterranean dishes cost about £5 ($9).

**NEW PICCADILLY RESTAURANT, 8 Denman St., W.1. Tel. 071/437-8530.**
**Cuisine:** ENGLISH/CONTINENTAL. **Tube:** Piccadilly Circus.
**$ Prices:** £3–£6 ($5.40–$10.80). No credit cards.
**Open:** Daily 11am–9:30pm.

Both the decor and menu here are straightforward. The long dining room is lined with tables on either side, and diners can choose from a large number of unadventurous but well-prepared English-style specialties such as chicken with mushroom sauce and steak risotto for around £3.50 ($5.40). For a pound less, try one of their many pizzas, or a pasta dish, such as ravioli. Add 95p ($1.70) for soup, plus £1.10 ($2) for apple pie or ice cream, and you'll have eaten a satisfying three-course meal for just about £5 ($9). The restaurant is located just off the bottom of Shaftesbury Avenue, a few feet from Piccadilly Circus, and doesn't have a liquor license; patrons are encouraged to bring their alcoholic beverage.

## SOHO'S CHINATOWN

Of the many fine restaurants in Soho's Chinatown, you should be aware of two particularly pleasing specialty kitchens:

**CHUEN CHENG KU, 17 Wardour St., W.1. Tel. 071/437-1398.**
**Cuisine:** CHINESE. **Tube:** Leicester Square.
$ **Prices:** £4–£7 ($7.20–$12.60). AE, DC, MC, V.
**Open:** Daily 11am–11:45pm; dumplings served until 5:45pm.

This huge restaurant serves a large selection (21 kinds) of steamed, fried, or boiled dim sum (dumplings), usually around lunchtime. Favorites include steamed pork buns and shrimp dumplings, both £1.50 ($2.70). It takes a few servings to get a good feed, and a fulfilling experience can be had for about £6 ($10.80).

**THE NEW CHAN MAY MAI, 25 Lisle St., W.1. Tel. 071/437-3602.**
**Cuisine:** CHINESE/MALAYSIAN. **Tube:** Leicester Square.
$ **Prices:** £3–£8 ($5.40–$14.40). No credit cards.
**Open:** Daily noon–midnight.

This is one of the most creative restaurants in Chinatown, dishing out fish with ginger, chicken satay, and other aromatic and flavorful specialties with a Malaysian bite. Begin with their wonderful minced crabmeat and sweetcorn soup, for £1.50 ($2.70).

## SOUTH KENSINGTON

**DAQUISE, 20 Thurloe St., S.W.7. Tel. 071/589-6117.**
**Cuisine:** POLISH. **Tube:** South Kensington.
$ **Prices:** £5–£7 ($9–$12.60): set lunch £5 ($9). No credit cards.
**Open:** Daily 10am–11pm.

Daquise is one of the best finds in South Kensington. Near the major museums and just steps from South Kensington Underground, this Polish restaurant features cabbage in many guises. Stuffed with meat, or served with veal escalope, it costs under £4 ($7.20). Their chlodiak soup (ham stock, beet root, cream, and pickled cucumber) may sound unusual, but it tastes great. A variety of Polish vodkas and beers is also served, and the friendly, if harried, staff encourages diners to nurse their drinks.

## THE CHAINS

**CRANKS**
**Cuisine:** VEGETARIAN.
$ **Prices:** £5–£8 ($9–$14.40). MC, V.
**Open:** Mon–Sat 10am–10:30pm.

When Cranks opened their first health-oriented vegetarian restaurant in the early 1960s, the British public laughed. Today, over half a dozen eateries continue to "crank out" innovative, high-quality cuisine at prices that have silenced all snickerers. Cheesy lasagne, lentil-and-spinach quiche, satay vegetables, and other tasty dishes are well presented, and served in modern, airy, and somewhat fancy settings. A wide selection of herb teas, at about £1 ($1.80) per pot, is available, as well as a good choice of reasonably priced organic wines.

Downtown locations include the following: Adelaide Street,

W.C.2 (tel. 071/379-5919), where the Strand meets Trafalgar Square; The Market, Covent Garden, W.C.2 (tel. 071/379-6508); Tottenham Street, W.1 (tel. 071/631-3912), two blocks from Goodge Street Underground off Tottenham Court Road; Barret Street, W.1 (tel. 071/495-1340), across Oxford Street from the Bond Street Underground; and Marshall Street, W.1 (tel. 071/437-9431), three blocks east of Regent Street in the heart of Soho.

**ED'S EASY DINER**

**Cuisine:** AMERICAN.

**$ Prices:** £3.50–£6.50 ($6.30–$11.70). No credit cards.

**Open:** Mon–Thurs 11:30am–midnight, Fri–Sat 11:30am–1am, Sun 11:30am–11pm.

Ed's Easys are reconstructions of 1950s-style American diners, complete with bobby-soxed waitresses and dime (5p) jukebox selectors. Despite the gimmick, this place flips one of the most authentic burgers in town; along with fries and a cola, or a milkshake, it will cost about £6 ($10.80).

Central London locations include: 12 Moor St., W.1 (tel. 071/439-1955), just off Cambridge Circus; and 362 King's Rd., S.W.3 (tel. 071/352-1956), past the fire station in Chelsea.

**RASA SAYANG RESTAURANT**

**Cuisine:** MALAYSIAN/SINGAPOREAN.

**$ Prices:** £5–£8 ($9–$14.40). AE, DC, MC.

**Open:** Daily noon–10:45pm (sometimes varies by location).

These spic-and-span establishments were some of the first Southeast Asian eateries in London. An unusual menu features dozens of meat and vegetarian dishes topped with traditional sauces. Coconut and fruit sauces are common, as are soups and satays. The restaurants are slightly lacking in atmosphere, but are well lit, contemporary in style, and often packed.

Central London locations include: 38 Queensway, W.2 (tel. 071/229-8417), diagonally across from the Bayswater Underground station; 10 Frith St., W.1 (tel. 071/734-8720), in the middle of Soho; and 3 Leicester Place, W.C.2 (tel. 071/427-4556), just southwest of Leicester Square.

## 3. SPECIALTY DINING

### LOCAL BUDGET BETS

#### FISH & CHIPS

Fast-food restaurants have taken their toll in London, but "chippies," as the British call them, are still easy to find. Nowadays, fish and chips are usually offered by Middle Eastern places, too, but the most

## FROMMER'S SMART TRAVELER: RESTAURANTS

VALUE-CONSCIOUS TRAVELERS SHOULD:

1. Look for budget restaurants hidden on side streets around Covent Garden and Soho—the festive atmosphere of these areas makes finding them fun.
2. Take special notice of establishments with a number of taxis parked outside—you can be sure the food is good and prices are low.
3. Beware of eateries with signs outside welcoming tourists in a dozen different languages.

authentic joints won't have a kebab in sight. Several kinds of fish are offered, but all taste similar and cod is the cheapest. Sitting down will raise the price of the meal considerably, so do as the locals do, and get it to "take away"—wrapped in a paper cone, doused with vinegar, and sprinkled with salt. The bill should never top £2.60 ($4.70).

Two of the most popular chippies include: **Johnnie's Fish Bar,** 494 King's Rd., S.W.10 (tel. 071/352-3876), just past the World's End Pub in Chelsea, open Monday through Saturday 11am to 11:30pm; and **North Sea Fish Bar,** 8 Leigh St., W.C.1 (tel. 071/387-5892), just southeast of Cartwright Gardens at Sandwich Street in Bloomsbury, open Monday through Saturday noon to 2:30pm, and again from 5:30 to 10:30pm.

## PUB GRUB

Pub food can vary from snacks at the bar to a complete restaurant meal, but it's usually cheap, good, and filling. Most pubs offer food, and there are so many pubs that if you don't like what you see in one, you can move on to the next. Don't be afraid to look at the food before committing—it's usually displayed under glass. When it's not, ask the barkeep for a menu. Popular items include Scotch eggs (a hard-boiled egg surrounded by meat and enclosed in dough), bangers and mash (sausages and mashed potatoes), meat pies (especially during colder months), and ploughman's lunch (bread, cheese, salad, and chutney). Wash it all down with a beer.

The best pubs make their own dishes and keep the food hot on hotplates. Others only offer factory-made pasties (meat-filled pastry) and microwave them on demand. Note that food and drink are ordered separately—they are run as separate enterprises and you must pay for each independently. A good pub lunch will seldom top

£3.50 ($6.30), and careful ordering can cut that amount almost in half.

Many popular pubs are listed in Chapter 9. Pubs known especially for their food include: **Black Friar,** 174 Queen Victoria St., E.C.4 (tel. 071/236-5650), near Blackfriars Underground in The City; **De Hems,** 11 Macclesfield St., W.1 (tel. 071/437-2494), in Soho's Chinatown; **The Sun,** 63 Lamb's Conduit St., W.C.1 (tel. 071/405-8278), between Russell Square and Holborn Underground stations, and the **Lamb and Flag,** 33 Rose St., W.C.2 (tel. 071/497-9504), by Covent Garden Market.

## CAFES

Cafés, or "caffs," are coming into fashion in London, and a host of Soho-based old-time java joints are once again at the center of this city's newfound café culture.

**BAR ITALIA, 22 Frith St., W.1. Tel. 071/437-4520.**

**Cuisine:** ITALIAN. **Tube:** Tottenham Court Road.

**$ Prices:** Cappuccino £1 ($1.80), pastry £1.25 ($2.25), sandwiches £1.50–£2.50 ($2.70–$4.50). No credit cards.

**Open:** Daily 7am–4am (sometimes later).

Soho's most authentic Italian café features great espresso served in a loud and busy atmosphere. Parma ham and cheese sandwiches are served at the bar, and can be eaten standing, or at one of the few tables, all of which are usually taken on weekends.

**MAISON BERTAUX, 28 Greek St., W.1. Tel. 071/437-6007.**

**Cuisine:** DESSERT. **Tube:** Leicester Square.

**$ Prices:** Coffee 70p ($1.25), pastry 65p–£1.25 ($1.15–$2.25). No credit cards.

**Open:** Mon–Sat 9am–7pm, Sun 9:30am–1pm and 3:30–6:30pm.

One of London's top French bakeries, Maison Bertaux seduces passersby with rich aromas and a window display packed with fresh pastries, buns, and brioches. Everything is prepared on the premises, and is served at small tables occupying two floors. Coffee, tea, and other drinks are available, along with meat-and-cheese-stuffed croissants and other light snacks.

**PATISSERIE VALERIE, 44 Old Compton St., W.1. Tel. 071/437-3466.**

**Cuisine:** DESSERT. **Tube:** Tottenham Court Road.

**$ Prices:** Coffee 70p ($1.25), pastry 70p–£1.75 ($1.25–$3.15). No credit cards.

**Open:** Mon–Sat 8am–7pm, Sun 10am–6pm.

This terminally crowded bakery is the Soho café to see and the place to be seen. Frequented by local film and theater types, Valerie is not the cheapest place for coffee and cake, but their chocolate gâteau is (almost) world-famous.

## LATE-NIGHT EATING

Unlike many other cities, London lacks healthy competition when it comes to after-hours snacking. The few places listed below form an almost complete directory of centrally located late-night London eateries.

**CANTON, 11 Newport Pl., W.C.2. Tel. 071/437-6220.**
**Cuisine:** CHINESE. **Tube:** Leicester Square.
**$ Prices:** £5–£10 ($9–$17.10). AE, DC, V.
**Open:** Mon–Thurs and Sun 11am–1am, Fri–Sat 11am–2am, sometimes later.

As the name suggests, this no-nonsense eatery specializes in Cantonese fare, served on two floors by a harried staff. The barbecued duck and pork are particularly recommended.

**THE CLIFTON, 126 Brick Lane, E.1. Tel. 071/247-2364.**
**Cuisine:** INDIAN. **Tube:** Aldgate East.
**$ Prices:** £4–£8 ($7.20–$14.40). AE, DC, MC, V.
**Open:** Daily noon–12:30am.

At least four Indian restaurants in the East End's Brick Lane serve meals to late-night eaters. The Clifton is the most famous any time of day, not because it's the best food on the street, but because it is the cheapest. The dining room is large and the menu features big portions of all the traditional favorites.

**HARRY'S, 19 Kingly St., W.1. Tel. 071/434-0309.**
**Cuisine:** ENGLISH. **Tube:** Piccadilly Circus or Oxford Circus.
**$ Prices:** £4–£6 ($7.20–$10.80). MC, V.
**Open:** Mon–Sat 5:30pm–6am

This ultratrendy hole-in-the-wall filled with after-hours clubbers is London's premiere late-night eatery. You might have to wait for a table at 3am, when weary-eyed patrons are ordering full English breakfasts and other caloric snacks. Tables downstairs, near the door, are most coveted, as they enable diners to see (and be seen by) everyone.

**UP ALL NIGHT, 325 Fulham Rd., S.W.10. No telephone.**
**Cuisine:** ENGLISH/AMERICAN. **Tube:** South Kensington.
**$ Prices:** £3–£5 ($5.40–$9). No credit cards.
**Open:** Daily noon–6am.

Insomniacs, third-shift workers, and assorted late-nighters pull their bentwood chairs up to wooden tables and munch on desserts, burgers, and breakfasts. This unassuming luncheonette-style burger joint is my favorite late-night restaurant in London.

## AFTERNOON TEA

As much as the tea itself, it's tradition that makes afternoon tea special. And the pot is usually served with a spread of sandwiches and sweets that more than make a meal. High tea is a pleasant and civilized leisure-class activity; few construction workers leave their sites for a cup of Darjeeling. Accordingly, an authentic tea is expensive, and usually served in top hotels, where a jacket and tie are required for men. An inexpensive restaurant advertising high tea is just an imitation.

**BROWN'S HOTEL, Albermarle and Dover sts., W.1. Tel. 071/493-6020.**
**Tube:** Green Park.
**$ Prices:** £11.50 ($20.70) per person. AE, DC, MC, V.
**Open:** Daily 3–6pm.

Serves the best set tea in London. You sit in one of the three wood-paneled, stained-glass lounges and feel like a millionaire. Tailcoated waiters fill your table with tomato, cucumber, and meat sandwiches, as well as scones and pastries. Choose from a variety of teas from India and Southeast Asia.

**RITZ HOTEL, Picadilly, W.1. Tel. 071/493-8181.**
**Tube:** Green Park.
**$ Prices:** £14 ($25.50) per person.
**Open:** Daily sittings at 3 and 4:30pm.

Probably the most famous afternoon tea in the world. There are two sittings daily and reservations are essential at least a week in advance.

**HEAL'S RESTAURANT, 196 Tottenham Court Road, W.1. Tel. 071/636-1666.**
**Tube:** Goodge Street.
**$ Prices:** £8 ($14.40) per person. AE, DC, MC, V.
**Open:** Mon–Sat 3–5:30 pm.

Located in the rear of Heal's building, this restaurant has a snazzy tea that outshines most hotel teas in both quality and price. The green-velvet-upholstered furniture is as luxurious as the smoked-salmon sandwiches and the scones with fresh cream. Like most good teas, it's all-you-can-eat.

## PICNIC SUPPLIES

There are plenty of supermarkets around offering the run-of-the-mill staples. Cold cuts and cheeses from the deli counter are usually cheaper than the prewrapped stuff that hangs in the cooler.

For some unusual picnic goodies, try the big and fascinating **Loon Fung Supermarket** at 42-44 Gerrard St., W.1 (tel. 071/437-7332), right in the heart of Soho's Chinatown. The most adventurous will try the black jelly fungus or the steamed, congealed chicken's blood. The rest of us will enjoy dried cuttlefish, a traditional snack that goes great with beer. Loon Fung is open daily from 10am to 7pm.

The Japanese Supermarket in the Japan Center, 66-68 Brewer St., W.1 (tel. 071/439-8035), off Regent Street near the Piccadilly Circus Underground, is worth a look for their precooked dishes and unusual Japanese sodas and snacks. It's open Monday through Friday from 10am to 7:30pm, Saturday from 10am to 6:30pm, and on Sunday from 10am to 6pm.

See "More Attractions: Parks and Gardens," in Chapter 6, for information on London's top picnic spots.

## 4. WORTH THE EXTRA BUCKS

**BAHN THAI, 21a Frith St., W.1. Tel. 071/437-8504.**
**Cuisine:** THAI. **Tube:** Tottenham Court Road.
**$ Prices:** £6–£15 ($10.80–$27). AE, MC, V.
**Open:** Lunch Mon–Fri noon–2:45pm; dinner Mon–Sat 6–11:15pm, Sun 6:30–10:30pm.

Right in the middle of Soho is one of the best Southeast Asian restaurants in London. Two floors of wooden tables, plants, and decorative wall hangings give this exceptional place a totally authentic feel. But it's the food you've come for, and you won't be disappointed. Excellent, unusual soups, seafood, and rice dishes are featured on the huge and creative menu. Frith Street is near Tottenham Court Road Underground, just south of Soho Square.

### FROMMER'S COOL FOR KIDS
#### RESTAURANTS

**Anwar's** *(see p. 96)* Gives kids a good introduction to Indian cooking. Since meals are served cafeteria-style, you can see the dishes before committing. Food here is both good and cheap. It is unlikely that your kid won't like it, and it won't cost you a bundle to find out.

**Ed's Easy Diner** *(see p. 100)* Faithfully re-creates an American 1950s-style American diner. The menu features giant burgers, authentic fries, and thick shakes. Need I say more?

**North Sea Fish Bar** *(see p. 101)* One of the best in the city for traditional fish and chips. Kids will love the crispy batter, and might even learn to like french fries doused with vinegar instead of ketchup.

**Porters Restaurant** *(see p. 106)* In the heart of bustling Covent Garden, a fun place to sample top-notch English meat pies. Sunday roasts are particularly appealing, when the entire restaurant takes on a festive atmosphere.

**The Star Cafe** *(see p. 91)* A playful English eatery located on a colorful Soho corner. Irish stew, beef casserole, a variety of meat pies, and other pastry-covered working-class English specialties will please the whole family.

**THE ENGLISH HOUSE, 3 Milner St., S.W.3. Tel. 071/584-3002.**

**Cuisine:** ENGLISH. **Tube:** South Kensington or Sloane Square.

$ **Prices:** £15–£30 ($27–$54); set lunch (Mon–Sat) £11.50 ($20.70); set dinner (Sun) £20 ($36). AE, DC, MC, V. **Reservations:** Recommended.

**Open:** Lunch daily 12:30–2:30pm; dinner Mon–Sat 7:30–11:30pm, Sun 7:30–10pm.

Set in a beautiful Chelsea back street, the English House looks like the ideal country home. As a fire roars in the cozy dining room, patrons are treated to beautifully prepared traditional English dishes, served by an expertly trained staff. Despite the fact that tables are too close together, dining here is romantic, and the meal will convince you that English food can be good.

**PORTERS RESTAURANT, 17 Henrietta St., W.C.2. Tel. 071/836-6466.**

**Cuisine:** ENGLISH. **Tube:** Covent Garden.

$ **Prices:** £7–£10 ($12.60–$17.10). MC, V. **Reservations:** Recommended.

**Open:** Lunch daily noon–3pm; dinner 5:30–11:30pm.

Just a block south of Covent Garden Market, Porters serves traditional English food with a flair. Their large, wood-and-fern restaurant offers over half a dozen meat pies, including steak-and-mushroom, which sells for £7 ($12.60). Weekends are best, when roast beef and Yorkshire pudding with gravy and roast potatoes is £8 ($14.40). As at most restaurants in the area, weekends are busy, so expect a wait at the well-stocked bar.

# CHAPTER 6

# WHAT TO SEE & DO IN LONDON



To paraphrase Dr. Johnson, the great English lexicographer: When one is tired of London, one is tired of life, for there is in London all that life can afford. There is so much to do and see in this vast city that even veteran tourists and locals regularly happen upon new finds. For the first-time visitor, the question is never what to do, but what to do *first.* Browse through the offerings, and take special note of opening hours. Careful planning will allow you to "bunch" attractions and make the most of your London stay.

Americans are famous for whizzing around Europe's major sights trying to squeeze in as many of the "hits" as their brief vacations will allow. Europeans (who are both geographically closer to one another, and enjoy longer holidays), often poke fun at the hectic pace of the American vacation. But when you've come a long way and only have a few days, moving at a fast clip is in order. If soaking up local culture in a Chelsea café is more your cup of tea, modifications to the itineraries below will have to be made.

## SUGGESTED ITINERARIES

### IF YOU HAVE 1 DAY

Most hotels start serving breakfast at 7:30am. Be there! After breakfast take the tube to Charing Cross or Embankment (they are within one block of each other) and cross into **Trafalgar Square,**

London's most famous square and the city's unofficial hub. Here the commercial **West End** meets **Whitehall,** the main street of government, and **The Mall,** the regal road that leads to Buckingham Palace. In the center of the square is **Nelson's Column.** The **National Gallery** is on the top end of the square, while the northeast side is dominated by the **Church of St. Martin-in-the-Fields.**

Turn down Whitehall, and go inside the **Banqueting House,** in the middle of the block, to view the magnificent ceiling painted by Rubens. Across the street from the Banqueting House, visit the home of the **Queen's Life Guards,** to see the Changing of the Guard Monday through Saturday at 11am and on Sunday at 10am and 4pm (not to be confused with the larger affair at Buckingham Palace).

Farther down Whitehall, in the middle of the street, you'll see the **Cenotaph,** dedicated to the citizens of the U.K. who died during wartime. Just opposite it is **10 Downing Street,** the official residence of the British prime minister.

At the foot of Whitehall lies Parliament Square, site of **Big Ben** and the spectacular **Houses of Parliament.** The famous **Westminster Abbey** is just across Parliament Square.

After a late lunch and a short rest, take the tube into The City and visit **St. Paul's Cathedral.**

### DID YOU KNOW . . . ?

- London's largest parks, including Hyde Park and Green Park, originally formed parts of royal estates.
- In the 1960s London launched two long-lasting fashions: long hair for men, miniskirts for women.
- London is the most populous city in Western Europe.
- There are almost a dozen national newspapers published in the capital.
- There are over 5,000 pubs in Greater London.
- The City of London only occupies about 1 square mile.
- According to tradition, only Cockneys are "real" Londoners; they were born within hearing range of the bell of St. Mary-le-Bow, a historic City church.
- Harrod's is the largest department store in Western Europe.
- London's Heathrow airport is the busiest in Europe.

## IF YOU HAVE 2 DAYS

Follow the itinerary described above, and have time to catch your breath! Take a break from your Whitehall stroll, cross beautiful St. James's Park, and arrive at **Buckingham Palace** at 11:30am for the **Changing of the Guard.**

Or: reverse your Whitehall walk and, starting in Parliament Square, end up at the National Gallery in Trafalgar Square. After visiting the gallery, continue north along Charing Cross Road, turn right on Long Acre, and visit trendy **Covent Garden.** In the afternoon of your second day, visit one of the museums listed in "Top Attractions," below.

### IF YOU HAVE 3 DAYS

Spend days 1 and 2 as described above. On your third day, visit **The City of London** and its host of interesting financial, legal, religious, and historical sights. Attractions include: the Stock Exchange; the Royal Exchange; the Old Bailey; St. Paul's Cathedral; and St. Bride's Church, on Fleet Street. Try to time your sightseeing so that you are at St. Bride's for a free lunchtime recital (Tuesday, Wednesday, and Friday at 1:15pm, or Sunday at 11am and 6pm).

In the afternoon of your third day, visit the **Museum of the Moving Image** on the South Bank, then stroll over to the adjacent **South Bank Arts Centre** for a late-afternoon drink.

### IF YOU HAVE 5 DAYS

Spend your first three days as described above. An extra couple of days will give you a chance to stop and to explore London's **historical neighborhoods** (most notably Chelsea and South Kensington), or to partake in the city's active cultural scene. If you like museums, make sure you make a pilgrimage to South Kensington. In addition to the **Victoria and Albert Museum,** there are no fewer than six other museums in this area, including the Natural History Museum, the Science Museum, the Geological Museum, and the Museum of Instruments. Also worth a stop is **Kensington Palace,** in Kensington Gardens.

## 1. THE TOP ATTRACTIONS

**BRITISH MUSEUM, Great Russell St., W.C.1. Tel. 071/ 636-1555.**

This museum houses an unmatched collection of antiquities—most of which are the spoils of empire-building. Important finds from Egypt, Greece, Rome, and Cyprus share this warehouse of history with spectacular collections from Asia and the Middle East. The Rosetta Stone, whose discovery in the 19th century enabled modern humans to understand Egyptian hieroglyphics, is found at the entrance to the Egyptian Sculpture Gallery. A set of sculptures from the Parthenon, known as the Elgin Marbles, is the most famous portion of the museum's extensive collection of Greek antiquities. Named for Lord Elgin, who took these treasures from Athens, the marbles and other treasures are hotly contested by foreign governments that want their cultural relics back. Amongst miles of thousand-year-old Mesopotamian jewelry, Babylonian astronomical instruments, and Assyrian artifacts, are some pretty exciting finds. Most fascinating, perhaps, are the contents of a number of Egyptian tombs, which include bandaged mummies.

To the right of the museum's entrance, on the ground floor, are the **British Library Galleries.** Rotating thematic displays come from the library's collection of over eight million books. Included in the permanent exhibit are two copies of the Magna Carta (1215), Shakespeare's First Folio (1623), and the Gutenberg Bible (ca. 1453), the first book printed using movable (hence, reusable) type. Autographed works by Bach, Mozart, and Handel are on display.

The adjacent **British Library Reading Room** was regularly used by Gandhi, Lenin, George Bernard Shaw, and others. Karl Marx wrote *Das Kapital* here. For tourists, admission is with a guide only, every hour on the hour from 11am to 4pm.

**Admission:** Main galleries, free; £1 ($1.80) donation requested. Special exhibitions £2 ($3.60) adults, £1 ($1.80) students, seniors, and children under 16.

**Open:** Mon–Sat 10am–5pm, Sun 2:30–6pm. **Tube:** Holborn or Russell Square.

**BUCKINGHAM PALACE, The Mall, S.W.1. Tel. 071/930-4832.**

Buckingham Palace is the site of England's best (but not only) **Changing of the Guard.** The highly touristed pageant takes place daily April through July at 11:30am, and on alternate days August through March. The ceremony is canceled during bad weather, and for major state events.

The popularity of the palace itself is not due to its great age or its architecture—it is neither old nor spectacular. But as the home to one of the world's last remaining monarchs, the building has strong symbolic interest. In 1837, Queen Victoria turned the palace into the sovereign's official residence. The huge Marble Arch was removed from the palace's forecourt and deposited in its present location, at the northeast corner of Hyde Park.

Unfortunately, Buckingham Palace is not open to visitors, so resign yourself to a glimpse of the Neo-Georgian East front, built in 1825 by John Nash, and redone in 1913 by Sir Aston Webb. When the queen is home, the Royal Standard is flown from the flagstaff on the building's roof.

**Tube:** Victoria, St. James's Park, or Green Park.

**HOUSES OF PARLIAMENT. Tel. 071/219-4272 for information.**

Located in the Palace of Westminster, the Houses of Parliament, along with their trademark clocktower, are the ultimate symbol of London. Originally built as a home for Edward the Confessor, before the Norman Conquest of 1066, the palace has gradually been altered and enlarged. Today, the spectacular 19th-century Gothic Revival building contains over 1,000 rooms and two

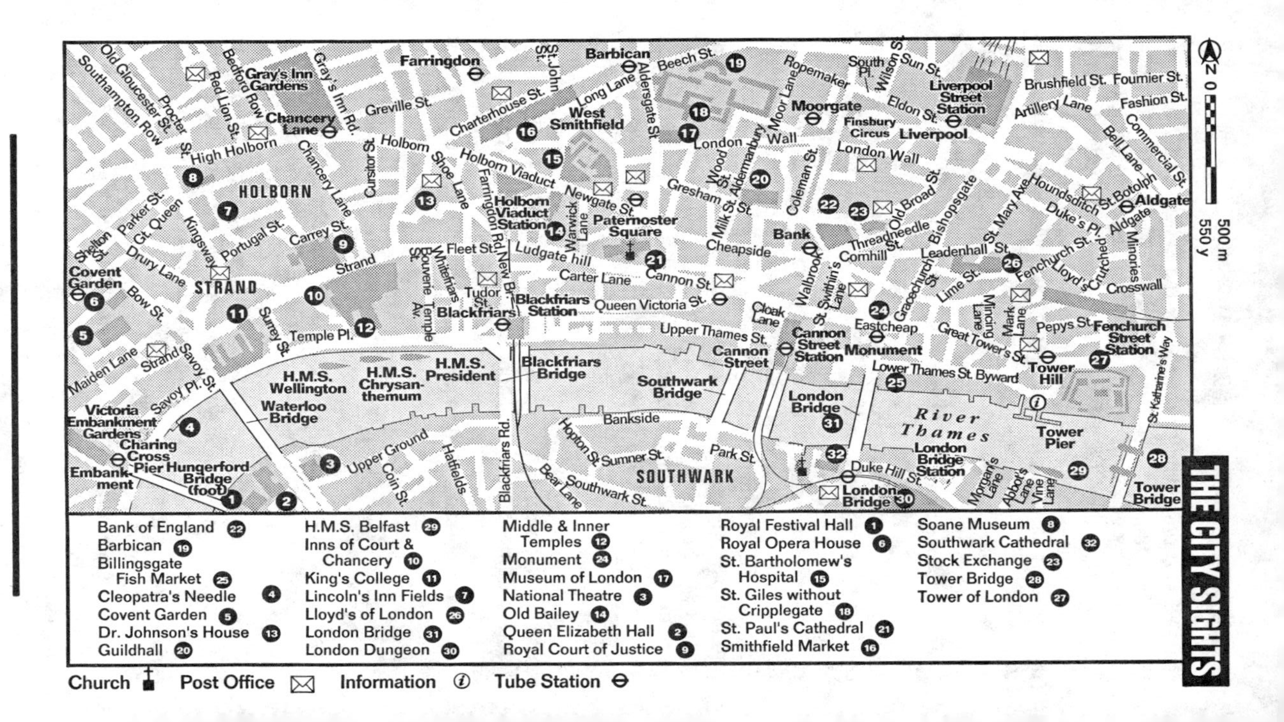


## IMPRESSIONS

*This—is London.*

—EDWARD R. MURROW, opening phrase for broadcasts from London during World War II

miles of corridors. The clocktower at the eastern end houses the world's most famous timepiece. **"Big Ben"** refers not to the clocktower, as many people assume, but to the largest bell in the chime, a 13½-tonner named for the first commissioner of works. Listen to the familiar chime, as it has inspired ostentatious doorbells around the world. At night a light shines in the tower whenever Parliament is in session.

Visitors may watch parliamentary debate from the Stranger's Galleries of Parliament's two houses. This can be very interesting and is especially exciting during debates on particularly controversial topics.

Rebuilt in 1950 after a German air-raid attack in 1941, the **House of Commons** remains small. Only 346 of its 650 members can sit at any one time, while the rest crowd around the door and the Speaker's Chair. The ruling party and the opposition sit facing one another, two sword lengths' apart, and on the table of the House sits the mace, a symbol of Parliament's authority.

The opulently furnished **House of Lords** has an almost sacrosanct feel. Debates here are not as interesting or lively as those in the more important Commons, but the line to get in is usually shorter, and a visit here will give you an appreciation for the pageantry of Parliament.

**Admission:** Free.

**Open:** The House of Commons, public admitted Mon–Thurs starting at 4pm, and Fri 9:30am–3pm; House of Lords, public admitted Mon–Thurs from about 3pm, and on some Fridays. Line up at St. Stephen's Entrance, just past the statue of Oliver Cromwell. Debates usually run into the night, and lines shrink after 6pm. **Tube:** Westminster.

**NATIONAL GALLERY, Trafalgar Square, W.C.2. Tel. 071/839-3321.**

Houses Britain's best collection of historical paintings by such masters as Rembrandt, Raphael, Botticelli, Goya, and others. The gallery's permanent collection, which is categorized by school, includes representative works from almost every major 13th- to 20th-century European artist. Temporary displays include special exhibits from the museum's own collection, as well as some of the world's top traveling shows.

Impressionist paintings by Monet, Rousseau, and Cézanne are particularly popular, as are works in the lower-floor galleries, which include damaged paintings by great artists as well as excellent forgeries.

Call ahead, and take advantage of one of the regularly scheduled guided tours or guest lecturers. Specially produced brochures, books, and events will help you focus on particulars of this truly extensive museum.

**Admission:** Free.

**Open:** Mon–Sat 10am–6pm, Sun 2–6pm. **Tube:** Charing Cross, Embankment, or Leicester Square.

**ST. PAUL'S CATHEDRAL, St. Paul's Churchyard, E.C.4. Tel. 071/248-2705.**

Dedicated to the patron saint of The City of London, St. Paul's is architect Sir Christopher Wren's masterpiece. Wren is buried in the cathedral's crypt, his tomb marked by the Latin inscription "Lector, si monumentum requiris, circumspice" ("Reader, if you seek his monument, look around you"). And what a monument! Over 515 feet long and 365 feet high (from curb to cross), the great Renaissance edifice is capped by one of the largest domes in Christendom. You can climb the 259 steps to the Whispering Gallery, located just below the dome. Acoustics here are such that even soft sounds can be heard on the other side of the dome, 107 feet away. A second steep climb brings you to the Stone Gallery, and presents you with a view of London that is unrivaled. The Golden Gallery is higher still: at the top of the dome, an additional 153-step climb.

Back on the ground, take a look at the American Memorial Chapel. Located within the ambulatory, the chapel was built with contributions from people all over Britain, and pays tribute to American soldiers who lost their lives during World War II.

St. Paul's Cathedral has been the setting for many important ceremonies, including the funerals of Admiral Lord Nelson (1806) and Sir Winston Churchill (1965), and the wedding of Prince Charles and Lady Diana Spencer in 1981.

**Admission:** Cathedral, free; £1 ($1.80) donation requested; crypt, £1.10 ($2); ambulatory, 60p ($1.10); galleries, £2 ($3.60). All entrances half price for children under 13.

**Open:** Cathedral, daily 7:30am–6pm; crypt and ambulatory, Mon–Fri 10am–4:15pm, Sat 11am–4:15pm, Sun for services only. **Tube:** St. Paul's.

**TATE GALLERY, Millbank, S.W.1. Tel. 071/821-1313.**

This is both London's main museum of modern art and the primary national gallery for British paintings. Local art connoisseurs complain about the museum's inability to attract major exhibitions, but even if they are not the most prestigious, shows here are usually of high quality. The Tate has an especially good collection of cubist works, as well as a wide selection of other contemporary styles. Excellent canvases by Monet, van Gogh, and Matisse are on display, as are four works by surrealist Salvador Dalí; his *Metamorphosis of Narcissus* is breathtaking.

The Clore Gallery is the museum's newest wing, and houses an extensive collection of J. M. W. Turner's oils and drawings. Over 300 works by Britain's most famous artist anchor the Tate's impressive collection of British art over the years.

**Admission:** Permanent Collection, free; temporary exhibits, £3 ($5.40) for adults, £1.50 ($2.70) for students, seniors, and children.

**Open:** Mon–Sat 10am–5:50pm, Sun 2–5pm. **Tube:** Pimlico.

**TOWER BRIDGE, E.1. Tel. 071/403-3761.**

Here's a lyrical London landmark you can't miss. From inside the colorful blue-and-white "flying" footbridges you can get a good idea of the city's layout, and a terrific view of London's unspectacular skyline. Below ground, the bridge's cantilever operating system and hydraulic machinery are open to view, displayed with detailed diagrams and historical photos. Unless you are particularly fond of heights or Victorian engineering, however, keep your pounds in your pocket as the best views are from the outside.

In summer, the bridge opens for shipping five times each day. Opening times change daily and are only announced one day in advance; call for information.

**Admission:** £2.50 ($4.50) for adults, £1 ($1.80) for seniors and children 5–15. Last tickets sold 45 minutes before closing.

**Open:** Apr–Oct, daily 10am–6:30pm; Nov–Mar, Mon–Sat 10am–4:45pm. **Tube:** Tower Hill.

**TOWER OF LONDON, E.C.3. Tel. 071/709-0765.**

Begun by William I (the Conqueror) soon after the Norman conquest of the British Isles in 1066, the complex has served as a fortress, a royal palace, a treasury, an armory, and a menagerie, but it is best remembered as a prison. The two young sons of Edward IV were murdered here in 1485, as was Henry VIII's second wife, Anne Boleyn. Today the closest the Tower comes to torture is the suffocating feeling you get on weekends when it seems like everyone in London is here.

The Tower of London is not a single tower at all, but a series of towers and buildings sharing the same compound. The oldest structure is the **White Tower,** which dates from 1078. Named for its whitewashed walls, this centrally situated tower is now home to an extensive collection of weapons and armor. Even if you're not fascinated by war, make it a point to see Henry VIII's anatomically exaggerated metal suit (you'll know it when you see it).

The White Tower faces the **Jewel House,** home to England's crown jewels—some of the most precious in the world. Located below ground, in fortified vaults, sparklers like the exquisite Koh-i-noor diamond, which adorns the Queen Mother's orb and sceptre, will make your eyes bulge.

The **Bloody Tower** is the compound's most infamous. According to popular legend, perpetuated by Shakespeare, the Bloody Tower was where the two little princes were murdered by the henchmen of Richard III. Sir Walter Raleigh also spent 13 years here before the executioner visited him.

Other buildings within the compound now house a variety of weapons, torture instruments, and related exhibits. Most are categorized by military campaign or era.

Before you leave, be sure to visit the **Chapel of St. John.** Dating from 1080, this is the first Norman chapel in London. Its heavy stone interior is interesting both architecturally and as a counterpoint to the instruments of brutality that have long surrounded it.

Upon entering the Tower of London, wait by the first gate for the excellent, and free, Beefeater-guided tour.

See "Special-Interest Sightseeing: For the History Buff," below, for information on attending the Tower's nightly Ceremony of the Keys.

**Admission:** £5.80 ($10.45) for adults, £3 ($5.40) for children; £1 ($1.80) less in winter.

**Open:** Mar–Oct, Mon–Sat 9:30am–5:45pm, Sun 2–5:30pm; Nov–Feb, Mon–Sat 9:30am–4:30pm. Beefeater tours given every half hour from 10:45am. **Tube:** Tower Hill.

**VICTORIA AND ALBERT MUSEUM, Cromwell Rd., S.W.7. Tel. 071/589-6371.**

Named after Queen Victoria and her consort, the V&A is an enormous treasure house devoted to the decorative arts. It is also the favorite London gallery of those in the know.

Truly huge, in both size and scope, the museum's 7 miles of galleries feature comprehensive collections of fine and applied arts covering many countries, periods, and styles. Islamic carpets, English furniture, Italian sculpture, and extensive collections of glass, ceramics, and ivories from India, China, and other parts of the world are all here, and methodically categorized. Highlights include the Great Bed of Ware, referred to by Shakespeare in *Twelfth Night,* and Raphael's famous *Cartoons,* ten immense tapestry patterns painted for Pope Leo in 1516. Most popular, perhaps, is the museum's incredible Dress Collection encompassing fashions from the 16th century to the present.

The Twentieth Century Primary Galleries, upstairs, feature temporary exhibitions of furniture, sculpture, and modern design.

**Admission:** Free (donation requested).

**Open:** Mon–Sat 10am–6pm, Sun 2:30–6pm. **Tube:** South Kensington.

**WESTMINSTER ABBEY, Dean's Yard, S.W.1. Tel. 071/222-5152.**

The Benedictine abbey, which housed a community of monks as early as A.D. 750, was called Westminster (West Monastery) after its location west of The City. In 1050, Edward the Confessor enhanced the site and moved his palace next door, beginning a tradition of church and state that continues to the present day. All of England's monarchs have been crowned in the abbey since the coronation of William I on Christmas Day in 1066. Most have also been married and buried here as well.

When not in use, the Coronation Chair (built in 1300) sits behind the High Altar. Incorporated into the chair is the Stone of Scone, which has been associated with Scottish royalty since the 9th century. Captured by Edward I in 1297, the Stone has been stolen back by Scottish nationalists several times (most recently in the 1950s), but always recovered.

Poet's Corner is the final resting place of some of Britain's most famous bards. Chaucer is buried here, as is the actor Laurence Olivier.

The abbey's Henry VII Chapel, with its exuberant architectural extravagances and exquisite intricate carvings, will take your breath away. Comprehensive "Super Tours" condense the abbey's 900-year history into 1½ hours but cost a whopping £6 ($10.80) per person.

**Admission:** Abbey, free; Royal Chapels, £2.20 ($3.95) for adults, £1.10 ($2) for students and children (free to Henry VII Chapel Wed 6–8pm, the only time that photography is permitted).

**Open:** Abbey, Mon–Sat 9am–5pm; Royal Chapels, Mon–Tues and Thurs–Fri 9am–4:45pm, Wed 9am–8pm, Sat 9am–2pm and 3:30–5:45pm. **Tube:** Westminster.

## FROMMER'S FAVORITE LONDON EXPERIENCES

**A Visit to the East End** Home to London's famous Cockneys, and gateway for most of the city's immigrants, the East End is best visited on Sunday, when a lively outdoor market takes over Petticoat Lane.

**Observing Parliamentary Debate** You wouldn't expect lawmakers to make catcalls and boo, but that's exactly what they do in the House of Commons. Debates here can be exciting, not sleep-inducing like they are back home.

**An Evening at a West End Theater** The variety is enormous, but it hardly matters which show you choose. The thrill of seeing top-notch live theater in London's famous West End is unparalleled.

**Afternoon Tea at the Ritz** It's not cheap, but it's not too expensive either, and for a short while you can be treated like royalty. Make reservations as far in advance as possible.

**A Pub Crawl in Soho** Perfect for "pubbing," Soho's crowded pub scene means you can experience a variety of atmospheres, and not have to stumble too far to reach the next one.

**Touring the Tower of London** Popular with tourists for good reason, the Tower of London is everything a good attraction should be: interesting, humorous, historical, educational, and fun.

**A Day Trip to the Country** Whether you go to Greenwich, Kew, Hampton Court, or Windsor, a day in England's rolling hills and open countryside will make you wish you never had to leave.

# 2. MORE ATTRACTIONS

## MUSEUMS & GALLERIES

In addition to the public institutions listed below, art lovers might consider visiting some **commercial galleries.** Although these enterprises are primarily interested in sales, works on display there can be admired free of charge. The largest cluster of galleries in the West End is in and around **Cork Street,** parallel to Bond Street. You can see an interesting range of contemporary British work as well as established international artists.

**THE MUSEUM OF THE MOVING IMAGE (MOMI), South Bank, S.E.1. Tel. 081/401-2636.**

This lively, "hands-on" celebration of film and television is not only one of the city's newest museums, it's also one of the best. Chronologically arranged exhibits are designed to captivate, and are staffed with outgoing, costumed actors who never step out of character. Visitors are encouraged to learn by reading the news from a TelePrompTer, creating their own animated strip, and playing with many interactive exhibits. The best thing about MOMI is that the museum itself is as entertaining as a top movie. Displays strike the perfect balance between technology and the culture it produced. The emphasis here is on things British, but MOMI's extraordinarily popular slant is right out of Hollywood.

**Admission:** £3.95 ($7.10) for adults, £2.75 ($4.95) for students, seniors, and children. AE, V.

**Open:** June–Sept Tues–Sun 10am–8pm; Oct–May Tues–Sat 10am–8pm, Sun 10am–6pm. **Tube:** Waterloo is closer, but the short walk over Hungerford Bridge from the Embankment Underground is much more scenic.

**MADAME TUSSAUD'S, Marylebone Rd., N.W.1. Tel. 071/935-6861.**

Eerily lifelike figures have made this century-old waxworks world-famous. The original moldings of Voltaire and members of the French Court, to whom Madame Tussaud had direct access, are fascinating. Unfortunately, however, this "museum" gives the lion's share of its space to images of modern superstars like Michael Jackson, and political figures like George Bush. The dungeon-level Chamber of Horrors, which features the likenesses of Charles

### IMPRESSIONS

*London, thou art the flower of Cities all.*
—WILLIAM DUNBAR (1465–1530)

Manson, Jack the Ripper, and the like, is the stuff tourist traps are made of. Despite the fact that Madame Tussaud's is expensive, and somewhat overrated, it attracts over 2.5 million visitors annually. If you go, get there early to get a jump on the crowds.

**Admission:** £5.20 ($9.35) for adults, £3.45 ($6.20) for children. No credit cards.

**Open:** July–Aug daily 9am–5:50pm; Sept–Jun, Mon–Fri 10am–5:30pm, Sat–Sun 9:30am–5:30pm. **Tube:** Baker Street.

**MUSEUM OF MANKIND, 6 Burlington Gardens, W.1. Tel. 071/437-2224.**

Home to the ethnographic department of the British Museum, the Museum of Mankind maintains exhibits relating to a variety of non-Western societies and cultures. The collections focus on the way people live, and include native houses, means of transport, clothes, tools, and the like. One of the world's greatest collections of African art can be found here, while changing exhibitions present themes from Australia, the Pacific islands, and South America. The museum is very accessible in both size and scope. Don't miss the 9-foot-high Easter Island statue brought back by Captain Cook.

**Admission:** Free.

**Open:** Mon–Sat 10am–5pm, Sun 2:30–6:30pm. **Tube:** Piccadilly Circus or Green Park.

**SIR JOHN SOANE'S MUSEUM, 13 Lincoln's Inn Fields, W.C.2. Tel. 071/405-2107.**

A fantastic array of antiquities, architectural drawings, and works by Hogarth, Turner, and Watteau are housed in the former home of the architect of the Bank of England. The house is jam-packed with objects, displayed in a seemingly haphazard manner. But enter the small room where Hogarth's *The Rake's Progress* is displayed and ask the guard to show you the room's secret. You will be convinced that there is a method to the madness.

Mercifully free of tourists, the house itself is more popular with art students than with loud gawkers. A mock-Gothic grotto and intriguing use of natural light are the architectural highlights of the museum. Statues and busts line the balconies above, while classical sculptures and Egyptian artifacts (including the sarcophagus of Seti I, Pharaoh of Egypt 1303–1290 B.C.) are displayed below.

**Admission:** Free.

**Open:** Tues–Sat 10am–5pm. **Tube:** Holborn.

**WALLACE COLLECTION, Hertford House, Manchester Square, W.1. Tel. 071/935-0687.**

Located in a large house, this museum features a fantastic collection of masterpieces by Rembrandt, Rubens, Murillo, and Van Dyck. Sitting on a pretty square behind Oxford Street, the house also contains a well-preserved selection of 18th-century furniture, ceramics, and armor. The collection's many clocks are also notable.

**Admission:** Free (donation requested).

**Open:** Mon–Sat 10am–5pm, Sun 2–5pm. **Tube:** Bond Street.

**COURTAULD INSTITUTE GALLERIES, Somerset House, The Strand, W.C.2. Tel. 071/580-1015.**

Originally assembled in the 1930s by textile mogul Samuel Courtauld, this intimate museum houses one of Europe's best collections of impressionist and post-impressionist paintings. Van Gogh's *Portrait of the Artist with a Bandaged Ear* is next to works by Renoir, Gauguin, Cézanne, and Manet.

**Admission:** £1.50 ($2.70) for adults, 50p ($.90) for students, children, and seniors.

**Open:** Mon–Sat 10am–5pm, Sun 2–6pm. **Tube:** Temple.

**NATIONAL POSTAL MUSEUM, King Edward Building, King Edward St., E.C.1. Tel. 071/432-3851.**

One of the world's best assemblages of postage stamps from Britain and other nations. Over 150 years of philatelic history are covered, from the "Penny Black" to current issues.

**Admission:** Free.

**Open:** Mon–Thurs 9:30am–4:30pm, Fri 9:30am–4pm. **Tube:** St. Paul's.

**SAATCHI COLLECTION, 98A Boundary Rd., N.W.8. Tel. 071/624-8299.**

In the world of contemporary art, this collection is unrivaled. Charles and Doris Saatchi are Britain's largest private collectors and their personal museum features rotating displays from their vast holdings. Enter through the unmarked metal gateway of a former paint warehouse.

**Admission:** Free.

**Open:** Fri–Sat noon–6pm only. **Tube:** St. John's Wood.

**INSTITUTE OF CONTEMPORARY ARTS [ICA], The Mall, S.W.1. Tel. 071/930-6393 for recorded information.**

A major publicly assisted forum for the expression of artistic ideas, ICA maintains a theater, cinema, café, bar, bookshop, and two galleries for the avant garde. Regularly scheduled talks usually relate to current exhibitions.

See "Fringe Theater," in Chapter 9, for more information on ICA.

**Admission:** Galleries, £1 ($1.80).

**Open:** Daily noon–8pm. **Tube:** Piccadilly Circus or Charing Cross.

## PARKS & GARDENS

The English take gardening seriously; planting and pruning are not joking matters. Consequently, London has a large number of well-kept parks and gardens right in the heart of the city.

## IMPRESSIONS

*In people's eyes, in the swing, tramp, and trudge; in the bellow and uproar; the carriages, motor cars, omnibuses, vans, sandwich men shuffling and swinging; brass bands; barrel organs; in the triumph and the jingle and the strange high singing of some aeroplane overhead was what she loved; life; London; this moment in June.*

—VIRGINIA WOOLF, *Mrs. Dalloway*

*This is a London particular. . . . A fog, miss.*

—CHARLES DICKENS, *Bleak House*

✪ **Hyde Park** (tel. 071/262-5484) is the large rectangular expanse that is most often associated with London and, accordingly, is one of the city's most popular greens. The aptly named Serpentine lake is the 340-acre park's most notable feature. The adjacent Serpentine Gallery (tel. 071/402-6075) is a small exhibition space featuring rotating contemporary art displays. It is open daily from 11am to 6pm.

As in other Royal Parks, wood-and-cloth chaise longues are scattered throughout, and there's a charge for their use. Fee collectors appear from nowhere to extract 55p ($1) from seated tourists who are usually ignorant of this cost of relaxation. Benches and the grass are free. On Sunday the park really comes alive, when artists hang their wares along the Bayswater Road fence, and the northeast corner, near Marble Arch, becomes "Speaker's Corner." Anyone can stand on a soapbox here and speak on any subject. Although this tradition is often touted as an example of Britain's tolerance of free speech, few people realize that this ritual began several hundred years ago when condemned prisoners were allowed some final words before they were hung on Tyburn gallows, which stood on the same spot! Take the tube to Hyde Park Corner.

Lying to London's north is a huge misshapen circle called **Regent's Park** (tel. 071/486-7905). Originally a private hunting ground of Henry VIII, today the park is London's playground, famous for its zoo, concerts, and open-air theater in the summer. A band plays free beside the lake twice daily from May through August. Get there by tube to Regent's Park, Baker Street, or Camden Town (to Camden Town for the zoo).

**Kensington Gardens** (tel. 071/724-2826), with its trademark Round Pond, merges with Hyde Park's westernmost side. Fronting Kensington Palace, the gardens are more formal and distinctive than those in the park. The famous statue of Peter Pan with attending bronze rabbits is the garden's most popular feature with children.

✪ **St. James's Park** (tel. 071/930-1793), opposite Buckingham Palace, is perhaps the most beautiful of London's greens. Swans, geese, and other species make their homes here, further validating the park's romantic status. A beautiful lake, plentiful benches, and a central location—near the West End—make this park perfect for picnicking. Take the tube to St. James's Park.

Adjacent **Green Park** (tel. 071/930-1793) is named for its absence of flowers (except for a short time in spring). But the ample shade from tall trees also makes this park a picnicker's paradise.

Founded in 1673, the **Chelsea Physic Garden,** 66 Royal Hospital Rd., S.W.3 (tel. 071/352-5646), is the oldest botanical garden in Europe. Behind its high walls is a rare collection of exotic plants, shrubs, and trees, many over 100 years old. An unusual rock garden contains stone from the Tower of London and basaltic lava from Iceland.

Originally founded by the Society of Apothecaries to grow plants for medicinal research, the garden has since expanded to include rare species from the New World. Admission is £2 ($3.60) for adults, £1 ($1.80) for students and children. Open from April through October only, on Wednesday and Sunday from 2 to 5pm. The resident English Gardening School holds lectures throughout the summer. Call for details. Take the tube to Sloane Square.

A yearlong program of events sponsored by the **Royal Horticultural Society,** Vincent Square, S.W.1 (tel. 071/834-4333), is capped by the spectacular Chelsea Flower Show, held every May on the grounds of the breathtakingly beautiful Chelsea Royal Hospital. Tickets for this rose of garden shows are becoming increasingly hard to obtain, but are available abroad from an overseas booking agent. Check with the British Tourist Authority (see "Information, Entry Requirements & Money," in Chapter 2, for addresses) to find out which agency will be handling ticket sales this year.

Finally, the **Museum of Garden History,** St. Mary-at-Lambeth, Lambeth Palace Rd., S.E.1 (tel. 071/261-1891), houses a collection of old tools, and maintains a small garden of rare flora collected by two 17th-century royal gardeners. Located south of the Thames, on the grounds of a former church, the museum is the perfect setting for afternoon tea, served daily. Admission is free. It's open Monday through Friday from 11am to 3pm and on Sunday from 10:30am to 5pm. Take the tube to Waterloo.

## LUNCHTIME CONCERTS IN CHURCHES

In addition to classical music performances in the major music halls, lunchtime concerts are regular scheduled in various churches throughout the city. Church concerts, usually given by young performers, are all free, though it is customary to leave a small donation. A full list of churches offering lunchtime concerts is available from the London Tourist Board.

**ST. BRIDE'S CHURCH, Fleet St., E.C.4. Tel. 071/353-1301.**

Concerts feature professional musicians or top students on Tuesday and Friday, while Wednesday is devoted to organ recitals. Get there early to explore the ancient crypt of this handsome Wren church.

**Admission:** Free.

**Open:** Concerts start at 1:15pm. **Tube:** Blackfriars.

**ST. JAMES'S CHURCH, 197 Piccadilly, W.1. Tel. 071/734-4511.**

One of the few churches outside The City of London to offer lunchtime recitals. You should also keep an eye out for the occasional inexpensive evening concerts here, usually scheduled during the summer months.

**Admission:** Free.

**Open:** Recitals Thurs–Fri at 1:10pm. **Tube:** Piccadilly Circus.

**ST. MARTIN-IN-THE-FIELDS, Trafalgar Square, W.C.2. Tel. 071/930-1862.**

At the weekly chamber-music recitals, works by Debussy and Schubert are favorites. This church is also known for its above-average choir; consider attending a full choral Sunday service.

**Admission:** Free.

**Open:** Recitals Mon–Tues 1:05pm. **Tube:** Embankment or Charing Cross.

## 3. COOL FOR KIDS

Babies are unwelcome in many restaurants, are not allowed in pubs, and signs barring baby carriages (called "prams") regularly decorate shop windows. But older children are often encouraged with discounts, and activities appealing to youngsters abound. **Kidsline** (tel. 071/222-8070) offers advice on current activities and entertainment happenings for youngsters, and **Circusline** (tel. 0522/681591) is a 24-hour updated recording on circuses around town. The listings magazines *Time Out* and *City Limits* feature special children's pages, and should be consulted for special events.

In addition to touring the **Tower of London,** seeing Buckingham Palace's **Changing of the Guard,** climbing to the top of **Tower Bridge** and **St. Paul's Cathedral,** and visiting the **Museum of the Moving Image,** I offer the following two suggestions:

**LONDON ZOO, in Regent's Park, N.W.1. Tel. 071/722-3333.**

The London Zoo has over 7,000 species. This 150-year-old

sanctuary features a giant panda, and has a worldwide reputation for breeding and conservation. The year-round children's zoo is augmented by a summertime "Meet the Animals" program, where camel and pony rides are offered.

**Admission:** £4.30 ($7.75) for adults, £3.50 ($6.30) for students, £2.60 ($4.70) for children 5–15.

**Open:** Apr–Oct, daily 9am–6pm; Nov–Mar, daily 10am–dusk (about 4pm). **Tube:** Camden Town.

**THE BRASS RUBBING CENTRE, in St. Martin-in-the-Fields Church, Trafalgar Square, W.C.2. Tel. 071/437-6023.**

Inside one of London's landmark churches, both adults and children can make rubbings of replicas of medieval church brasses. It is interesting, historical, and even artistic.

**Admission:** Free. Brass rubbings cost from 50p (90¢).

**Open:** Mon–Sat 10am–6pm; Sun noon–6pm.

# 4. SPECIAL-INTEREST SIGHTSEEING

## FOR EVERYONE

**FREUD MUSEUM, 20 Maresfield Gardens, Hampstead, N.W.3. Tel. 071/435-2002.**

Located in the psychoanalyst's former home. Although Freud lived here less than a year, after fleeing from the Nazis in 1938, he was able to re-create his Viennese consulting room, where you can view his famous couch. Six rooms remain as they were at the time of his death, decorated with antiques and memorabilia. Some are graphically sexual.

**Admission:** £2 ($3.60) for adults, £1 ($1.80) for students, free for children under 12.

**Open:** Wed–Sun noon–5pm. **Tube:** Finchley Road.

**HIGHGATE CEMETERY, Swain's Lane, Hampstead. Tel. 081/340-1834.**

Swain's Lane divides London's Highgate Cemetery in two. The old, overgrown "Egyptian" west side filled up years ago and is now accessible only by guided tour (hourly in summer). The most famous resident of the east side (where you can roam freely) is Karl Marx, whose grave is topped by a huge bust. The Chinese government helps pay for the upkeep of Marx's grave, a site still popular with Communist government delegations sightseeing in London.

**Admission:** East side, free; west side, a £4 ($7.20) donation is requested when joining a tour, run by the Friends of Highgate Cemetery (tel. 071/348-0808).

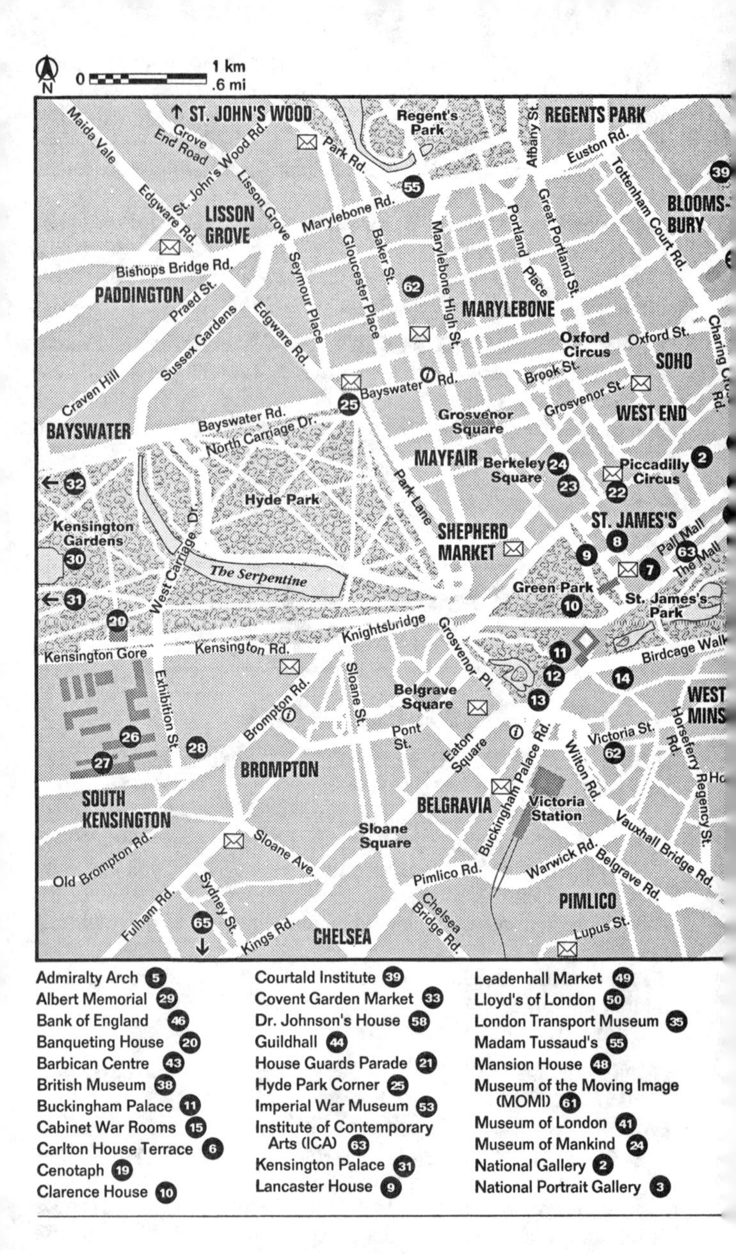


**Open:** Apr–Sept daily 10am–5pm, Oct–Mar daily 10am–4pm
**Tube:** Archway.

## FOR THE LITERARY ENTHUSIAST

As the former capital of the English-speaking world, London boasts a rich literary tradition. Geoffrey Chaucer lived above Aldgate, in

# INNER LONDON AND SPECIAL-INTEREST SIGHTSEEING

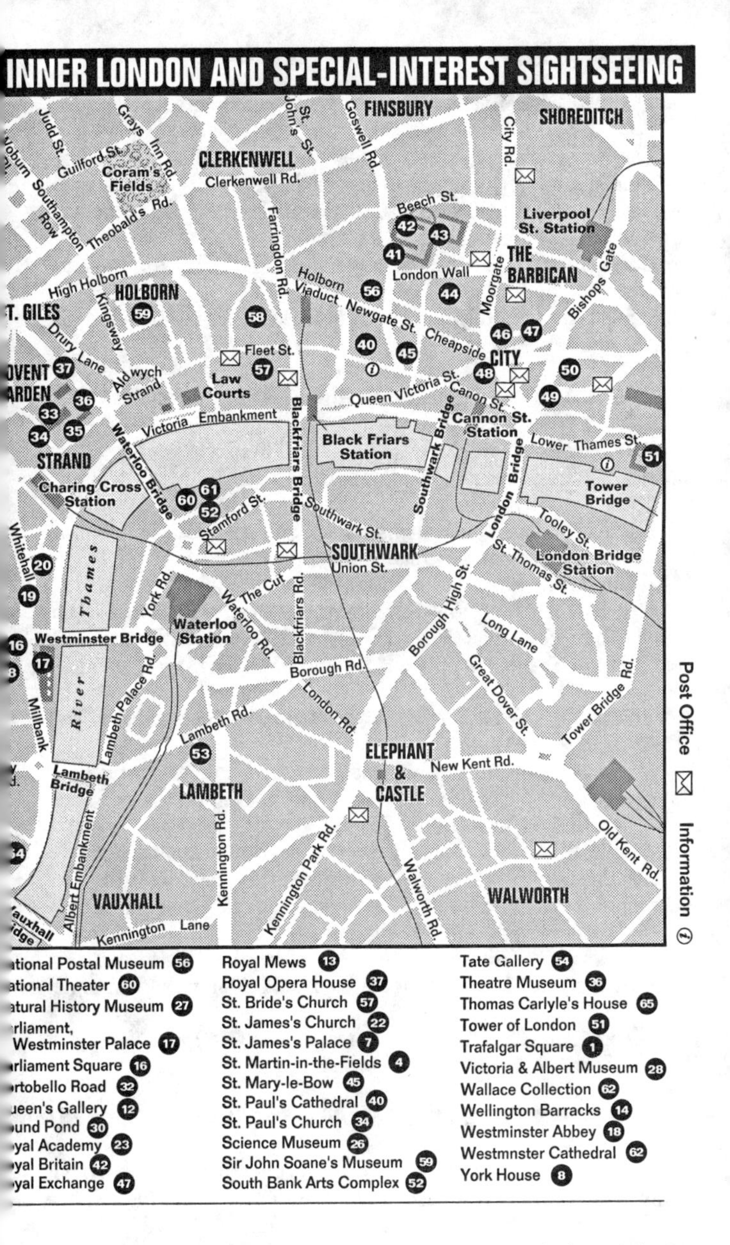


the easternmost part of The City, until 1386, and playwright Joe Orton lived on Noel Road in Islington until his death in 1967. Oscar Wilde, Dylan Thomas, George Orwell, D. H. Lawrence, Shaw, Kipling, Blake—the list of writers who made London their home goes on and on. Unfortunately, a little blue plaque is usually all that's left to mark the past, but there are some exceptions.

**DR. JOHNSON'S HOUSE, 17 Gough Square, Fleet St., E.C.4. Tel. 071/353-3745.**

The house where famous lexicographer Samuel Johnson (1709–84) lived and worked, compiling the world's first English dictionary, is now a shrine to him. His original dictionary is on display in the long attic where it was produced.

**Admission:** £1.70 ($3.05) for adults, £1 ($1.80) for students, seniors, and children.

**Open:** May–Sept, Mon–Sat 11am–5:30pm; Oct–Apr, Mon–Sat 11am–5pm. **Tube:** Blackfriars.

**KEATS'S HOUSE, Wentworth Place, Keats Grove, N.W.3. Tel. 071/435-2062.**

Romantic poet John Keats (1795–1821) lived and worked in this unassuming home in tranquil Hampstead Heath. "Ode to a Nightingale" was penned here, and a first edition is displayed along with books, diaries, letters, and memorabilia, and some original furnishings. A trip to his house is highly recommended.

**Admission:** Free.

**Open:** Apr–Oct, Mon–Fri 2–6pm, Sat 10am–1pm and 2–5pm, Sun 1–5pm; Nov–Mar Mon–Fri and Sun 2–5pm, Sat 10am–1pm and 2–5pm. **Tube:** Hampstead.

**THOMAS CARLYLE'S HOUSE, 24 Cheyne Row, S.W.3. Tel. 071/352-7087.**

This 18th-century town house, located on a beautiful back street in Chelsea, is one of the best in London for its beauty and authenticity. Carlyle, a Scottish writer, lived here 47 years, until his death in 1881. His house remains virtually unaltered, to the extent that some of the rooms are without electric light. The surrounding neighborhood is now one of the most expensive residential areas in the city; the sublime silence of this enclave creates a wonderful counterpoint to the bustle of nearby King's Road.

**Admission:** £2 ($3.60) for adults, £1 ($1.80) for children under 17.

**Open:** Apr–Oct, Wed–Sun 11am–5pm. **Closed:** Nov–Mar. **Tube:** Sloane Square.

**DICKENS'S HOUSE, 48 Doughty St., W.C.1. Tel. 071/405-2127.**

Home to one of London's most famous novelists for a short, but prolific period, this row house on the outskirts of Bloomsbury is one of the most touristed houses in London. Dickens only lived here from 1837 to 1839, but in that time he produced some of his best-loved works, including *The Pickwick Papers, Nicholas Nickleby,* and *Oliver Twist.* The author's letters, furniture, and first editions are in glass display cases, adjacent to rooms that have been restored to their original appearance.

**Admission:** £1.50 ($2.70) for adults, £1 ($1.80) for students and seniors, 50p (90¢) for children.

**Open:** Mon–Sat 10am–5pm. **Tube:** Russell Square.

**THE OLD CURIOSITY SHOP, 13-14 Portsmouth St., W.C.2. Tel. 071/405-9891.**

It's debatable whether or not this is the one that Dickens wrote about, but it hardly matters. The amazing Tudor shop dates from 1567, and from the looks of it, you can't dispute its age. Make sure you climb the rickety stairs and see the shop's original fireplace.

**Admission:** Free (no purchase necessary).

**Open:** Apr–Oct, Mon–Fri 9am–5:30pm; Nov–Mar, daily 9am–5pm. **Tube:** Holborn.

## FOR THE HISTORY BUFF

It is hard to find much "history" on the streets of London because most of the old buildings have been either demolished or stashed away in the Museum of London (see "For the Architecture Lover," below). But history can be experienced firsthand by observing age-old ceremonies that are carried out as faithfully today as they were hundreds of years ago. Aside from the aforementioned Changing of the Guard, and a visit to the Houses of Parliament, plan in advance to attend the **Ceremony of the Keys** at the Tower of London. Every night for the past 700 years, the gates of this ancient complex have been ceremoniously locked. You can watch the half-hour-long ritual if you request permission in writing at least one month in advance. Tickets are free. Write to the Resident Governor, Constable's Office, HM Tower of London, London EC 3N 4AB. Include an International Reply Coupon.

**THE CABINET WAR ROOMS, Clive Steps, King Charles St., S.W.1. Tel. 071/930-6961.**

In the British Government's World War II underground headquarters, the Cabinet Room, Map Room, Churchill's Emergency Bedroom, and the Telephone Room (where calls to Roosevelt were made) have been restored to their 1940s appearance.

Taped tours, costing £1.50 ($2.70), take visitors around the 21-room complex in about an hour.

**Admission:** £3 ($5.40) for adults, £2 ($3.60) for students, £1.50 ($2.70) for children under 16.

**Open:** Daily 10am–5:50pm (last admission, 5:15pm). **Tube:** St. James's Park or Westminster.

## FOR THE ARCHITECTURE LOVER

In the United States, a 150-year-old structure is almost always a national treasure. In London, it very well may be another fish-and-chips shop. Successive eras have produced distinctive architectural styles, all still extant on the streets of London.

**MUSEUM OF LONDON, 150 London Wall, E.C.2. Tel. 071/600-3699.**

Roman reconstructions, a Stuart merchant's house, and a Victorian shop help illustrate the city's impressive past. In addition to displaying finds from London's archeological digs, the museum presents a good multimedia film presentation on the infamous fire of 1666.

**Open:** Tues–Sat 10am–6pm, Sun 2–6pm.

**Admission:** Free. **Tube:** St. Paul, Barbican, or Moorgate.

**THE ARCHITECTURAL ASSOCIATION, 36 Bedford Square, W.C.1. Tel. 071/636-0974.**

This is London's best architectural college. Its two galleries show major contemporary works.

**Admission:** Free.

**Open:** Mon–Fri 10am–7pm, Sat 10am–3pm. **Tube:** Tottenham Court Road.

## ROMAN LONDON

Every once in a while excavation for the purposes of constructing a new building reveals remnants of old London. These finds are routinely removed to the Museum of London (see above), so that little remains of the original city of Londinium. An exception is parts of the old Roman Wall, beside the Museum of London. Built by the Emperor Hadrian in A.D. 122, the crumbling wall was originally part of Cripplegate fort. It is located between the Tower of London and the Tower Hill Underground station.

Other Roman finds are located in the British Museum (see "Top Attractions," above) and in the nearby town of Bath (see Chapter 10).

## THE MIDDLE AGES

In the centuries after the Norman Conquest (1066), London became a great and powerful city. Its medieval monuments became symbols of the city's economic and military might. Westminster Abbey and The Tower of London are the most obvious architectural examples.

**GUILDHALL, off Gresham St., E.C.2. Tel. 071/606-3030.**

The seat of The City of London's local government, Guildhall (1411) is The City's most important Gothic secular structure. Twice restored (after the Great Fire and the Blitz), the hall is still the site of city council meetings, presided over by the Lord Mayor. Meetings are held at 1pm on the third Thursday of each month. They are open to the public.

**Admission:** Free.

**Open:** Daily 10am–5pm. **Tube:** Bank.

**SOUTHWARK CATHEDRAL, Montague Close, S.E.1. Tel. 071/407-2939.**

Founded in 1106, most of the church's edifice dates from the 15th century. Inside this Gothic masterpiece is a wooden effigy of a knight dating from 1275, as well as a memorial to Shakespeare.

Lunchtime concerts are regularly staged on Mondays and Tuesdays. Call for exact times and schedules.

**Admission:** Free.

**Open:** Daily 8am–6pm. **Tube:** London Bridge.

## TUDOR & STUART LONDON

**Inigo Jones** and **Christopher Wren** were two of London's most celebrated architects. Both men designed in the English Renaissance style using Italian and French models, both of which were inspired by the architecture of classical Greece and Rome. Jones's **Banqueting House** (see Chapter 8) and **St. Paul's Church,** overlooking Covent Garden Market, are excellent examples of the era. Wren's most famous work is **St. Paul's Cathedral,** but his **Royal Hospital** in Chelsea and **Kensington Palace** in Kensington are equal testaments to his ingenuity.

## GEORGIAN LONDON

Whole areas built in the 18th century celebrate the Georgian period's distinct style. Notice the huge windows fronting houses on Cartwright Gardens, Bedford Square, and other squares around Bloomsbury. The Horse Guards buildings on Whitehall date from this period as well.

**ST. MARTIN-IN-THE-FIELDS, Trafalgar Square, W.C.2. Tel. 071/930-1862.**

This famous London church is known for its spire-topped classical portico—the style most often copied by churches in the New World. A look at the church's grand interior can be combined with a visit to the Brass Rubbing Centre (see "Cool for Kids," above), or with a lunchtime concert (see "Lunchtime Concerts in Churches," above).

**Admission:** Free.

**Open:** Daily 7:30am–7:30pm. **Tube:** Charing Cross or Embankment.

## VICTORIAN LONDON

London's most striking buildings are pure Victoriana. And although the variety of styles from this era prevents one from making architectural generalizations, my favorite buildings are unabashedly flamboyant ones such as **St. Pancras Station** (take the tube to Euston), the **Houses of Parliament,** and the **Royal Courts of Justice** on the Strand (the latter is open Monday through Friday from 10:30am to 4:30pm; take the tube to Aldwych or Temple).

**Albert Bridge,** which connects Chelsea with the South Bank, was built during the 1870s, and is an excellent example of suspension engineering. It is said that soldiers crossing the bridge have to break-step so the vibrations of marching do not injure the span. At night, thousands of white lights make Albert Bridge one of London's prettiest.

## THE 20TH CENTURY

There are so many ugly 20th-century buildings in London that Prince Charles has taken an interest in actively fighting against the city's further architectural decline. There are, fortunately, some stunning exceptions.

**WESTMINSTER CATHEDRAL, Ashley Place, S.W.1. Tel. 071/834-7452.**

Westminster Cathedral, the headquarters of the Catholic church in Britain, was completed in 1903. Just a stone's throw from Victoria Station, this spectacular Byzantine-style building stands in stark contrast to the contemporary office buildings surrounding it. The interior marble columns and detailed mosaics are equally majestic. Take a look at the excellent rendering of the cathedral's interior, hung on the wall just inside the front door.

**Admission:** Free.

**Open:** Daily 7am–10pm. **Tube:** Victoria.

**THE LLOYDS OF LONDON BUILDING, Lime St., E.C.3. Tel. 071/623-7100.**

Designed by Richard Rogers (co-architect of Paris's Pompidou Center), the Lloyds of London Building opened in 1986 to much critical attention. All the "guts" of the building (elevators, water pipes, electrical conduits) are on the exterior, and cranes are permanently affixed to the roof, ready to help with further expansion should it become necessary. At night, special lighting lends an extraterrestrial quality to the site. You can visit the Lloyds exhibition inside, and get a bird's-eye view of the Underwriting Room of this famous insurer.

**Admission:** Free.

**Open:** Mon–Fri 10am–2:30pm. **Tube:** Monument or Bank.

# FOR THE VISITING AMERICAN

**Grosvenor Square,** W.1, has strong U.S. connections and is known to some as "Little America." John Adams lived on the square when he was the American ambassador to Britain, a statue of Franklin Roosevelt stands in the center of the square, General Eisenhower headquartered here during World War II, and the entire west side is occupied by the U.S. Embassy.

The former **home of Benjamin Franklin,** 36 Craven St., W.C.2 (steps from Trafalgar Square), is just one of many houses formerly occupied by famous Americans. For a complete list, pick up *Americans in London* (Queen Anne Press, 1988), by Brian Morton, an excellent anecdotal street guide to the homes and haunts of famous Americans.

## 5. ORGANIZED TOURS

Although the image of a tour group is repugnant to most independent travelers, the benefits of guided tours are almost always worth their accompanying stigma. This is especially true of a walking tour, or a short motorized sightseeing tour with a knowledgeable guide. To this end, I make the following suggestions:

### WALKING TOURS

London's most interesting streets are best explored on foot, and several high-quality and inexpensive walking-tour companies will help you find your way. The best are offered by ✪ **City Walks and Tours,** 9-11 Kensington High St., W.8 (tel. 071/837-2841), featuring over a dozen itineraries led by scholars who are truly interested in their subjects. Brochures listing itineraries can be picked up at London Tourist Board information offices, or you can call for daily itineraries. No reservations are necessary—just show up at the appointed time and place. Tours are priced at £4.50 ($8.10) for adults, £3.50 ($6.30) for students and seniors, free for children under 14. Several money-saving multiwalk cards are available.

One of London's most popular walks follows the route from Trafalgar Square to Parliament Square, and is outlined in Chapter 7. Other enjoyable walks are also described in that chapter, as well as in *Frommer's Touring Guide to London* (Prentice Hall Travel).

### BUS TOURS

If your time is more limited than your budget, a comprehensive bus tour may be your best bet. These tours guarantee that you will catch all the sights, even though you may not have the foggiest idea of where they are in relation to one another. At £9 ($16.20) per person, the **London Regional Transport** (tel. 071/227-3456) panoramic tours are cheapest. Tours depart frequently from Piccadilly Circus and Victoria Street (Victoria Station). From June 10 to September 22, tours run daily from 9am to as late as 7pm; the rest of the year, daily from 10am to 5pm. Tickets are cheapest when bought in advance at Piccadilly Circus or in Victoria Station's Travel Information Centre.

Do-it-yourselfers should purchase a **Travelcard** (see "Getting Around," in Chapter 3) and climb aboard a famous red double-decker bus. Two of the more scenic bus routes are: bus no. 11, which passes King's Road, Victoria Station, Westminster Abbey, Whitehall, Horse Guards, Trafalgar Square, the National Gallery, the Strand, Law Courts, Fleet Street, and St. Paul's Cathedral; and no. 53, which passes Regent's Park Zoo, Oxford Circus, Regent Street, Piccadilly Circus, the National Gallery, Trafalgar Square, Horse Guards, Whitehall, and Westminster Square.

# 6. SPORTS & RECREATION

Touring a city means more than just hitting the top sights and eating in foreign restaurants. It means involving yourself in the daily life of the locals. There is no better way to get to know the natives than to watch them at play. In addition to informing you about the availability of sports you know well, the listings below feature some special activities that are particularly British.

Questions pertaining to any London sport, either spectator or participatory, will be answered free of charge by **Sportsline** (tel. 071/222-8000), Monday through Friday from 10am to 6pm.

## SPECTATOR SPORTS

### CRICKET

Each summer, two London-area cricket grounds host a number of "tests" against rival teams. India, Australia, and other former colonies each provide formidable competition. Check the newspapers or call Sportsline (see above) or the tourist board for information on current matches.

**LORD'S CRICKET GROUND, St. John's Wood Rd., N.W.8. Tel. 071/289-1611.**

England's most important matches are played here. Games here are society events, but Americans and other middle class are welcome, if seats are available, and you can afford a ticket.

**Admission:** £15–£35 ($27–$63).

**Open:** Box office Mon–Fri 9:30am–5:30pm. **Tube:** St. John's Wood.

**OVAL CRICKET GROUND, The Oval Kennington, S.E.11. Tel. 071/582-6660.**

The cricket ground of the people, the Oval is less stodgy (and less pretty) than Lord's. Home to Surrey CCC, this field hosts matches during summer months only.

**Admission:** £15–£25 ($27–$45).

**Open:** Box office Mon–Fri 9:30am–5pm. **Tube:** Oval.

### FOOTBALL

England's soccer (called "football") season runs from August to April and attracts fiercely loyal crowds. Games usually start at 3pm and are great to watch, but the stands can get rowdy. Think about splurging for seats. Centrally located first-division football clubs include: **Arsenal,** Arsenal Stadium, Avenell Rd., N.5 (tel. 071/226-0304), tube to Arsenal; **Tottenham Hotspur,** 748 High Rd., N.17

(tel. 081/801-3323), tube to Seven Sisters; and **Chelsea,** Stamford Bridge, Fulham Rd., S.W.6 (tel. 071/381-6221), tube to Fulham Broadway. Tickets cost £6 to £16 ($6.80–$23.80), and games are usually played on Saturday.

## RACING

There is no horse racing in London proper, but **Ascot, Epsom,** and **Sandown** are within easy reach. Less serious bettors may want to try one of the greyhound dog tracks below, for an exciting alternative night out. Races run throughout the year.

**CATFORD STADIUM, Ademore Rd., S.E.26. Tel. 081/690-2261.**

There is a party atmosphere at Catford, one of London's busiest tracks. Don't expect champagne and caviar here; this is one of the working class's last refuges. There are usually ten races on Monday, Wednesday, and Saturday, the first one beginning at 7:30pm.

**Admission:** £2–£3 ($1.80–$5.40). **BritRail:** Catford.

**WEMBLEY STADIUM, Wembley. Tel. 081/902-8833.**

The soccer field is partitioned every Monday, Wednesday, and Friday to make way for the dogs. The first race usually begins at 7:30pm.

**Admission:** £2.50–£4 ($4.50–$7.20). **Tube:** Wembley Park.

## RUGBY

**Twickenham,** Whitton Rd., T.W.2 (tel. 081/892-8161), is the headquarters of the amateur Rugby Football Union where local and international games are played. The season lasts from September to April. Big games are expensive and sell out far in advance, but tickets for smaller matches start from £5 ($9). Take the tube to Richmond, then the Southern Railway.

## TENNIS

Center court seats for the ✪ **Wimbledon Championships** are sold by lottery half a year in advance. Unfortunately, there is no system in place allowing foreigners to participate in the draw, but Keith Prowse, Inc. (with an office in New York), offers Wimbledon packages, which include accommodations. Also, a (very) few center court seats are sold on the day of the match. To get these seats, camping out in line the night before might be in order; prices range from £16 to £30 ($28.80 to $54).

Tickets for the outside courts, where you can see all the stars in earlier rounds of play, are usually available at the gate. Ground entrance for these outside courts costs £8 ($14.40), reduced to £4 ($7.20) after 5pm. For further information, call the **All England**

**Lawn Tennis and Croquet Club** (tel. 081/946-2244). To get there, take the tube to Wimbledon.

## PARTICIPATORY SPORTS

### CHESS

Amateurs and grand masters lock horns at the **King's Head Chess Club,** at the King's Head Pub, 33 Moscow Rd., W.2 (tel. 071/229-4233). Sets and clocks can be rented from the bar for £1 ($1.80) plus a £5 ($9) returnable deposit, and there's always someone looking for a game. The club is open during pub hours. Tube to Bayswater.

### FITNESS GYMS

**CHELSEA SPORTS CENTRE, Chelsea Manor St., S.W.3. Tel. 071/352-6985.**

A community fitness center, this trilevel spa has a pool and a weight room available at bargain prices. To use the weights, guests must first take a half-hour "induction," costing £3.50 ($6.30). Other facilities include a squash court, aerobics classes, a sauna, and a solarium.

**Prices:** Weights £2 ($3.60) per session; pool £1.50 ($2.70). Call for prices on other facilities.

**Open:** Weight room Mon–Sat 8am–10pm, Sun 8am–6:30pm; pool Mon, Wed, and Thurs 7:30am–7pm, Tues 7:30am–7pm and 8 to 10pm, Fri 7:30am–10pm, Sat 8am–10pm, Sun 8am–6:30pm. **Tube:** Sloane Square.

**CENTRAL YMCA, 112 Great Russell St., W.C.1. Tel. 071/637-8131.**

Snazzy for a Y, this top facility includes a swimming pool, weight room, sauna, and solarium. Beauticians, massage therapists, and other specialized staff members are also on hand.

**Prices:** £3.50 ($6.30) per day, £25 ($45) per week.

**Open:** Mon–Fri 8am–10:30pm, Sat–Sun 10am–10pm. **Tube:** Tottenham Court Road.

### HORSEBACK RIDING

**Richard Briggs Riding Stables,** 63 Bathurst Mews, W.2 (tel. 071/723-2813), and **Ross Nye,** 8 Bathurst Mews, W.2 (tel. 071/262-3791), are the places to go if you want to join a group horseback ride around Hyde Park. Briggs charges £22 ($39.60) per hour, Ross Nye costs £19 ($34.20), and both get booked up early for weekends. No galloping or jumping is allowed. Get there by tube to Lancaster Gate or Paddington.

### ICE SKATING

**QUEEN'S ICE SKATING CLUB, Queensway, W.2. Tel. 071/229-0172.**

Weekend disco nights are especially crowded at this large indoor rink right in the heart of Bayswater. The basement-level rink can handle about 1,000 skaters, and often does.

**Admission:** £2.50–£4 ($4.50–$7.20).

**Open:** There are three sessions daily; call for exact times. **Tube:** Bayswater or Queensway.

**BROADGATE ICE, 3 Broadgate, E.C.2. Tel. 071/588-6565.**

You can also glide to the hits at England's only open-air rink. This tiny but modern rink is surrounded by wine bars and features a state-of-the-art sound system that will knock your skates off.

**Admission:** £4 ($7.20) including skate rental.

**Open:** Nov–Apr Mon–Fri 11am–3pm and 4–8pm, Sat–Sun 11am–2pm and 3–6pm. **Tube:** Liverpool Street.

## SNOOKER

**CENTRE POINT SNOOKER CLUB, under Centre Point, New Oxford St., W.C.1. Tel. 071/240-6886.**

Exit the Tottenham Court Road tube, look on the wall next to the tallest building around, and you're sure to see the sign pointing into the dungeon that is the Centre Point Snooker Club. Snooker is played on a pocketless table that is both longer and wider than the table used for standard American pool. This game can seem complicated to the uninitiated. The club is open 24 hours, a policy that helps perpetuate the sport's seedy image.

**Cost:** £4 ($7.20) per hour.

**Open:** Daily 24 hours. **Tube:** Tottenham Court Road.

# CHAPTER 7

# STROLLING AROUND LONDON



Despite heavy traffic, never-ending construction, and confusing streets, London is a walker's city. The walking tours outlined below are designed to acquaint you with different parts of the city and the divergent aspects of city life. For alternative itineraries, consult *Frommer's Touring Guide to London* (Prentice Hall Travel), or take one of the excellent guided walks offered daily by **City Walks and Tours** (tel. 071/837-2841; see Chapter 6).

## WALKING TOUR 1 — Political London

**Start:** Trafalgar Square.
**Finish:** Parliament Square.
**Time:** 1½ hours, not including museum stops.
**Best Times:** When the museums are open, Monday to Saturday between 10am and 5:30pm, Sunday between 2 and 5:30pm.
**Worst Times:** Early Sunday, when the museums are closed.

Whitehall, a single, long road that connects Trafalgar Square with Parliament Square, is London's primary street for government. The entire length of the road was once fronted by the Old Palace of Whitehall (Westminster Palace), until it burned down in 1698. Today, the Home and Foreign Offices have a Whitehall address, as do a host of other government buildings. The official residence of the prime minister is just steps away on Downing Street, and the spectacular Houses of Parliament are at the end of the block, towering over Parliament Square.

Start your tour in Trafalgar Square, which is easily reached by tube to the Charing Cross or Embankment Underground stations (each within one block of the other). Watch out for speeding cars and cross the street into:

1. **Trafalgar Square.** You are now standing in the heart of London. To the east is The City, London's financial center. To the north are Leicester Square and the commercial West End, London's entertainment and shopping areas. To the west is The Mall, the royal road that leads to Buckingham Palace. And to the south is Whitehall, the city's thoroughfare of government. In the center of the square is:
2. **Nelson's Column,** one of the most famous monuments in

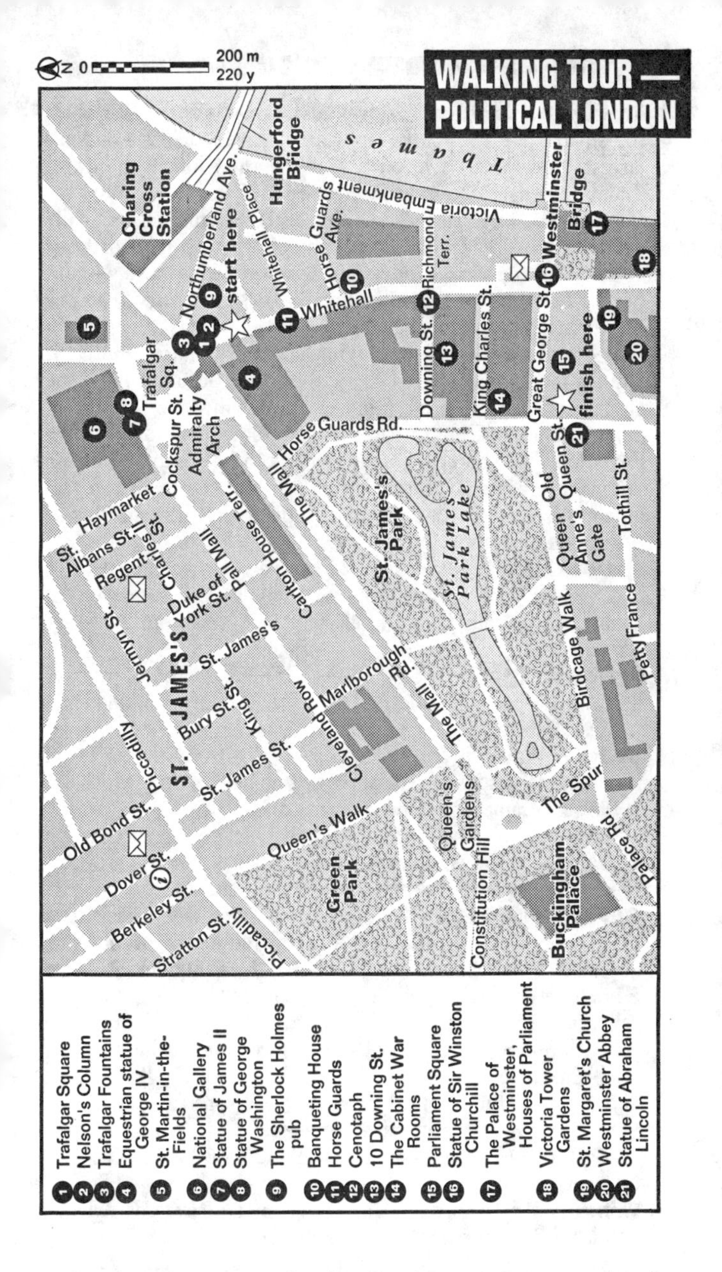


London. Commemorating the victorious naval commander who died at the Battle of Trafalgar (1805), the 145-foot column is topped by the figure of Lord Nelson. The statue itself stands 16 feet high, and is made of stone. It is so heavy it had to be hoisted up in three different pieces. At the base of the column are the famous:

**3. Trafalgar Fountains.** Surrounded by oversize bronze lions, the square and the fountains are the annual site of London's largest New Year's Eve party. Of the three other statues in Trafalgar Square, the most interesting is of:

**4. George IV,** on horseback. This equestrian statue was originally intended to top Marble Arch, which stands at the northeast corner of Hyde Park. One wonders why the king rides without boots, on a horse without stirrups or saddle. Look to the northeastern corner of the square, toward:

**5. St. Martin-in-the-Fields.** This popular London church is famous for its spire-topped classical portico. Begun in 1722, the church contains several famous tombs, including those of painters Thomas Chippendale, William Hogarth, and Sir Joshua Reynolds. The church's grand interior can be combined with a visit to the Brass Rubbing Centre (*see p. 123*), or with a free lunchtime concert (*see p. 122*). Occupying the entire north side of the square is the:

**6. National Gallery.** (*See p. 112.*) Designed by William Wilkins in 1832–38, the gallery houses Britain's best collection of historical paintings by world-class masters. The museum's entrance is guarded by the:

**7. James II Statue,** sculpted by Grinling Gibbons, one of England's greatest. Made in 1686, this one of London's best statues. Also outside the gallery is the:

**8. George Washington Statue.** A gift from the state of Virginia, the statue is a replica of the one by Houdon, which sits in the state capital building in Richmond.

With your back toward the National Gallery, cross Trafalgar Square, and begin your walk down Whitehall.

---

**REFUELING STOP** If you're ready for a light snack or a pint, make your second left turn off Whitehall, into Great Scotland Yard. Cross Northumberland Avenue to **9. The Sherlock Holmes** pub, 10 Northumberland Street (*see p. 180*). In the upstairs dining room of this popular "theme" pub you will find a re-creation of Holmes's fictional living room at 221b Baker Street. The head of the hound of the Baskervilles and other relevant "relics" decorate the downstairs bar.

---

Back on Whitehall, continue walking for 3 blocks. On your left you will see:

**10. Banqueting House,** on the corner of Horseguards Avenue. Modeled on Sansovino's Library in Venice, and completed by Inigo Jones in 1622, this opulent eating hall is the only extant part of the Old Palace of Whitehall, which stretched almost the entire way from Trafalgar Square to Parliament Square. Commissioned by Charles I, the interior ceiling was painted by Rubens in 1635, and portrays the benefits of wise rule. Ironically, that same king was beheaded outside Banqueting House in 1649. You can enter Tuesday through Saturday from 10am to

5:30pm, Sunday from 2pm to 5:30pm. Admission is £1 ($1.80). Directly across Whitehall from Banqueting House is:

11. **Horse Guards,** home to the Queen's ceremonial guards. Two brightly suited mounted guards stand watch—solely for the benefit of tourists—daily from 10am to 4pm. There is a small, relatively crowd-free changing-of-the-guard ceremony here Monday to Saturday at 11am, Sunday at 10am. The best show is probably the guard dismount, which takes place daily at 4pm.

Farther down Whitehall, in the middle of the street, you'll see the:

12. **Cenotaph,** dedicated to the citizens of the U.K. who died during the two world wars. Often surrounded by flowers and wreaths, the monument was built by Sir Edwin Lutyens in 1919. Just opposite it is:

13. **10 Downing Street,** the official residence of the British prime minister. Unlike most of the big government buildings on Whitehall, which were built in the 19th century, Downing Street is small in scale, lined with homes dating from 1680 to 1766. Number 10, down on the left-hand side, has been home to prime ministers since 1731. Number 11 is the office and home of the Chancellor of the Exchequer. Although they look small, these rather plain fronts hide sizable rooms and offices. Due to a rise in terrorist threats, we can no longer enter Downing Street, but must content ourselves to the view from behind police barricades.

Turn right at the next corner, and leave Whitehall for a short walk down King Charles Street. At the far end of the street are:

14. **The Cabinet War Rooms.** (*See p. 127.*) Here, in the British government's World War II underground headquarters, you can see the Cabinet Room, Map Room, Churchill's Emergency Bedroom, and the Telephone Room (where calls to Roosevelt were made). They have all been restored to their 1940s appearance, accurate down to an open cigarette pack on the table.

Return to Whitehall, turn right, and continue one block into:

15. **Parliament Square.** Laid out in the 1860s by Charles Barry, the designer of the new Houses of Parliament, the square was remodeled earlier this century when the center of the square was turned into a traffic island. Several statues sit around the square; most depict British prime ministers and generals. The first one you will encounter is the:

16. **Statue of Sir Winston Churchill.** Sculpted in 1973 by Ivor Roberts-Jones, the bronze statue is fitted with a small electrical current to discourage pigeons from sitting on the prime minister's head.

It's probably hard for you to concentrate on statues when one of the world's most famous buildings, and a spectacular architectural wonder as well, is towering above you.

17. **The Palace of Westminster,** now occupied by the **Houses of Parliament,** is a stunning example of Victorian engineering.

(*See p. 110–112 for complete information.*) The site has been home to royalty and government since Edward the Confessor occupied a palace here, before the Norman Conquest of 1066. The oldest remaining part of the building is **Westminster Hall,** a rectangular banqueting room, noted for its magnificent oak hammerbeam roof. Rebuilt in 1394–1402 for Richard II, the hall was regularly used for high treason trials, including those of Anne Boleyn, Sir Thomas More, Guy Fawkes, and Charles I. Oliver Cromwell was proclaimed lord protector here (his statue stands outside), and more recently, this is where Sir Winston Churchill lay in state. Unfortunately, since a bomb killed an MP in 1979, entrance to Westminster Hall is difficult; tickets are available, on a limited basis, from your embassy (*see Chapter 3 for information*). Rebuilt after a fire in 1834, the current 19th-century Gothic Revival building contains over 1,000 rooms and two miles of corridors. The 316-foot-high Clock Tower is the palace's most striking feature. Inside is **Big Ben,** a 28-thousand-pound bell that first chimed in 1858.

Just past the Houses of Parliament, on your left-hand side, fronting the Thames is:

**18. Victoria Tower Gardens.** Filled with benches, this small park is a great place for a picnic. At the park's entrance is a replica of Rodin's *Six Burghers of Calais*. The large bronze statue depicts the men who surrendered to Edward III in order to save their city from destruction in the Hundred Years War. Exiting the park, and turning back to Parliament Square, you face:

**19. St. Margaret's Church,** a grand 15th-century structure that is often initially mistaken for Westminster Abbey. St. Margaret's is in fact the parish church of the House of Commons, and is most famous for its beautiful and enormous east window, a stained-glass masterpiece made to commemorate the marriage of Catherine of Aragon to Prince Arthur, the brother of Henry VIII. Sir Walter Raleigh, Samuel Pepys, and John Milton, among others, are buried here. Behind the church, on the south side of Parliament Square, is:

**20. Westminster Abbey.** (*See p. 115–116 for complete information.*) Originally called Westminster (West Monastery) after its location west of The City, this was the site of a Benedictine abbey as early as A.D. 750. The present building was started by Henry III in 1245, and now contains his tomb. The main structure was completed by the end of the 14th century; Henry VII's Chapel was built during the beginning of the 16th century, the west towers were constructed in 1735, and the exterior underwent a drastic restoration in the 19th century.

Back on Parliament Square, take a close look at the many statues. Do you recognize anyone? You may be surprised to find the statue of:

**21. Abraham Lincoln,** on the side of the square farthest from the

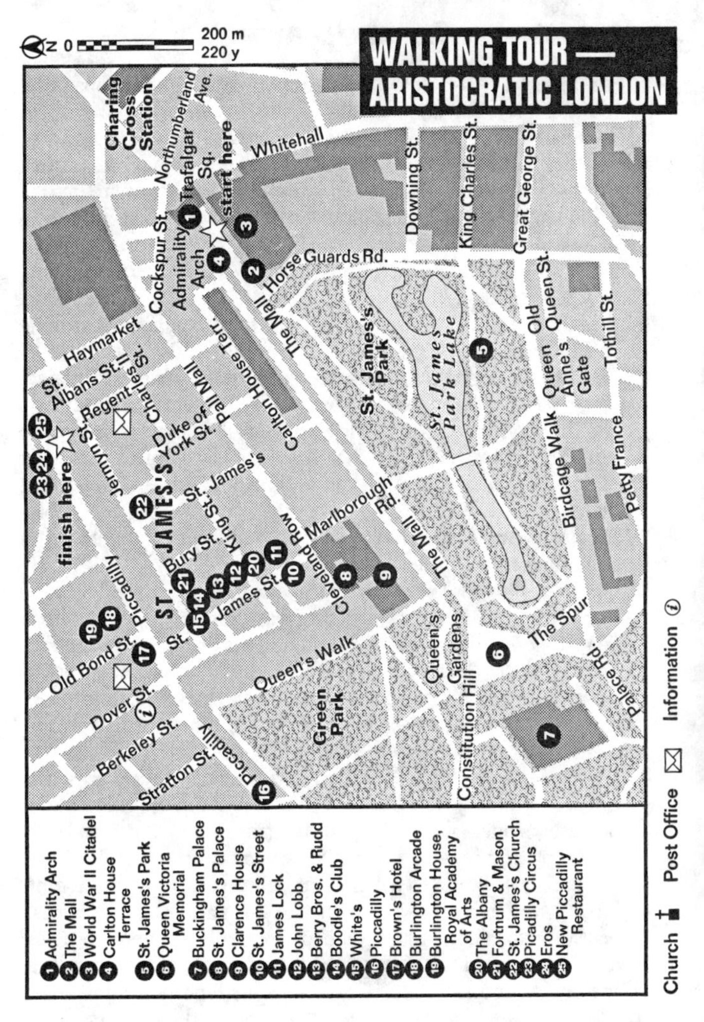


Parliament, the only depiction of a non-Briton on the square. It was donated by the city of Chicago, and is an exact replica of the one in Lincoln Park.

## WALKING TOUR 2 — Aristocratic London

**Start:** Trafalgar Square.
**Finish:** Piccadilly Circus.
**Time:** Approximately 2 hours, not including shopping stops.
**Best Times:** Mornings, when you can be at Buckingham Palace in time for the Changing of the Guard (usually at 11:30am).

**Worst Times:** After 6pm and on Sundays, when the shops of St. James's and Piccadilly are closed.

The small corner of London nestled between Green Park and St. James's Park has long been a favorite of the aristocracy. St. James's Palace was a royal residence as early as 1660, and Queen Victoria made Buckingham Palace her home when she took the throne in 1837.

Start your tour in Trafalgar Square (*see Walking Tour 1, above*), and proceed through:

1. **Admiralty Arch,** on the eastern side of the square, the striking entranceway to:
2. **The Mall,** a straight half-mile strip that connects Trafalgar Square with Buckingham Palace. Closed to traffic on Sundays and during important state visits, The Mall takes its name from a similarly named ball game that was once played on a long court here. Near the entrance to The Mall, Admiralty Arch is flanked by the:
3. **World War II Citadel,** on the south side, a bomb-proof communications center, and:
4. **Carlton House Terrace,** to the north. Built in 1837 by John Nash, the large Regency structure was home to prime ministers Gladstone and Palmerston. It also housed the offices of the Free French forces from 1940 to 1945, under the leadership of Charles de Gaulle. The Terrace now houses the Institute of Contemporary Arts (*see p. 119 for complete information*). Bordering the entire south side of The Mall is:
5. **St. James's Park,** the oldest of London's Royal Parks, was opened by Henry VIII in 1532. One of London's prettiest parks, St. James's once contained an aviary, from which Birdcage Walk, on the other side of the park, takes its name. From 1662 to 1990, the park was home to a family of pelicans. Although these big birds have been removed to the Regent Park Zoo, St. James's centrally located wrench-shaped lake still supports over 20 species of waterfowl. After a stroll (and maybe even a picnic) in the park, continue along The Mall to its terminus at the:
6. **Queen Victoria Memorial.** Now enclosed by an iron fence, in the center of a busy traffic circle, the massive 1911 statue depicts the queen with golden horses. Just behind the Memorial is:
7. **Buckingham Palace,** originally home to the Duke of Buckingham, and later converted into a royal residence by George IV. (*See p. 110 for complete information on the palace and the Changing of the Guard.*) John Nash, one of London's most prolific architects, led the renovation. Rebuilding was far from finished when Queen Victoria took up residence in 1837. Successive modifications have enlarged the palace to almost 600 rooms. Although tourists only have a good view of the rather plain neo-Georgian east front (added by Sir Aston Webb in 1913), the best view is said to be from the back, where the queen's famous garden parties are held. The Changing of the

Guard is performed by five rotating regiments of the Queen's Foot Guards.

Backtrack 1 block up The Mall, turn left on Stable Yard Road, and after one more block, turn right, around the corner of:

8. **St. James's Palace.** Built in the 1530s by Henry VIII, this pretty, but understated, palace has lent its name to the fashionable area that surrounds it. Since it was originally built in the 16th century, the Tudor residence has been successively modified by illustrious craftsmen and architects including Grinling Gibbons and Christopher Wren. Although it is no longer home to the reigning monarch, foreign ambassadors to London are still called "ambassadors to the Court of St. James's."

   Walk to the front of the palace, just ahead of you. Although you cannot enter it:

9. **Clarence House,** the residence of the Queen Mother, is located through the big front gates, just behind the palace. Here, facing the south end of St. James's Street, guards in tall, black bearskin hats stand guard with bayoneted machine guns—weapons that have only relatively recently replaced the sword. With your back to the palace gates, walk up:

10. **St. James's Street,** one of the city's most opulent roads. This short stretch is home to some of London's most famous gentlemen's clubs. For centuries, these bastions of aristocracy have provided lodging, food, drink, and good company for the well-heeled. Only recently have women been admitted. None displays its name; if you don't know where they are, you probably weren't meant to. On the right-hand side are many shops boasting storefronts that haven't changed substantially since the 18th century. These are some of the most exclusive stores anywhere. For instance:

11. **James Lock,** 6 St. James's Street, has long supplied handmade hats to wealthy, aristocratic ladies and gentlemen. Heads are measured for made-to-order hats that can take up to 2 months to create. It is said that the traditional bowler was invented here, and it can still be purchased for about £90 ($162). You might just want to window shop. Nearby is:

12. **John Lobb,** 9 St. James's Street, the world's fanciest shoemakers. Members of the royal family have been coming here for handcrafted footwear for more than 200 years; their exact foot measurements are all kept here. To make sure the shoe fits, John Lobb will take a cast of your foot, and create the shoe around it. The simplest styles start from about £800 ($1,440), and you will have to wait about half a year. A few doors down is:

13. **Berry Bros. & Rudd,** a wine shop that has changed little since it first opened as a grocery store in 1699. As you have probably guessed, however, this is no ordinary liquor store. Behind the dark black exterior are an enormous pair of scales, wheelback Windsor chairs, and, curiously, no wine—the bottles are kept downstairs in the cellars. The list is extensive, however, and in addition to an excellent selection of French, German, and

American wines, the store sells malts, cognacs, sherries, and vintage ports that date back to the turn of the century.

Continue walking up St. James's Street, until you reach:

**14. Boodle's Club,** 28 St. James's Street, on the right-hand side, flanked by two towerlike wings. You might be able to steal a peek into this old gentlemen's club—a gathering place for politicians and gentry since 1783—through the large, street-level windows.

Further up St. James's, two doors past Jermyn Street, is:

**15. White's,** one of London's most famous clubs for wealthy gentlemen. Founded in 1775 as a chocolate house—in the years when cocoa was fashionable and expensive—White's began as a club for Tories, conservatives who supported George III. Continue walking up St. James's to its end at:

**16. Piccadilly,** a main street reputedly named for a 17th-century dressmaker who invented a type of frilly collars called "picadills." Once the address of many of London's largest aristocratic mansions, Piccadilly is now one of the city's major commercial thoroughfares. Just ahead, nestled between Albermarle and Dover streets is:

**17. Brown's Hotel,** an ultratraditional, oak-paneled hostelry of the rich and famous.

---

**REFUELING STOP** If you're in the area between 3pm and 6pm, and like to get a taste of the aristocratic lifestyle, enter **Brown's Hotel** (tel. 071/493-6020) for the best set tea in London. While you relax in an overstuffed chair under stained-glass windows, tailcoated waiters will serve you an endless supply of sandwiches and scones. If you can, make advance reservations (*see p. 104*).

---

Cross Piccadilly, turn right, and almost immediately on your left you will see the:

**18. Burlington Arcade,** one of London's first malls. There are no chain-stores here, however. This elegant Regency shopping arcade has been filled with small, expensive boutiques since 1819. Tailcoated watchmen, called "beadles," continue to enforce the promenade's conservative code of behavior, making sure visitors don't run, yell, or whistle. Next to the arcade is:

**19. Burlington House,** home of the Royal Academy of Arts (tel. 071/734-9052), England's oldest fine arts society. Founded in 1768, the academy boast a collection including works by Constable, Gainsborough, Reynolds, Stubbs, and Turner, and sculpture by Michelangelo. The society is best known for its annual summer exhibition, in which contemporary works are displayed and (often) sold. The academy is open Monday to Saturday from 10am to 6pm, and costs £2.80 ($5.05) for adults, £1.90 ($3.40) for students and seniors, and £1.40 ($2.50) for children under 18. Beside Burlington House is:

20. **The Albany,** a 1770 Georgian apartment building, with a reputation as London's most prestigious address.

Cross Piccadilly. Directly across from the Burlington House, at the corner of Duke Street, is:

21. **Fortnum & Mason,** 181 Piccadilly, a fancy department store famous for its food hampers and ground-floor food market. Founded in 1705, Fortnum's is reputed to be the oldest extant shop in Piccadilly. Look on the building's exterior and notice the Royal Warrants: coats of arms awarded by the royal family to show that they shop here, too. Higher up on the wall is an ornately decorated glockenspiel. If you arrive on the hour you can see the clock put on a show.

Continue down Piccadilly one block to:

22. **St. James's Church,** a postwar reconstruction of one of Sir Christopher Wren's prettiest designs. Enter the courtyard and notice the outdoor pulpit atop a short flight of carved stairs. Inside, the church boasts a beautifully carved baptismal font and organ case, by master sculptor Grinling Gibbons. Our tour ends 3 blocks ahead at:

23. **Piccadilly Circus,** a confusing confluence of the West End's major thoroughfares. Best at night, when the enormous neon advertising signs are in full glow, the circus is best known for its center-island **statue of Eros.** Cast in 1893, this small aluminum angel is not the cherub of love, but was made to represent Christian charity, in honor of Victorian philanthropist Lord Shaftesbury.

---

**A FINAL REFUELING STOP** If you'd like to end your tour with lunch or dinner, head for the **24. New Piccadilly Restaurant,** 8 Denman Street (tel. 071/437-8530). Located one block north of Piccadilly Circus, just off the bottom of Shaftesbury Avenue, this no-nonsense English restaurant offers good, inexpensive meals in one of London's most heavily touristed areas. There is no liquor license; patrons are encouraged to bring their own. (*See p. 98 for complete details.*)

---

## WALKING TOUR 3 — Legal London

**Start:** Trafalgar Square.
**Finish:** St. Paul's Cathedral.
**Time:** About 2 hours, not including museum stops.
**Best Times:** Weekdays, when the streets and Inns of Court are full of activity.
**Worst Times:** Weekends, when The City becomes a virtual ghost town.

England's fascinating, but sometimes complex, legal system is centered around four powerful legal societies; Lincoln's Inn, Gray's Inn, Middle Temple, and Inner Temple. Called "Inns of Court," the origins of these important fraternities are shrouded in history.

Until the 18th century, many lawyers were forced to decline professional advancements and judgeships, because they could not afford to throw the requisite banquet for their fraternity. The enforcement of these traditions allowed the class-conscious inns to keep wealthy landholders in the highest positions. It wasn't at all covert. In the early 17th century, a mandate by James I actually denied admission to the Inns of Court to anyone who was not a gentleman by descent.

Although they are no longer the sole dispensers of legal education, the powerful societies still provide lectures to aspiring barristers, and maintain complete control over admissions to the bar. Before they are allowed to practice, law students are required to serve an apprenticeship for two years at one of the four Inns of Court.

This walk will take you along one of London's oldest and busiest thoroughfares, through several churches, and into several sanctuaries of law—some of the most mysterious and least-known parts of the city.

Start your tour in Trafalgar Square (*see Walking Tour 1, above*), and walk east along the right-hand side of the:

1. **Strand,** meaning "sandy bank." This long stretch used to hug the Thames, in the days before the Embankment narrowed the river. The Strand has been long been the address of fancy homes and pretty churches, and has been associated with lawyers for over six centuries. As you begin your walk, you'll notice the:
2. **Adelphi and Vaudeville theatres,** on your left, known for musicals and dramas, respectively.

   Stay on the right, however, where one of the first buildings you will encounter, just past Carting Lane, is the:
3. **Savoy Hotel.** This was London's most prestigious hostelry when it first opened in 1889. Notice the long driveway, into and out of which taxis continually move. This may be the only place in London where cars drive on the right-hand side. The adjacent:
4. **Savoy Theatre** was home to several of Gilbert and Sullivan's first comic operas.

   Two blocks ahead, just past Lancaster Place (which crosses Waterloo Bridge) is:
5. **Somerset House,** a huge Palladian structure dating from 1776, housing the Internal Revenue Ministry and the:
6. **Courtauld Institute Galleries,** a small museum with one of the best collections of impressionist and post-impressionist art in Europe. (*See p. 119 for complete information.*)

   After exiting the galleries, return to the Strand, and almost immediately you come upon the church:
7. **St. Mary-le-Strand,** lodged on an island in the middle of the street. Consecrated in 1724, the exterior Ionic portico hides a baroque interior, complete with intricate floral moldings. Fa-

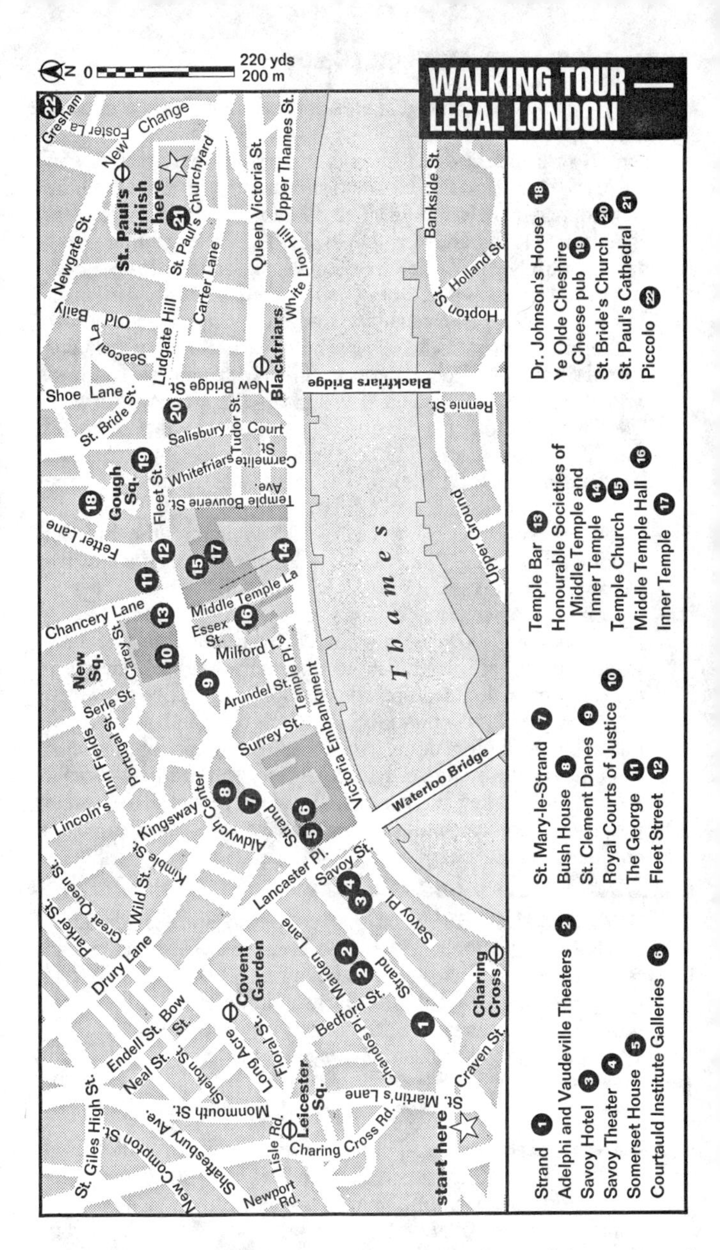


mous parishioners included Sir Isaac Newton and the parents of Charles Dickens, who were married here in 1809.

Opposite the church, under the arches of Aldwich, on the north (left) side of the Strand is:

**8. Bush House,** a 1935 building that has been home to BBC Radio's World Service since 1940.

About 3 blocks ahead stands another center-island church, that of:

9. **St. Clement Danes.** Although it survived the Great Fire of 1666, the church was condemned soon afterward, and rebuilt by Christopher Wren in 1682. The 50-foot baroque steeple was added in 1719 by architect James Gibbs. After suffering heavy damage during the Battle of Britain, the interior was renovated, and the church was rededicated in honor of the Royal Air Force. The building's exterior remains damaged by shrapnel, a reminder of the hits it took from German bombs. The interior contains several Shrines of Remembrance, filled with names of airmen who died in action. Included are many Americans who were killed while fighting for Britain. The Welsh slate floors are inlaid with 750 brass badges of RAF squadrons. Lexicographer Samuel Johnson spent a lot of time in this church, as evidenced by the statue of him that stands out front.

Just outside the church, it's hard to ignore the hulking building in front of you, with its elaborate ornamentation. It's not a grand cathedral, it's the:

10. **Royal Courts of Justice,** one of London's most architecturally stunning Victorian buildings. Construction of the Law Courts, as they are also called, was begun in 1874. The design is the result of an architectural competition won by George Street, an expert in 13th-century Gothic styles. Inside the main hall of this highest English court is a small exhibition of the legal costumes worn by judges and barristers. You are free to walk around the building and peek into the courtrooms. Here, and in the halls, you can still see lawyers and judges dressed in ermine-trimmed robes and full-bottomed wigs.

---

**REFUELING STOP** Take time out to rub elbows with judges and lawyers and pop into **11. The George,** 213 Strand, an old timbered inn opposite the Royal Courts of Justice. This bilevel pub serves traditional ales on the ground floor and full lunches upstairs. It is known for its particularly good carved meats, served with the requisite potatoes and two veg.

---

Just past the Law Courts, the Strand becomes:

12. **Fleet Street,** named for a river—now covered—which used to flow from Hampstead. Fleet Street is synonymous with journalism, and was once home to the printing facilities and offices of most of London's newspapers. Since the *Daily Telegraph* and the *Daily Express* left their respective buildings several years ago, there are no longer any newspapers headquartered here. The monument in the middle of the street is:

13. **Temple Bar,** which marks the entrance to The City of London, and stands at the point in the road where the Strand becomes Fleet Street. Topped by a dragon and surrounded by statues of royalty, the Bar was erected in 1880, and is actually a memorial

to two previous gates that occupied this spot for hundreds of years. The monument, and much of the area surrounding you, is named for its proximity to Temple Church, an ancient church belonging to the order of the Knights Templar (*see below*).

On your right, about 50 yards up Fleet Street, is a pretty half-timbered house at number 17. Turn right under the house (Inner Temple Lane), and walk through the gateway into the grounds of the:

14. **Honourable Societies of Middle Temple and Inner Temple.** This single compound used to house the Knights Templar, a powerful religious brotherhood popular in the Middle Ages. The site is now home to two of London's four Inns of Court. The 14th-century inns were so called because they provided room and board to the students. Today, tradition still requires legal apprentices to eat with their fraternity 24 times before they are admitted to the bar. Practicing barristers must also continue to eat with the society, at least three times during each law term, in order to maintain their membership. Although they overlap somewhat, the Inner Temple has most of its buildings to the left of the walk you are now standing on, while most of Middle Temple's buildings are to your right.

Walk about 40 yards and turn left after the doorway marked no. 2. Just through this passageway, on your right, is:

15. **Temple Church,** an unusual round church designed using both Norman and Gothic models. Styled after the Dome of the Rock, in Jerusalem, this stone church was consecrated in 1185 and is one of the oldest in London. Inside, the nine life-size statues lying on the church floor are effigies of rich patrons of the Templars. A few steps south of the church is:

16. **Middle Temple Hall,** which dates from 1570, and was long the site of Middle Temple's mock trials. The hall used to keep regular visiting hours, but has recently been closed to the public. Try knocking on the door. If the guard is in he might let you sneak a peek. Inside is London's most fantastic double hammerbeam oak roof, and the walls are almost completely covered with coats of arms of former Middle Temple members. It is said that this hall hosted the first performance of Shakespeare's *Twelfth Night,* in 1601, a show which, most probably, was attended by the Bard himself. Queen Elizabeth I was also in the audience, and later gave the hall an oak table made of a single 29-foot plank. It still sits at the hall's far end.

To the east of Middle Temple Hall, just across the lawn, are the buildings of:

17. **Inner Temple,** the society with which Margaret Thatcher was associated, before turning to politics.

Exit the temple grounds the same way you came in. Cross Fleet Street, turn right, and take the second left after Fetter Lane, onto Johnson Court. Just steps ahead is Gough Square, site of:

18. **Dr. Johnson's House.** (*See p. 126 for complete information.*) Now a museum, this is the house where journalist and

lexicographer Samuel Johnson (1709–84) lived and worked, compiling the world's first English dictionary.

---

**REFUELING STOP** **19. Ye Olde Cheshire Cheese** pub, located on the north (left) side of Fleet Street, in a narrow passageway called Wine Office Court, has been serving since 1667. This historical wooden pub is where Dr. Johnson took his tipple, and is a sightseeing attraction in its own right. You'll have to duck through the low doors which, along with the long bar and wooden benches, are unchanged since the 17th century. (*See p. 180–181 for complete information.*)

---

Crossing Fleet Street once again, you soon arrive at:

**20. St. Bride's Church,** hiding on your right, in a courtyard just before Ludgate Circus. Look at the tiered spire. It's said that this stunning steeple was the inspiration for the traditional wedding cake, first created by a baker across the way. On December 30, 1940, German bombs destroyed the church and revealed the ruins of seven previous reconstructions on the same site. Most of what was uncovered is now on display in a small museum downstairs. If you arrive at 1:15pm on Tuesday, Wednesday, or Friday, stop in for a free classical-music concert (*see p. 121–122 for full details*).

Our walk now takes us across busy Ludgate Circus, for the ¼-mile walk up Ludgate Hill to The City of London's most spectacular masterpiece:

**21. St. Paul's Cathedral,** the only building in London that would not be out of place in Rome or Venice. (*See p. 113 for complete information.*) If you have the strength, climb the stairs to the uppermost gallery, and you will be rewarded with an unrivaled view of London. Looking west, you can trace your steps all the way back to Trafalgar Square.

---

**A FINAL REFUELING STOP** If you're in the mood for a quick bite before heading back to the West End or continuing on to the Tower of London, stop in at **22. Piccolo,** 7 Gresham Street, a simple sandwich bar with a cheap and extensive menu. The shop is two blocks northeast of St. Paul's, just off Martin's Le Grand Street, between St. Paul's Underground and the Museum of London. (*See p. 94–95 for complete information.*)

---

# CHAPTER 8

# SHOPPING A TO Z

Even the most jaded capitalist may be awed by the sheer quantity of shops in London. In breadth and depth of merchandise, London rivals New York as the best shopping city in the world. In fact, the range and variety of goods is so staggering that a quick jump into a store can easily turn into an all-day shopping spree. Everything you never even knew you needed is available here, and several distinct shopping areas—each with its own personality—make shopping fun.

## LONDON SHOPPING AREAS

The **West End** is the heart of London shopping, and mile-long **Oxford Street** is its main artery. The sidewalks are terminally congested here, and with good reason. A solid row of shops stretches as far as the eye can see. If you only have one day to shop, spend it here. At its midsection, Oxford Street is crossed by **Regent Street,** a more elegant thoroughfare lined with boutiques, fine china shops, and jewelers.

At Piccadilly Circus, Regent Street meets **Piccadilly,** which, along with **St. James's Street, Jermyn Street,** and the **Burlington Arcade,** make up one of the swankiest shopping regions in the entire world.

Anchored by Harrods department store, **Brompton Road** in Knightsbridge features a good variety of fashionable, touristy stores for both men and women.

**Sloane Street** is one of London's fanciest for high fashion. Connecting Knightsbridge with Chelsea, this sparkling street is lined with designer shops like Joseph, Giorgio Armani, Valentino, and Kenzo.

**King's Road** bisects Chelsea and straddles the fashion fence between trend and tradition. In the 1970s, this was the center of punk fashion. Things have quieted down somewhat, but the chain-store boutiques are still mixed with a healthy dose of the avant garde.

Young fashion also flourishes on **Kensington High Street** in general, and in Hyper-Hyper and the Kensington Market in particular. See listings below for information on specific shops.

### Hours

Stores are usually open Monday through Saturday from 10am to 6pm, but most stay open at least one extra hour one night during the week. Shops in Knightsbridge usually remain open until around 7pm

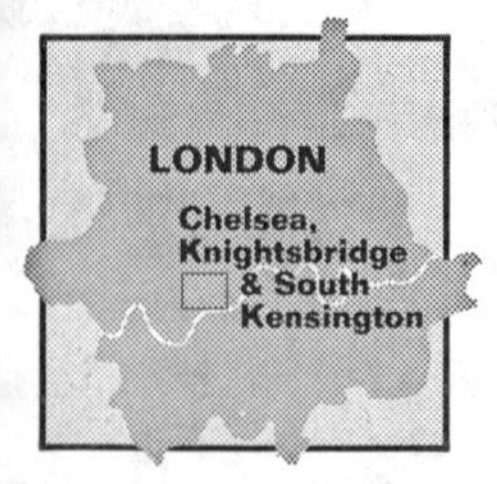


- Antiquarius 7
- Beauchamp Place 5A
- Brompton Arcade 3
- Brompton Road shopping area 2
- Chelsea Antique Market 10
- Chenil Galleries 9
- Harrod's 5
- Hyper-Hyper 1
- Kensington Studio High Street 1
- Kensington Market 1
- KIng's Road shopping area 6
- R. Soles 8
- Sloane Street shopping area 4

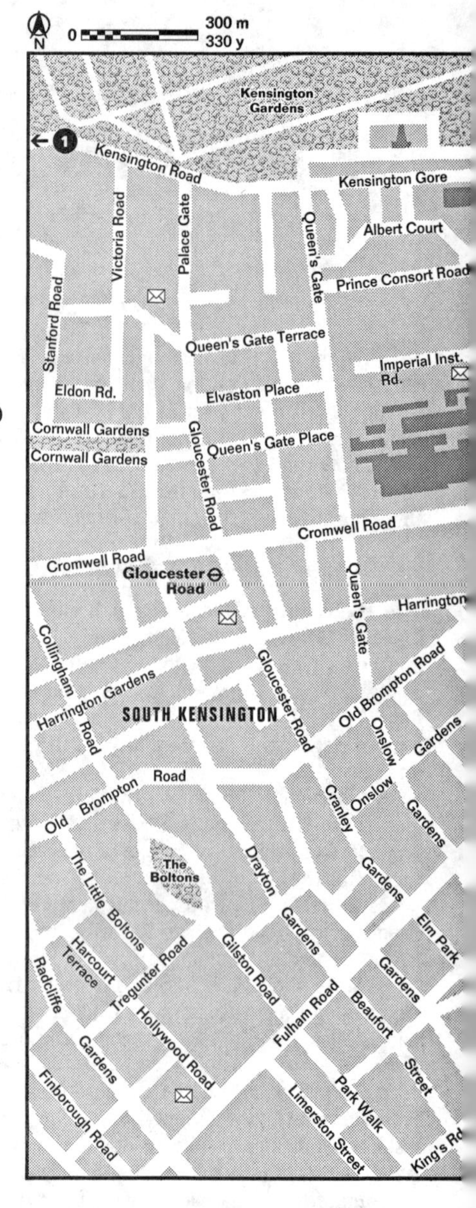


on Wednesdays, while stores in the West End are open late on Thursdays. Some shops around touristy Covent Garden stay open until 7 or 8pm nightly. By law, most stores are closed Sunday. If you are planning on visiting a particular store, it would be wise to call before heading out.

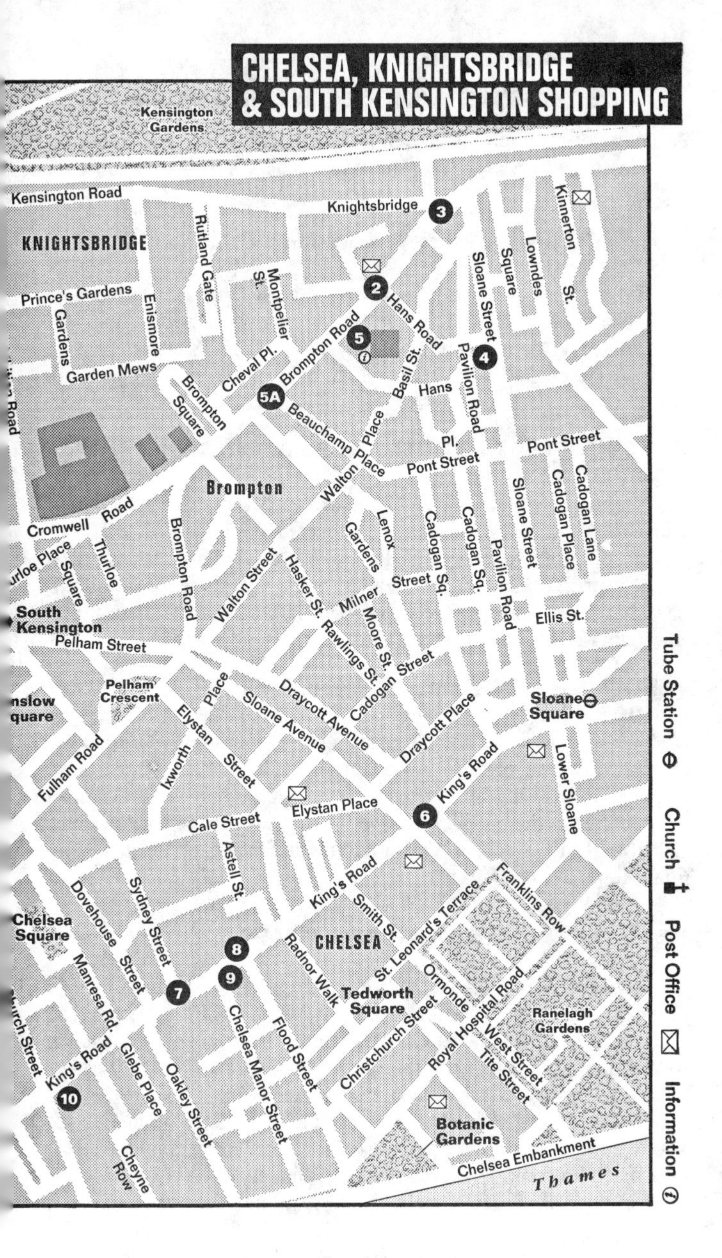


## Reclaiming Value-Added Tax (VAT)

As an incentive to shop, foreign tourists can reclaim taxes on some high-priced items. See "Saving Money on Shopping" in Chapter 2 for details on reclaiming Value-Added Tax (VAT).

## BEST BUYS & WHERE TO FIND THEM

As you stroll through the city, unusual specialty shops will undoubtedly catch your eye. A few you might especially want to look for include:

**THE BACK SHOP, 24 New Cavendish St., W.1. Tel. 071/ 935-9120.**

The Back Shop claims to stock the largest range of products for backache sufferers in Europe. Vibrating pillows, supports, massage oils, and other comfort-inducing devices are sold. Accepts AE, DC, MC, V. Open: Mon–Fri 10am–6pm, Sat 10am–2pm. Tube: Bond Street.

**ANYTHING LEFT HANDED, 56 Beak St., W.1. Tel. 071/ 437-3910.**

"Righties" will be amazed at how much they take for granted when they visit this unusual shop located off Regent Street, four blocks south of Oxford Circus. Practical gifts include scissors, rulers, kitchenware, corkscrews, mugs, and books—all made for the southpaw. No credit cards are accepted. Open: Mon–Fri 10:30am–5pm, Sat 10am–2pm. Tube: Oxford Circus.

**THE FILOFAX CENTRE, 21 Conduit St., W.1. Tel. 071/ 499-0457.**

Nothing was more representative of the booming 1980s than the Filofax loose-leaf organizers found under almost every yuppie arm. They're not cheap, but they are handy and, here at the British headquarters, you can pick up every insert ever made for the filers. Accepts AE, DC, MC, V. Open: Mon–Fri 9:30am–6pm, Sat 10am–6pm. Tube: Oxford Circus.

## TRADITIONAL SALES

January sales are as British as Christmas pudding (which is usually reduced by 30% after the holiday). All the big department stores start their annual sales just after Christmas, and the smaller shops usually follow suit. For Londoners, the January sales are a rite, and tourists are not immune to the fever and passion they induce. Several department stores (chiefly Harrods and Selfridges) compete for all-night lines by offering one or two particularly remarkable specials. Be aware, however, that some goods, shipped in especially for the sales, are not of as high a quality as those offered the rest of the year.

## MARKETS

Outdoor markets are where knowledgeable Londoners and bargain-hunting tourists shop for food, clothing, furniture, books, antiques, crafts, and, of course, junk. Dozens of markets cater to different communities, and for shopping or just browsing they offer a unique and exciting day out. Few stalls officially open before sunrise. Still, flashlight-wielding professionals appear quite early, snapping up gems before they reach the display table. During wet weather, stalls may close early. See below for detailed information on specific London markets.

## ANTIQUES

In addition to looking in the outdoor markets listed below, serious and casual antiques hunters should check out three stall-filled "malls" along Chelsea's King's Road. **Antiquarius,** 131 King's Rd. (tel. 071/351-5353), features over 100 sellers hawking everything from books and prints to scientific instruments, glass, and jewelry. **Chelsea Antique Market,** 245 King's Rd. (tel. 071/352-5689), has been around since 1964 and is known for good prices on records, period clothing, and assorted bric-a-brac. **Chenil Galleries,** 181 King's Rd. (tel. 071/351-5353), is more upscale, and specializes in oil paintings, furniture, and an eclectic collection of 19th-century applied arts and crafts.

The shops are open Monday through Saturday from 10am to 6pm and are closest to the Sloane Square and South Kensington tube stations.

## BOOKS

London is the best place in the world for books—new, used, and antiquarian. A great many of the city's 1,000 or so booksellers are clustered together in and around **Charing Cross Road,** each specializing in a subject. Look for entire shops devoted to art, science fiction, religion, medicine, cookery, crime, government, sport, and travel. Browsers should start at Leicester Square Underground and work their way north along Charing Cross Road. Don't ignore side streets like St. Martin's Court and Cecil Court.

To find the specialist shop that interests you, look in the telephone directory, ask at a tourist board information office, or ask a local bookseller. The list below includes some of the city's largest departmental bookshops as well as two good travel bookstores.

**DILLONS THE BOOKSTORE, 82 Gower St., W.C.1. Tel. 071/636-1577.**

An extremely helpful staff, terrific indexing, and almost a quarter of a million books makes Dillons one of the best bookshops in the world. Selling new books exclusively, this store seems to stock almost every book in print. Accepts MC, V. Open: Mon and Wed–Fri 9am–7pm, Tues 9:30am–7pm, Sat 9:30am–5:30pm. Tube: Goodge Street.

**FOYLES, 119 Charing Cross Rd., W.C.2. Tel. 071/437-5660.**

Easily the largest bookseller on the strip, London's famous Foyles features an extensive selection of top sellers, along with a good collection of hard-to-find titles. Accepts AE, V. Open: Mon–Wed and Fri–Sat 9am–6pm, Thurs 9am–7pm. Tube: Leicester Square or Tottenham Court Road.

**HATCHARDS, 187 Piccadilly, W.1. Tel. 071/437-3924.**

This chain carries all the latest releases along with the most popular fiction and nonfiction titles.

Conveniently located branches include 390 Strand, W.C.2 (tel. 071/379-6264), and 63 Kensington High St., W.8 (tel. 071/937-0858). Accepts AE, MC, V. Open: Mon–Fri 9am–6pm, Sat 9am–5pm. Tube: Piccadilly Circus or Green Park.

**EDWARD STANFORD, 12 Long Acre, W.C.2. Tel. 071/836-1321.**

One of the best travel bookshops in the world, Edward Stanford is known for its exhaustive collection of travel guides and travel literature, as well as tons of maps and atlases. Accepts MC, V. Open: Mon and Sat 10am–6pm, Tues–Wed and Fri 9am–6pm, Thurs 9am–7pm. Tube: Leicester Square.

**LONDON TOURIST BOARD BOOKSHOP, in the Tourist Information Centre, Victoria Station Forecourt, S.W.1. Tel. 071/730-3488.**

Shelves here are stocked exclusively with books on Britain in general and London in particular, including all the applicable selections from the Frommer series. Look here for detailed guides to shopping and walking as well as specialized information for gay, student, disabled, and other travelers. Accepts V. Open: Easter–Oct daily 9am–8pm; the rest of the year, Mon–Sat 9am–7pm, Sun 9am–5pm. Tube: Victoria.

## DEPARTMENT STORES

Department stores are the city's most famous shopping institutions, and a handful stand out as top tourist attractions as well.

**HARRODS, 87-135 Brompton Rd., S.W.1. Tel. 071/730-1234.**

By many estimates, Harrods is the largest department store in the world, selling everything from pins to pianos. The store claims that anything in the world can be bought here, and it may be true; whenever I'm too lazy to find it cheaper elsewhere, I do indeed find it here. Even if you're not in a shopping mood, the incredible ground-floor food halls are definitely worth a visit. Accepts AE, DC, MC, V. Open: Mon–Tues and Thurs–Sat 9am–6pm, Wed 9:30am–7pm. Tube: Knightsbridge.

**SELFRIDGES, 400 Oxford St., W.1. Tel. 071/629-1234.**

Selfridges seems almost as big as, and more crowded than, its chief rival, Harrods. Opened in 1909 by Harry Selfridge, a salesman from Chicago, this department store revolutionized retailing with its variety of goods and dynamic displays. The ground-floor perfumerie is one of London's best, while upper floors are well stocked with top designer fashions. Accepts AE, DC, MC, V. Open: Mon–Wed and Fri–Sat 9:30am–6pm, Thurs 9:30am–8pm. Tube: Marble Arch or Bond Street.

**LIBERTY, 210-220 Regent St., W.1. Tel. 071/734-1234.**

London's prettiest department store enjoys a worldwide reputation for selling fine textiles in unique surroundings. In addition to colorful clothing separates boasting the famous Liberty imprint, this old-world store features an incomparable Asian department, and fashions by well-known designers. Accepts AE, DC, MC, V. Open: Mon–Wed and Fri–Sat 9:30am–6pm, Thurs 9:30am–7:30pm. Tube: Oxford Circus.

**MARKS & SPENCER, 458 Oxford St., W.1. Tel. 071/935-7954.**

England's largest and best-known department store chain is headed by this flagship store in the heart of Oxford Street. Mid-priced British designs run the gamut from traditional to trendy, though the store is most famous for its excellent underwear and intimate apparel departments. No credit cards are accepted. Open: Mon–Fri 9am–8pm, Sat 9am–6pm. Tube: Marble Arch.

## FASHION

### DISCOUNT

**A SHOP CALLED SALE, 28 Bedfordbury, W.C.2. Tel. 071/240-9730.**

Shoppers with designer tastes and chain-store budgets will appreciate this unusual upscale surplus shop. Men's and women's clothes by top contemporary designers are displayed on two floors, and are often more than half their original price. The store is located on a small street off New Row. No credit cards are accepted. Open: Mon–Fri 11am–7pm, Sat 11am–6pm. Tube: Covent Garden.

**DESIGNER SALE STUDIO, 241 King's Rd., S.W.3. Tel. 071/351-4171.**

Krizia, Armani, and other high-fashion designer womenswear are sold here for one-third or more off their original ticket price. Much of the stock is made up of hits from last season, though current samples and timeless accessories are also usually on hand. Accepts AE, DC, MC, V. Open: Mon–Fri 10am–7pm, Sat 10am–6pm. Tube: Sloane Square.

**70, Lamb's Conduit St., W.C.1. Tel. 071/430-1533.**

Primarily an outlet for men's clothes, it sells overstock from top designers' less conservative lines Giorgio Armani, Jean Paul Gaultier, and François Gibaud labels are common here, and sold by knowledgeable salespeople in contemporary surroundings. Accepts AE, MC, V. Open: Mon–Sat 10am–5:30pm. Tube: Holborn.

## CONTEMPORARY

The following listings are "warehouse" shops, each encompassing dozens of small individually owned and managed stalls.

**HYPER-HYPER, 26-40 Kensington High St., W.8. Tel. 071/938-4343.**

Hyper-Hyper lets young British designers run their own stands as a stepping-stone to the big time. This bilevel shop is not cheap, but chock full of England's most interesting and esoteric fashions, it's definitely worth a visit. Some stalls accept credit cards.

Open: Mon–Wed and Fri–Sat 10am–6pm, Thurs 10am–7pm. Tube: High Street Kensington.

**KENSINGTON MARKET, 49-53 Kensington High St., W.8. Tel. 071/937-1572.**

Located diagonally across the street from Hyper-Hyper, this market's downscale, individually operated stalls are on the cutting edge of street fashion. Look for the latest nightclub fashions, hard-impact postpunk designs, period clothing, and chunky "heavy metal" accessories. Even after a recent reorganization, the multilevel shop is labyrinthine, and often packed. Some stalls accept credit cards.

Open: Mon–Sat 10am–6pm. Tube: High Street Kensington.

**THE GARAGE, 350 King's Rd., S.W.3. Tel. 071/352-6488.**

Occupying the cavernous interior of one of Chelsea's most unusual buildings, this former ambulance station is now filled with a good variety of fashion-oriented stalls. The selection is eclectic—leisure suits are sold next to track suits—with an emphasis on hip casual wear. Some stalls accept credit cards.

Open: Mon–Tues and Thurs–Fri 10am–6pm, Wed and Sat 10am–7pm. Tube: Sloane Square or South Kensington.

## SHOES

There are so many shoe stores in London, they almost outnumber pubs and churches. In general, check Brompton Road and Sloane Street for high fashion, King's Road for trendy styles, and Oxford Street for midpriced popular footwear. Below are some top selections.

**BALLY, 246 Oxford St., W.1. Tel. 071/629-6045.**

Swiss-based Bally sells both traditional and fashionable styles for both men and women. Their well-staffed and -stocked shops are particularly known for soft leathers and excellent quality. Accepts AE, DC, MC, V. Open: Mon–Wed and Fri–Sat 9:30am–6:30pm, Thurs 9:30am–8pm. Tube: Oxford Circus.

**NATURAL SHOE STORE, 21 Neal St., W.C.2. Tel. 071/836-5254.**

Not every shoe here is the most beautiful in the world, but they are the most comfortable. The shop carries the full line of Dexter shoes, as well as others with specialized contours, arches, and soles. Accepts AE, DC, MC, V. Open: Mon–Tues and Sat 10am–6pm, Wed–Fri 10am–7pm. Tube: Covent Garden.

**R. SOLES, 178A King's Rd., S.W.3. Tel. 071/352-8798.**

This jam-packed shop is not only one of Chelsea's trendiest shoe stores, it's also one of the city's best booteries. Accepts AE, DC, MC, V. Open: Mon–Sat 9:30am–7pm. Tube: Sloane Square.

## MUSIC

Because their mainstream and alternative selections are so great, several excellent and huge music department stores have taken their toll on London's mom-and-pop specialty record shops.

**HMV, 150 Oxford St., W.1. Tel. 071/631-3423.**

In addition to a competent ground-floor pop department, HMV is known for its particularly vast collection of international music and spoken-word recordings, downstairs. Look for contemporary sounds from Europe, Africa, India, and the Caribbean. Accepts AE, DC, MC, V. Open: Mon–Wed and Fri–Sat 9:30am–7pm, Thurs 9:30am–8pm. Tube: Tottenham Court Road or Oxford Circus.

**TOWER RECORDS, 1 Piccadilly Circus, W.1. Tel. 071/439-2500.**

A veritable warehouse of sound, Tower maintains a complete catalogue of current releases on record, tape, and compact disc. The various formats are independently organized and include good selections of pop, jazz, bluegrass, folk, country, sound tracks, and more. Downstairs you'll find a good variety of international music magazines. Accepts AE, MC, V. Open: Mon–Sat 9am–midnight. Tube: Piccadilly Circus.

**VIRGIN MEGASTORE, 14 Oxford St., W.1. Tel. 071/631-1234.**

In many ways the best record supermarket, Virgin is particularly strong with new releases. Customers can listen to the selections on headphones before committing. Since its early days, the store has expanded to include videos, a Virgin Atlantic airline ticket office, and a café. Accepts AE, MC, V. Open: Mon–Sat 9:30am–8pm. Tube: Oxford Circus or Tottenham Court Road.

## OUTDOOR MARKETS

**PORTOBELLO MARKET, along Portobello Rd., W.11.**

Portobello Market is the grandaddy of them all, famous for its overflow of antiques and bric-a-brac along a road that never seems to end. As at all antiques markets, bargaining is in order here. Saturday between 8am and 4pm is best, as the market consists mainly of fruit and vegetable stalls during the week. Tube: Notting Hill Gate; ask anyone for directions from there.

**CAMDEN PASSAGE MARKET, off Upper St., N.1.**

The Market at Camden Passage is smaller than Portobello, and usually cheaper, too. Wednesday and Saturday are the best days to pick up bargain jewelry, trinkets, and antiques. Open: Daily 8:30am–3pm. Tube: Angel.

**CAMDEN MARKETS, along Camden High St., N.W.1.**

Don't confuse Camden Passage (above) with the Camden Markets. This trendy collection of stalls, in parking lots and empty spaces all the way to Chalk Farm Road, specializes in original fashions by young designers, and junk from people of all ages. Cafés and pubs (some offering live music) line the route, making for an enjoyable day out. When you've had enough of shopping here, turn north and walk along the peaceful and pretty Regent's Canal. Open: Sat–Sun 8am–6pm only. Tube: Camden Town.

**BRIXTON MARKET, Electric Ave., S.W.9.**

Brixton is the heart of African-Caribbean London, and the Brixton Market is its soul. Electric Avenue (immortalized by Jamaican singer Eddie Grant) is lined mostly with exotic fruit and vegetable stalls. But continue to the end and turn right, and you will see a terrific selection of the cheapest secondhand clothes in London. Take a detour off the avenue through the enclosed **Granville Arcade** for African fabrics, traditional West African teeth-cleaning sticks, reggae records, and newspapers oriented to the African-British community. Open: Mon–Tues and Thurs–Sat 8am–5:30pm, Wed 8am–1pm. Tube: Brixton.

**PETTICOAT LANE MARKET, Middlesex St., E.1.**

Located in the East End, this is London's best market for inexpensive fashions. A terrific variety of new, contemporary styles hang on racks all along the street. Tourists also flock here to see real Cockneys and try jellied eel, the local delicacy. Open: Sun 9am–2pm only.

## TOILETRIES

**THE BODY SHOP, 32 Great Marlborough Su., W.1. Tel. 071/437-5137.**

Now famous internationally, this British-based chain sells oils, lotions, shampoos, and a terrific variety of organically based beauty aids to the health-conscious. Their range of "cruelty-free" cosmetics, creams, and coverings are biodegradable and not tested on animals. Accepts AE, DC, MC, V. Open: Mon–Wed and Sat 9:30am–6pm, Thurs 9:30am–7:30pm, Fri 9:30am–7pm. Tube: Oxford Circus.

**CRABTREE & EVELYN, 6 Kensington Church St., W.8. Tel. 071/937-9335.**

Fans of Beatrix Potter and Laura Ashley are undoubtedly also loyal to this purveyor of fanciful English-design toiletries. Pastel-colored soaps, powders, and potpourri are all gift quality and beautifully packaged. Accepts AE, MC, V. Open: Mon–Wed, and

Fri–Sat 9:30am–6pm, Thurs 9:30am–7pm. Tube: High Street Kensington.

**NEAL'S YARD REMEDIES, 2 Neal's Yard, W.2. Tel. 071/379-7222.**

London's best shop for packaged herbal medications, aroma therapy oils, homeopathic hair remedies, and other nonprescription medications. The store is located at the end of a short cul-de-sac off Short's Gardens, two blocks north of Covent Garden Market. No credit cards are accepted. Open: Mon–Tues and Thurs–Fri 10am–6pm, Wed and Sat 10am–5:30pm, Sun 11am–4pm. Tube: Covent Garden.

## TRADITIONAL BRITISH GOODS

**THE SCOTCH HOUSE, 2 Brompton Rd., S.W.1. Tel. 071/581-2151.**

Good-quality sweaters and vests begin at about £45 ($81) and increase in price depending on quality and complexity of design. The emphasis here is on hand-knit Shetlands and cashmeres, as well as machine-made woolens. Kilts, hats, socks, and scarves can be bought off the rack, or made to order with your desired pattern. Accepts AE, MC, V. Open: Mon–Wed and Fri 10:30am–6:30pm, Thurs 10:30am–7pm, Sat 10:30am–5:30pm. Tube: Covent Garden.

**JAMES SMITH & SONS, 53 New Oxford St., W.C.1. Tel. 071/836-4731.**

Few things are more British than the umbrella, and James Smith & Sons is one of London's premier purveyors. Traditional "brollies" come in nylon or silk, and are stretched over wood or metal frames. Prices start from about £25 ($45), and a fancy umbrella or cane can set you back £300 ($540) and more. Accepts MC, V. Open: Mon–Fri 9am–5:30pm, Sat 10am–4pm. Tube: Tottenham Court Road.

**THE TEA HOUSE, 15A Neal St., W.C.2. Tel. 071/240-7539.**

In addition to teapots, tea balls, and assorted paraphernalia, this wonderful-smelling shop sells over 70 varieties of tea from India, China, Japan, and the rest of the world. Available loose or in bags, traditional English blends make excellent, light, and inexpensive gifts. Accepts AE, DC, MC, V. Open: Mon–Sat 10am–7pm. Tube: Covent Garden.

**FRANK JOHNSON, 187 Ferndale Rd., S.W.9. Tel. 071/733-1722.**

Darts fans and curious others will want to visit this most British of sports shops. All types of darts and components are sold along with their associated paraphernalia. Boards can be shipped home right from the store. Accepts AE, MC, V. Open: Mon–Tues and Thurs–Sat 9:30am–6pm, Wed 9:30am–1pm. Tube: Brixton.

**WATERFORD WEDGWOOD, 173 Piccadilly, W.1. Tel. 071/629-2614.**

Waterford crystal and Wedgwood china share the same table under the roof of this upscale shop. There's a good selection of fine cut-glass vases, platters, and objets d'art, available in a wide range of prices. Complete sets of the famous powder-blue-and-white Jasper china are available, along with many other styles and patterns. Accepts AE, DC, MC, V. Open: Mon–Fri 9am–6pm, Sat 9am–4pm. Tube: Piccadilly Circus or Green Park.

**THE LONDON WEATHER CENTRE SHOP, 284 High Holborn, W.C.1. Tel. 071/836-4311.**

It's somehow fitting that a shop concerning itself with the elements should thrive in a country that is famous for its fascination with the weather. Thermometers, barometers, anemometers, and a variety of other weather gauges are sold here, along with books, charts, games, mugs, T-shirts, and other related goods. Accepts MC, V. Open: Mon–Fri 9am–5pm. Tube: Holborn.

CHAPTER 9

# LONDON NIGHTS



London is a cultural cornucopia. As the sun sets and a hush descends on the rest of the land, the capital's theaters, clubs, and pubs swing into action.

The term "West End," when applied to theater, refers to commercial theaters around Shaftesbury Avenue and Covent Garden. Currently, there are about 40 such houses where comedies, musicals, and dramas are regularly staged. Tickets cost from £10 to £25 ($18 to $45), and are usually most expensive for musicals since demand for them is highest. But discounts are available for the wise tourist.

## DISCOUNT TICKETS

The **Society of West End Theatre** (tel. 071/836-0971) operates a **discount ticket booth** in Leicester Square, where tickets for many shows are available at half price, plus a £1.25 ($2.25) service charge. Tickets are sold only on the day of performance, and there is a limit of four per person. You cannot return tickets, and no credit cards are accepted. The booth is open Monday through Saturday from noon on matinee days (which vary with individual theaters), and from 2:30 to 6:30pm for evening performances. All West End theaters are closed Sunday.

Blockbuster shows can be sold out months in advance, but if you just have to see *Phantom of the Opera,* one of the many high-commission **ticket agencies** can help you out. Always check with the box office first for any last-minute returns. Free West End theater guides listing all the current productions are distributed by tourist offices, hotels, and ticket agencies.

If you have an International Student ID Card, you are eligible to purchase tickets to top shows at drastically reduced prices. Not all theaters participate in this program, so call first for availability. Those

### IMPRESSIONS

*London; a nation, not a city.*

—Benjamin Disraeli

that do participate offer their student-priced seats on a standby basis half an hour before the performance.

Classical music is also in abundance in London, with top-rated musicians performing almost every night of the year. A broad variety of venues ensures a good selection, running the gamut from tiny trios to grand orchestras. Keep an eye on the weekly listings in *Time Out* and *City Limits* magazines—both available at most newsagents—for a comprehensive roundup of the week's events.

Rock-and-roll may not have been invented here, but the English perfected a style and sound that took the world by storm. London still boasts an excellent music scene, and several accessible, centrally located clubs stage up-and-coming acts almost nightly.

# 1. THE PERFORMING ARTS

## MAJOR PERFORMING ARTS COMPANIES

### OPERA

Not until the 1946 premiere of Benjamin Britten's *Peter Grimes* did British opera get a serious reception. But since that time, opera schools have opened, seasons have come into being, and a host of great composers have lifted British opera onto the world stage. London's two busy opera companies—The English National Opera and the Royal Opera—are highly regarded and regularly joined by visiting stars.

As always, check the weekly listings magazines *Time Out* and *City Limits* for major programs as well as current fringe offerings.

**THE ENGLISH NATIONAL OPERA, London Coliseum, St. Martin's Lane, W.C.2. Tel. 071/836-3161.**

The English National Opera (ENO) is an innovative company that continually thrills enthusiasts and rocks traditionalists. Operas are always sung in English, and many productions have been transported to Germany, France, and the United States. The ENO performs in the 2,350-seat London Coliseum. Their season lasts from August to May.

**Tickets:** £4–£35 ($7.20–$63). AE, DC, MC, V.

**THE ROYAL OPERA, in the Royal Opera House, Bow St., Covent Garden, W.C.2. Tel. 071/240-1066.**

England's most elite opera company sings the standards in their original languages. Projected "supertitles" translate the libretto. International stars from New York and Rome are regularly featured.

**Tickets:** £3–£100 ($5.40–$180). AE, DC, MC, V.

# LONDON NIGHTS

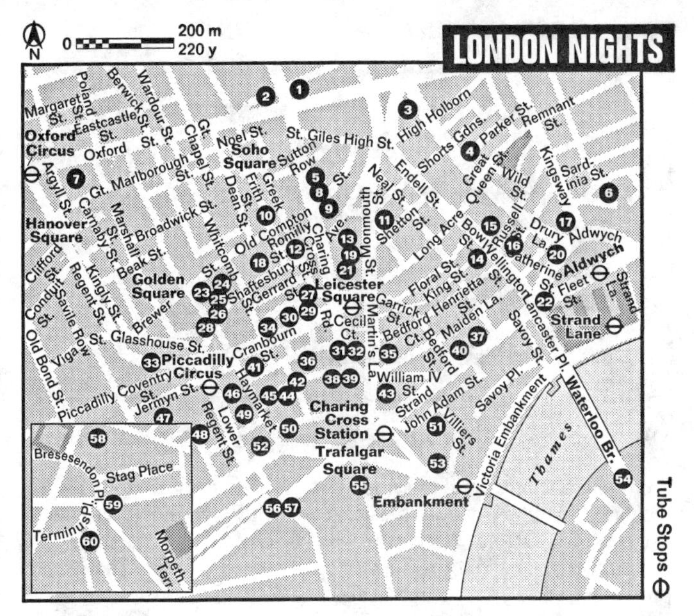


**THEATERS:**

- Adelphi 40
- Albery J. Garrick 32
- Aldwych 17
- Ambassadors 13
- Apollo 26
- Apollo Victoria 60
- Arts Theatre Club/Unicorn Theatre 21
- Cambridge Theatre 11
- Cannon Planton Street 44
- Comedy 45
- Dominion 1
- Duke of Yorks 39
- Dutchess 22
- Fortune 15
- Globe 25
- Her Majesty's 52
- ICA 57
- London Coliseum 43
- London Palladium 7
- New London 4
- Lyric 28
- Odeon Mezzanine 38
- Palace 12
- Phoenix 5
- Piccadilly 33
- Players Theatre 51
- The Playhouse 53
- Prince Edward 10
- Prince of Wales 41
- Queen's 24
- Royal Opera House 14
- Royalty 6
- Shaftesbury 3
- St. Martins 19
- Strand 20
- Theatre Royal Drury Lane 16
- Theatre Royal Haymarket 50
- Vaudeville 37
- Victoria Palace 59
- Westminster 58
- Whitehall 55
- Windhams 31

**CINEMAS:**

- Cannon Haymarket 49
- Cannon Oxford Street 2
- Cannon Piccadilly 47
- Cannon Shaftesbury Avenue 9
- Curzon Phoenix 8
- Curzon West End 18
- Empire 30
- ICA 56
- Lumiere 35
- Metro Cinema 23
- National Film Theatre 54
- Odeon 36 46
- Odeon West End 42
- Plaza 48
- Premiere 34
- Prince Charles 27
- Warner West End 29

## THE MAJOR CONCERT & PERFORMANCE HALLS

**Sadler's Wells Theatre** 071/278-8916
**Barbican Centre** 071/638-8891
**London Coliseum** 071/836-3161
**Royal Albert Hall** 071/589-3203
**The Royal Opera House** 071/240-1066
**South Bank Arts Centre** 071/928-8800
**Wigmore Hall** 071/935-2141

## CLASSICAL MUSIC

From chamber concerts to symphonies, a handful of London stages regularly feature classical music. The British Music Information Centre, 10 Stratford Place, W.1 (tel. 071/499-8567), is the city's clearinghouse and resource center for "serious" music. The center provides free telephone and walk-in information on current and upcoming events. Free recitals are offered weekly, usually on Tuesdays and Thursdays at 7:30pm; call for exact times. Take the tube to Bond Street.

All of London's major orchestras, including the **Royal Philharmonic Orchestra** and the **English Chamber Orchestra,** perform in the South Bank Centre's Royal Festival Hall, among other venues. Tickets usually cost from £6 ($10.80) and, when available, reduced-price student standbys are sold two hours before the performance.

**LONDON SYMPHONY ORCHESTRA, Barbican Centre, Silk St., E.C.2. Tel. 071/638-8891.**

London's top orchestra is currently under the musical direction of the charismatic Michael Tilson Thomas. Summer schedules usually include a series of "pops" concerts. Reduced-price student standby tickets are sometimes available 30 minutes prior to showtime.

**Tickets:** £5–£25 ($9–$45). AE, DC, MC, V.

## THEATER COMPANIES

Two major London-based companies are subsidized by the British government. They regularly work with the country's top actors and playwrights, staging some of the best productions in the city.

**NATIONAL THEATRE, South Bank, S.E.1. Tel. 071/928-2252.**

Three separate theaters are housed under the single concrete roof of the National, on the south bank of the river Thames. The Olivier and the Lyttelton are larger stages, and usually alternate between classical productions and more contemporary works. The smaller Cottesloe Theatre is ideally suited to experimental plays and less-popular mainstream productions. Free music recitals are usually held in the foyer on evenings before performances.

Three dozen of each theater's best seats are sold on the morning of the performance. Other unsold tickets are available on the day of the show on a standby basis—for as little as £7 ($12.60). Box office open: Mon–Sat 10am–8pm. Tube: Waterloo.

**Tickets:** £6–£16 ($10.80–$28.80). AE, DC, MC, V.

**ROYAL COURT THEATRE, Sloane Square, S.W.1. Tel. 071/730-1745.**

Experimental drama and new comedy by young playwrights are the specialties of the Royal Court. Whatever the current production, you've probably never heard of it. But if history is to be your guide, chances are it's terrific, and you should go . . . if you can get a ticket, that is. Box office open: Mon–Sat 10am–8pm. Tube: Sloane Square.

**Tickets:** £5–£15 ($9–$27). AE, DC, MC, V.

## DANCE

Dance in London is really cheap. The major houses all offer inexpensive standby seats (sold on the day of performance only), while prices at fringe theaters rarely top £5 ($9).

**CONTEMPORARY DANCE THEATRE, at The Place, 17 Duke's Rd., W.C.1. Tel. 071/387-0031.**

This showplace usually offers good performances and cheap tickets. The space is small, and, as you can see from the mirrors and bars, is used by a dancing school during the day. Box office open: Mon–Fri (and Sat performance days) noon–6pm. Tube: Euston.

**Tickets:** £7–£10 ($12.60–$18). MC, V.

**ROYAL BALLET, in the Royal Opera House, Bow St., Covent Garden, W.C.2. Tel. 071/240-1066.**

London's top troupe performs for a high-class crowd on one of the prettiest stages in the city.

**Tickets:** £3–£100 ($5.40–$180). AE, DC, MC, V.

**LONDON FESTIVAL BALLET, in the South Bank Centre, South Bank, S.E.1. Tel. 071/928-8800.**

During summer months only, the London Festival Ballet's season runs from mid-June to the beginning of August. The company also plays other venues, including the Dominion Theatre, Tottenham Court Road, W.1 (tel. 071/580-9562). Box office open: Daily 10am–10pm. Tube (for South Bank Centre): Waterloo.

**Tickets:** £7–£14 ($12.60–$25.20). AE, MC, V.

## MAJOR CONCERT HALLS & ALL-PURPOSE AUDITORIUMS

**BARBICAN CENTRE, Silk St., E.C.2. Tel. 071/638-8891.**

Reputedly the largest arts complex in Europe, the Barbican is so mazelike that yellow lines have been painted on the sidewalk to help visitors negotiate their way from the Underground to the box office. The architecture of sprawling centre has long been the object of critical attention, most of it negative.

Even its detractors, however, agree that the Barbican has an excellent concert hall. This acoustically superior space is home to both the London Symphony Orchestra and the English Chamber Orchestra. Festivals and other large-scale events are often held when the orchestras are quiet.

Free student concerts are performed in the foyer on Level 5, weekdays from 5:30 to 7:30pm. The program, which alternates between classical and jazz, is repeated on Sundays from 12:30 to 2:30pm. Box office open: Daily 9am–8pm. Tube: Barbican or Moorgate.

**Tickets:** £5–£25 ($9–$45); reduced-price student standby tickets sometimes available. AE, DC, MC, V.

**LONDON COLISEUM, St. Martin's Lane, W.C.2. Box office tel. 071/836-3161;** recorded information tel. 071/836-7666.

Home to the English National Opera, the Coliseum is one of London's most architecturally spectacular houses. During summer, and other times when the Opera is off or out of town, visiting companies (often dance) perform. Box office open: Mon–Sat 10am–9pm. Tube: Leicester Square or Charing Cross.

**Tickets:** Opera £4–£35 ($7.20–$63). AE, DC, MC, V.

**ROYAL ALBERT HALL, Kensington Gore, S.W.7. Tel. 071/589-3203.**

Despite its infamous echo, the 10,000-seat Royal Albert books top symphonies, big-name rock bands, and the occasional boxing match, among other events. The BBC Henry Wood Promenade Concerts, held from mid-July to mid-September, are usually the year's highlight, packing in over 60 concerts in as many days. Box office open: Mon–Sat (and Sun performance days) 10am–6pm. Tube: Knightsbridge or Kensington High Street.

**Tickets:** £5–£40 ($9–$72). MC, V.

**THE ROYAL OPERA HOUSE, Bow St., Covent Garden, W.C.2. Tel. 071/240-1066;** for unsold seat information tel. 071/836-6903.

Home to both the Royal Opera and the Royal Ballet, this posh theater is rich in history, having first hosted an opera in 1817. When available, good seats are astronomically expensive, but there are several budget options:

At about £3 ($5.40) the upper-level benches are a bargain. Usually available on the day of the performance, these restricted-view seats are pretty far from the stage.

Standing room, in the rear of the stalls, is available after all the seats have been sold. At about £9 ($16.20), it's a relatively inexpensive way to see a production in one of the world's foremost theaters.

Finally, about five dozen orchestra seats are sold beginning at

10am on the day of the show. Line up before dawn if Pavarotti or Placido Domingo is in town. Box office open: Mon–Sat 10am–8pm. Tube: Covent Garden.

**Tickets:** £3–£100 ($5.40–$180). AE, DC, MC, V.

**SADLER'S WELLS THEATRE, Rosebery Ave., E.C.1. Tel. 071/278-8916.**

This is one of the busiest stages in London, and also one of the best. Host to top visiting opera and dance companies from around the world, the theater offers great sight lines and terrific prices. Seats are available from 10:30am at the advance box office across the road. Box office open: Mon–Sat 10:30am–6:30pm; until 7:30pm on performance nights. Tube: Angel.

**Tickets:** £5–£27 ($9–$48.60). AE, DC, MC, V.

**SOUTH BANK ARTS CENTRE, South Bank, S.E.1. Box office tel. 071/928-8800;** recorded information 071/633-0932.

The South Bank Arts Centre, London's flagship performing arts complex, includes three well-designed, modern concert halls. **Royal Festival Hall** is the usual site for major orchestral performances. Smaller **Queen Elizabeth Hall** is known for its chamber-music concerts, and the intimate **Purcell Room** usually hosts advanced students and young performers making their professional debut. All three stages are lit almost every night of the year, and it's not all classical music: ballet, jazz, pop, and folk concerts are also staged here.

The foyer of the Royal Festival Hall is one of the city's hardest-working concert halls in and of itself. Regular, free, informal lunchtime music recitals are scheduled here, in front of the Festival Buffet café, daily from noon to 2pm. A Friday evening Commuter Jazz series is also held here during summer months only from 5:15 to 6:45pm. Box office open: Daily 10am–10pm. Tube: Waterloo is closest, but short walk over Hungerford rail Bridge from Embankment Underground is more scenic.

**Tickets:** £5–£50 ($9–$90); discounted student standby seats sometimes available. AE, DC, MC, V.

**WIGMORE HALL, 36 Wigmore St., W.1. Tel. 071/935-2141.**

Considered by many to be the best auditorium in London for both intimacy and acoustics. Buy the cheapest seats, as it really doesn't matter where you sit. Box office open: Mon–Sat 10am–8:30pm; Sun 45 minutes before performance. Tube: Bond Street or Oxford Circus.

**Tickets:** £4–£16 ($7.20–$28.80). Discounted student standby tickets sometimes available. AE, DC, MC, V.

## THEATERS

Attending a play in London is almost a requirement for tourists. More theatrical entertainment is offered here than in any other city, usually at prices far below those in New York. About 40 West End stages compete for audiences with comedies, musicals, and dramas. Many of the major theaters offer reduced-price tickets to documented students on a standby basis. When available, these tickets are sold 30 minutes prior to curtain time; line up early for popular shows.

**ADELPHI, Strand, W.C.2. Tel. 071/836-7611.**
Box office open: Mon–Sat 10am–8pm. Tube: Charing Cross.
**Tickets:** £10–£23 ($18–$41.40); £10 ($18) student standby. AE, DC, MC, V.

**ALBERY, St. Martin's Lane, W.C.2. Tel. 071/867-1115.**
Box office open: Mon–Sat 10am–8pm. Tube: Leicester Square.
**Tickets:** £9–£23 ($16.20–$41.40); £12 ($21.60) student standby. AE, DC, MC, V.

**ALDWYCH, The Aldwych, W.C.2. Tel. 071/836-6404.**
Box office open: Mon–Sat 10am–8pm. Tube: Covent Garden.
**Tickets:** £9–£20 ($16.20–$36). AE, DC, MC, V.

**AMBASSADORS, West St., W.C.2. Tel. 071/836-6111.**
Box office open: Mon–Sat 10am–8pm. Tube: Leicester Square.
**Tickets:** £7–£17 ($12.60–$30.60); £8 ($14.40) student standby. AE, DC, MC, V.

**APOLLO, Shaftesbury Ave., W.1. Tel. 071/437-2663.**
Box office open: Mon–Sat 10am–8pm. Tube: Piccadilly Circus.
**Tickets:** £6–£17 ($10.80–$30.60). AE, MC, V.

**APOLLO VICTORIA, Wilton Rd., S.W.1. Tel. 071/828-8665.**
Box office open: Mon–Sat 10am–8pm. Tube: Victoria.
**Tickets:** £9–£23 ($16.20–$41.40). AE, DC, MC, V.

**ARTS THEATRE, 6 Great Newport St., W.C.2. Tel. 071/836-3132.**
Box office open: Mon–Sat 10am–8pm. Tube: Leicester Square.
**Tickets:** £8–£18 ($14.40–$32.40); £8 ($14.40) student standby. MC, V.

**CAMBRIDGE, Earlham St., W.C.2. Tel. 071/379-5299.**
Box office open: Mon–Sat 10am–8pm. Tube: Covent Garden.
**Tickets:** £8–£16 ($14.40–$28.80). AE, MC, V.

**DRURY LANE THEATRE ROYAL, Catherine St., W.C.2. Tel. 071/836-8108.**
Box office open: Mon–Sat 10am–8pm. Tube: Holborn or Covent Garden.
**Tickets:** £8–£23 ($14.40–$41.40). AE, MC, V.

**DUKE OF YORK'S, St. Martin's Lane, W.C.2. Tel. 071/836-5122.**
Box office open: Mon–Sat 10am–8pm. Tube: Leicester Square.
**Tickets:** £10–£15 ($18–$27); £5 ($9) restricted view; £8 ($14.40) student standby. AE, MC, V.

**FORTUNE, Russell St., W.C.2. Tel. 071/836-2238.**
Box office open: Mon–Sat 10am–8pm. Tube: Leicester Square.
**Tickets:** £8–£16 ($14.40–$28.80); £8 ($14.40) student standby. AE, MC, V.

**GLOBE, Shaftesbury Ave., W.1. Tel. 071/437-3667.**
Box office open: Mon–Sat 10am–8pm. Tube: Piccadilly Circus.
**Tickets:** £8–£17 ($14.40–$30.60). AE, MC, V.

**HAYMARKET THEATRE ROYAL, Haymarket, S.W.1. Tel. 071/930-9832.**
Box office open: Mon–Sat 10am–8pm. Tube: Piccadilly Circus.
**Tickets:** £8–£17 ($14.40–$30.60). AE, DC, MC, V.

**HER MAJESTY'S, Haymarket, S.W.1. Tel. 071/839-2244.**
Box office open: Mon–Sat 10am–8pm. Tube: Piccadilly Circus.
**Tickets:** £9–£22 ($16.20–$39.60). AE, MC, V.

**LONDON PALLADIUM, Argyll St., W.1. Tel. 071/437-7373.**
Box office open: Mon–Sat 10am–8pm. Tube: Oxford Circus.
**Tickets:** £7–£19 ($12.60–$34.20). AE, MC, V.

**LYRIC SHAFTESBURY AVENUE, Shaftesbury Ave., W.1. Tel. 071/437-3686.**
Box office open: Mon–Sat 10am–8pm. Tube: Piccadilly Circus.
**Tickets:** £6–£17 ($10.80–$30.60); £8 ($14.40) student standby. AE, MC, V.

**MAYFAIR THEATRE, Stratton St., W.1. Tel. 071/629-3036.**
Box office open: Mon–Sat 10am–8pm. Tube: Green Park.
**Tickets:** £10–£12 ($18–$21.60); £8 ($14.40) for students at all times. AE, DC, MC, V.

**NEW LONDON, Drury Lane, W.2. Tel. 071/405-0072.**
Box office open: Mon–Sat 10am–8pm. Tube: Covent Garden.
**Tickets:** £8–£21 ($14.40–$37.80). AE, DC, MC, V.

**PALACE, Shaftesbury Ave., W.1. Tel. 071/434-0909.**
Box office open: Mon–Sat 10am–8pm. Tube: Leicester Square.
**Tickets:** £6–£22 ($10.80–$39.60). AE, DC, MC, V.

**PHOENIX THEATRE, Charing Cross Rd., W.C.2. Tel. 071/867-1044.**
Box office open: Mon–Sat 10am–8pm. Tube: Leicester Square.
**Tickets:** £13–£26 ($23.40–$46.80); £13 ($23.40) student standby. AE, DC, MC, V.

**PICCADILLY THEATRE, Denman St., W.1. Tel. 071/867-1118.**

Box office open: Mon–Sat 10am–8pm. Tube: Piccadilly Circus.
**Tickets:** £11–£21 ($19.80–$37.80); £11 ($19.80) student standby. AE, MC, V.

**PRINCE EDWARD, Old Compton St., W.1. Tel. 071/734-8951.**
Box office open: Mon–Sat 10am–8pm. Tube: Leicester Square.
**Tickets:** £10–£23 ($18–$41.40). AE, MC, V.

**PRINCE OF WALES, Coventry St., W.1. Tel. 071/839-5972.**
Box office open: Mon–Sat 10am–8pm. Tube: Leicester Square.
**Tickets:** £18–£26 ($32.40–$46.80). AE, MC, V.

**QUEEN'S, Shaftesbury Ave., W.1. Tel. 071/734-1166.**
Box office open: Mon–Sat 10am–8pm. Tube: Leicester Square.
**Tickets:** £8–£17 ($14.40–$30.60); £8 ($14.40) student standby. AE, MC, V.

**ST. MARTIN'S, West St., W.C.2. Tel. 071/836-1443.**
Box office open: Mon–Sat 10am–8pm. Tube: Leicester Square.
**Tickets:** £7–£15 ($12.60–$27). AE, MC, V.

**SHAFTESBURY THEATRE, Shaftesbury Ave., W.C.2. Tel. 071/379-5399.**
Box office open: Mon–Sat 10am–8pm. Tube: Holborn.
**Tickets:** £7–£21 ($12.60–$37.80). AE, DC, MC, V.

**VAUDEVILLE, Strand, W.C.2. Tel. 071/836-9987.**
Box office open: Mon–Fri 10am–8pm, Sat 10am–8:30pm. Tube: Charing Cross.
**Tickets:** £8–£17 ($14.40–$30.60). AE, DC, MC, V.

**VICTORIA PALACE, Victoria St., S.W.1. Tel. 071/834-1317.**
Box office open: Mon–Sat 10am–8pm. Tube: Victoria.
**Tickets:** £8–£19 ($14.40–$34.20); £10 ($18) student standby. AE, MC, V.

**WESTMINSTER THEATRE, Palace St., S.W.1. Tel. 071/834-0283.**
Box office open: Mon–Sat 10am–8pm. Tube: Victoria.
**Tickets:** £9–£16 ($16.20–$28.80); £8.50 ($15.30) student standby. AE, MC, V.

**WHITEHALL THEATRE, Whitehall, S.W.1. Tel. 071/867-1119.**
Box office open: Mon–Sat 10am–8pm. Tube: Charing Cross.
**Tickets:** £10–£16 ($18–$28.80); £9 ($16.20) student standby. AE, DC, MC, V.

**WYNDHAMS, Charing Cross Rd., W.C.2. Tel. 071/867-1116.**
Box office open: Mon–Sat 10am–8pm. Tube: Leicester Square.

**Tickets:** £7–£17 ($12.60–$30.60); £8 ($14.40) student standby. AE, DC, MC, V.

## FRINGE THEATER

Some of the best theater in London is performed on the "fringe"—at the dozens of "fringe" theaters devoted to "alternative" plays, revivals, contemporary dramas, and even musicals. These shows are often more exciting than established West End productions; they are also consistently lower in price. Expect to pay from £4 to £7 ($7.20–$12.60). Most theaters offer discounted seats to students and seniors.

Fringe theaters are not bunched together like the big stages of the West End. In fact, most are not in central London; they are scattered throughout city neighborhoods and patronized primarily by locals. Check the weekly listings in *Time Out* and *City Limits* for theater listings, schedules, and show times. Some of the more popular and centrally located fringe theaters are listed below. Call for details on current productions.

**ALMEIDA THEATRE, 1 Almeida St., N.1. Tel. 071/359-4404.**

Home to the annual Festival of Contemporary Music from mid-June to mid-July, the Almeida is also known for its adventurous stagings of new and classic plays. The theater's legendary status means consistently good productions at higher-than-average prices. Performances are usually held Monday through Saturday. Box office open: Mon–Sat 10am–6pm. Tube: Angel.

**Tickets:** £7–£13 ($12.60–$23.40). MC, V.

**GATE NOTTING HILL, in the Prince Albert Pub, 11 Pembridge Rd., W.11. Tel. 071/229-0706.**

This tiny room above a pub in Notting Hill is one of the best alternative stages in London. Popular with local cognoscenti, the theater specializes in translated works by foreign playwrights. Performances are usually held nightly at 7:30pm, with a second late show at 10:15pm Thursday through Saturday. Box office open: Mon–Fri 11am–6pm, Sat 2–6pm. Tube: Notting Hill Gate.

**Tickets:** £4–£6 ($7.20–$10.80). No credit cards.

**HALF MOON THEATRE, 213 Mile End Rd., E.1. Tel. 071/791-1141.**

The Half Moon caters to its East End audience with plays that often tackle contemporary social issues. The theater enjoys a loyal neighborhood following and often works closely with the surrounding community. New works are commissioned by the theater and often border on performance art. Box office open: Mon–Sat 10am–6pm. Tube: Stepney Green.

**Tickets:** £2–£7 ($3.60–$12.60). MC, V.

**ICA THEATRE, The Mall, W.1. Tel. 071/930-3647.**

In addition to a cinema, café, bar, bookshop, and two galleries, the Institute of Contemporary Arts (ICA) has one of London's top theaters for experimental work. The fact that ICA is subsidized by the government usually means good, high-quality performances. Box office open: Daily noon–8pm. Tube: Charing Cross or Piccadilly Circus.

**Tickets:** £5–£6 ($9–$10.80). AE, DC, MC, V.

**THE KING'S HEAD, 115 Upper St., N.1. Tel. 071/226-8561.**

Arguably London's most famous fringe venue, the King's Head is also the city's oldest pub-theater. Despite its tiny stage, the popular theater is heavy on musicals; some that originated here have gone on to become successful West End productions.

Both matinee and evening performances are usually held Sunday through Friday. Evening performances only on Saturdays. Box office open: Mon–Fri 10am–6pm, Sat 10am–8pm, Sun 10am–4pm. Tube: Angel.

**Tickets:** £5–£8 ($9–$14.40). No credit cards.

**SOHO POLY THEATRE, 16 Riding House St., W.1. Tel. 071/636-9050.**

This centrally located theater stages serious drama by new English and European playwrights. Box office open: Mon–Sat 10am–5:30pm. Tube: Oxford Circus.

**Tickets:** £5–£7 ($9–$12.60). MC, V.

**YOUNG VIC, 66 The Cut, S.E.1. Tel. 071/928-6363.**

Adjacent to the Old Vic, a major venue that once was home to the National Theatre, the New Vic endeavors to give new talent a stage. The seating, around a central stage, is as unusual as the theater's eclectic variety of productions. Box office open: Mon–Sat 10am–6pm. Tube: Waterloo.

**Tickets:** £5–£9 ($9–$16.20). MC, V.

## 2. THE CLUB & MUSIC SCENE

### CABARET

London's best-kept secret? Cabaret: usually a combination of song, dance, comedy, and sex. Basically, anything goes and uniformly low prices make this one of London's best bets. *Note:* Many cabarets are closed during the Edinburgh Festival in August.

In addition to the clubs listed below, keep an eye out for performances at the **Alley Club,** in the Horse and Groom, 128 Great Portland St., W.1 (tel. 071/646-1324); **Chuckle Club,** 15 Bressenden Place, S.W.1 (tel. 071/828-7827); and **The Guilty Pea,** in The Wheatsheaf, 25 Rathbone Place, W.C.1 (tel. 071/986-6881). Check the weekly listings magazines for current offerings.

**THE COMEDY STORE, 28A Leicester Square, W.C.2. Tel. 071/839-6665.**

London's premier comedy club features top acts from Britain and the world. The house troupe performs Wednesdays, standup alternates with music on Thursdays, and big names play the weekend gigs. Performances: Wed–Thurs 9pm; Fri–Sat 8pm and midnight; Sun 8:30pm. Tube: Leicester Square.

**Admission:** £7 ($12.60).

**TATTERSHALL CASTLE COMEDY CABARET, Victoria Embankment, W.C.1. Tel. 071/839-6548.**

New and established acts show their stuff on the moored boat P.S. *Tattershall Castle,* anchored opposite the Embankment tube station. Shows are inexpensive, and usually full of laughs. Performances: Showtimes vary, call club for details. Tube: Embankment or Charing Cross.

**Admission:** £3.50 ($6.30).

**ORANJE BOOM BOOM, at De Hems Dutch Coffee Bar, Macclesfield Street, W.1. Tel. 071/701-6605.**

This West End coffee shop is typical of the smaller venues where good, off-beat cabaret often lurks. Performances: Usually Wednesdays. Call club for details. Tube: Leicester Square.

**Admission:** £4 ($7.20).

## ROCK

Since the British rock explosion in the 1960s, London hasn't let up on the number of clubs featuring homegrown talent. The West End in general, and Soho in particular, has a number of intimate places featuring every kind of music known to bandkind. Archaic drinking laws require most late-opening clubs to charge admission, which unfortunately often gets pricey. As usual, check the weekly listings magazines *Time Out* and *City Limits* for up-to-the-minute details.

**MARQUEE, 105-107 Charing Cross Rd., W.C.2. Tel. 071/437-6603.**

Pink Floyd, David Bowie, Led Zeppelin, the Who, and practically every other rocker you've ever heard of started out playing at Marquee. After more than 30 years and a change of address, this is still *the* place to hear the bands of the future. Bar prices are refreshingly closer to pub than club. Open: Daily 7–11pm. Tube: Tottenham Court Road.

**Admission:** £4–£7 ($7.20–$12.60). No credit cards.

**ROCK GARDEN, 6-7 Covent Garden Plaza, W.C.2. Tel. 071/240-3961.**

Less hip, but with lots of zip is the fashion-unconscious Rock Garden. Because this small basement club overlooks touristy Covent Garden Market, most of the 250 or so revelers are usually foreigners.

The quality of music varies, as the club's policy is to give new talent a stage. But Dire Straits, Police, and many others played here before fame visited them, and triple and quadruple bills ensure a good variety. Open: Mon–Sat 7:30pm–3am, Sun 7:30pm–midnight. Tube: Covent Garden.

**Admission:** £4–£8 ($7.20–$14.40); you can save £1 ($1.80) by arriving before 11pm on the weekends. MC, V.

**WAG, 35 Wardour St., W.1. Tel. 071/437-5534.**

The split-level Wag club is one of the trendiest live-music places in town. The downstairs stage usually attracts newly signed, cutting-edge rock bands, while dance disks spin upstairs. The door policy can be selective, but if it's your kind of music, you're probably dressed for the part. Open: Mon–Sat 10:30pm–4:30am. Tube: Leicester Square or Piccadilly Circus.

**Admission:** £5–£10 ($9–$18). No credit cards.

## IN CAMDEN TOWN & KENTISH TOWN

Many of London's best noise polluters are in Camden Town and adjacent Kentish Town, just east of Regent's Park.

**THE BULL & GATE, 389 Kentish Town Rd., N.W.5. Tel. 071/485-5358.**

Smaller, cheaper, and often better than its competitors, the Bull & Gate is the unofficial headquarters of London's pub rock scene. Independent and unknown rock bands are often served back-to-back by the half dozen. Open: Pub hours; music Mon–Sat 8–11pm. Tube: Kentish Town.

**Admission:** £3–£4 ($5.40–$7.20). No credit cards.

**CAMDEN PALACE, 1A Camden Rd., N.W.1. Tel. 071/387-0428.**

Features a variety of music from punk to funk. When the bands stop, records spin, and feet keep moving to the beat. Open: Mon–Thurs, Sat 9pm–2:30am; Fri 8pm–2:30am. Tube: Mornington Crescent or Camden Town.

**Admission:** £5–£10 ($9–$18). AE, MC, V.

**DINGWALL'S, Camden Lock, Chalk Farm Rd., N.W.1. Tel. 071/267-4967.**

Popular for live-music weekends that feature anything from heavy metal to R&B. The club's adventurous booking policy pleases an unpretentious crowd. Open: Mon, Wed 8pm–2am; Tues, Thurs–Sat 10pm–3am; Sun 9pm–1am. Tube: Camden Town or Chalk Farm.

**Admission:** £2–£6 ($3.60–$10.80). No credit cards.

**TOWN & COUNTRY CLUB, 9-17 Highgate Rd., N.W.5. Tel. 071/265-3334.**

This huge ex-theater with a large dance floor, good seating, and a great, varied line-up of bands is one of London's best clubs. All-day festivals are not unheard-of here, and on weekends, after 1am, there is free bus service to Trafalgar Square.

Open: Mon–Thurs 7–11:30pm, Fri–Sat 7pm–2am. Tube: Kentish Town.

**Admission:** £6–£11 ($10.80–$19.80). AE, DC, MC, V.

## JAZZ

You can get information on jazz concerts and events from the **Jazz Centre Society** (tel. 071/240-2430) and the listings magazines. Free jazz is offered every Sunday from 12:30 to 2:30pm on level 5 of the Barbican Centre, Silk St., E.C.2 (tel. 071/638-4141); tube to Barbican or Moorgate.

**BASS CLEF, 35 Coronet St., N.1. Tel. 071/729-2476.**

Many jazz-loving Londoners swear by this intimate, accessible place. The small club features jazz, Latin, and African music, as well as alternative dance nights. Open: Tues–Sat 8pm–2am, Sun 8pm–midnight. Tube: Old Street.

**Admission:** Free–£7 ($12.60); usually free Tues. AE, DC, MC, V.

**BRAHMS & LISZT, 19 Russell St., W.C.2. Tel. 071/240-3661.**

This wine bar presents live jazz nightly in the cellar. Local combos provide a good background to conversation. Bar prices are reasonable for a place within sight of Covent Garden Market. Open: Mon–Sat until 1am, Sun until 10:30pm. Tube: Covent Garden.

**Admission:** Free until 9:30pm; £4.50 ($8.10) after. No credit cards.

**THE 100 CLUB, 100 Oxford St., W.1. Tel. 071/636-0933.**

An austere underground club, The 100 usually hosts jazz nights on Monday, Wednesday, Friday, and Saturday. The stage is in the center of a smoky basement—looking just the way a jazz club is *supposed* to look. Open: Mon and Wed 8pm–midnight; Tues, Thurs, and Sun 7:30–11pm; Fri–Sat 8pm–1am. Tube: Tottenham Court Road.

**Admission:** £4–£7 ($7.20–$12.60). Student discount available. No credit cards.

**PIZZA EXPRESS, 10 Dean St., W.1. Tel. 071/437-9595.**

One of the city's most popular jazz rooms finds an unlikely location in the basement of a chain restaurant. The house band shares the stage with visiting musicians. Dinner is compulsory, but inexpensive and tasty. Open: Mon–Sat 8:30pm–1am, Sun 8pm–midnight. Tube: Tottenham Court Road.

**Admission:** £5–£7 ($9–$12.60), plus food. AE, DC, MC, V.

**RONNIE SCOTT'S, 47 Frith St., W.1. Tel. 071/439-0747.**

Ronnie Scott's is the capital's best-known jazz room. Top names from around the world regularly grace this Soho stage, but fans be forewarned: The place is pricey. Call for events and show times. Open: Mon–Sat 8:30pm–3am, Sun 8–11pm. Tube: Leicester Square.

**Admission:** Usually £10–£13 ($18–$23.40), plus a bar minimum. AE, DC, MC, V.

## DANCE CLUBS & DISCOS

The hippest Londoners go to "one-nighters," weekly dance events held at established clubs. The very nature of this scene demands frequent fresh faces, outdating recommendations before ink can dry on a page. Weekly listings magazines contain the latest. Discount passes to dance clubs are sometimes available just inside the front door of Tower Records on Piccadilly Circus. Otherwise, expect to part with a mint to get in. Once inside, beware: £4 ($7.20) cocktails are not uncommon.

**THE HIPPODROME, Charing Cross Rd., W.C.2. Tel. 071/437-4311.**

Located near Leicester Square, the popular Hippodrome is London's big daddy of discos, with a great sound system and lights to match. Very touristy, fun, and packed on weekends. Open: Mon–Sat 9pm–3:30am. Tube: Leicester Square.

**Admission:** £8–£13 ($14.40–$23.40). AE, DC, MC, V.

**SHAFTESBURY'S, 24 Shaftesbury Ave., W.1. Tel. 071/734-2017.**

Just north of Piccadilly Circus, this smaller mainstream disco features plenty of seating, a good dance floor, and, most important, great sound. Open: Tues–Sat 9pm–3am. Tube: Piccadilly Circus.

**Admission:** £5–£9 ($9–$16.20).

### GAY DISCOS

**BANG, at Busbys, 157 Charing Cross Rd., W.C.2. Tel. 071/734-6963.**

Loud music, a large dance floor, and a trendy crowd makes Bang one of the best dance spots in the city. Open: Mon 10pm–3am, Sat 11pm–4am. Tube: Tottenham Court Road.

**Admission:** £4–£6 ($7.20–$10.80).

**HEAVEN, Villiers St., W.C.2. Tel. 071/839-3852.**

Hands down, this is the most famous gay club in the city. A stage, where live bands sometimes perform, overlooks a huge dance floor. The crowd varies, but the sound system is always great. The club entrance is on a small street between Charing Cross and Embankment Underground stations. Open: Tues–Wed, Fri–Sat 10pm–3am. Tube: Embankment or Charing Cross.

**Admission:** £5–£9 ($9–$16.20).

# 3. THE PUB SCENE

There is nothing more British than a pub. The public house is exactly that, the British public's place to meet, exchange stories, tell jokes, and drink. Many people have tried to build something that looks like a pub outside Britain, but all fail to capture the unique feel of the real McCoy. It is indicative of this book's American perspective that we list pubs under "London Nights"; to the British these institutions are all-day affairs. There is not the same taboo about spending an afternoon drinking in England as there is in America. And on Sunday afternoons the whole family might go to the pub! (Note, however, that children under 14 are not allowed in pubs at all, and no one under 18 may legally drink alcohol.)

Beer is the main drink sold in pubs; don't even try to order a martini in most places. Sold in Imperial half-pints and pints (20% larger than U.S. measures), the choice is usually between lager and bitter, and the locals usually opt for the latter. Expect to pay between £1.20 ($2.15) and £1.75 ($3.15) for a pint. Many pubs serve particularly good "real" ales, distinguishable at the bar by handpumps that must be "pulled" by the barkeep. Real ales are natural "live" beers, allowed to ferment in the cask. Unlike lagers, English ales are served at room temperature and may take some getting used to. For an unusual and tasty alternative to barley pop, try cider, a flavorful fermented apple juice that's so good you'll hardly notice the alcohol—until later.

As a rule, there is no table service in pubs, and drinks (and food) are therefore ordered at the bar. Tipping at a pub is unusual, and should be reserved for exemplary service.

All pubs used to close in the afternoons, but a recent change in the law, toasted by most, now allows pubs to stay open from 11am to 11pm Monday through Saturday, and from noon to 3pm and 7 to 10:30pm on Sunday. Not all pubs take advantage of this new freedom, however; some still close daily between 3pm and 7pm.

Carpeted floors, etched glass, and carved-wood bars are the hallmarks of most pubs. But each one looks different, and each has its particular flavor and clientele. Greater London's 5,000-plus pubs ensure that you never have to walk more than a couple of blocks to find one, and part of the enjoyment of "pubbing" is discovering a special one on your own. But a few tried and true are listed below to help you on your way.

**FERRET AND FIRKIN, 114 Lots Rd., S.W.10. Tel. 071/ 352-6645.**

David Bruce's Ferret and Firkin, in Chelsea, offers the best pub night out in London. The beer served here is brewed in the basement and really packs a punch. But the best thing about this pub is the nightly piano player whose amplified instrument turns the place into a raucous singalong party. You don't have to be under 30 to crowd in here, but only the younger revelers will know all the words. Nine other Firkin pubs are just as fun and flavorful. Unfortunately, most are difficult to reach. Tube: Sloane Square, then bus 11 or 22 down King's Road.

**FROG & FIRKIN, 41 Tavistock Crescent, W.11. Tel. 071/ 727-9250.**

Just outside of Bayswater's northwestern corner is the Frog &

Firkin, a carbon copy of the Ferret in Chelsea (see above). Tube: Westbourne Park.

**LAMB & FLAG, 33 Rose St., W.C.2. Tel. 071/836-4108.**

The Lamb & Flag is an old timber-framed pub in a short cul-de-sac off Garrick Street in Covent Garden. The pub was dubbed the "Bucket of Blood" by the poet Dryden after he was almost beaten to death here (no doubt for being too witty at someone else's expense). The pub can be hard to find, but its great atmosphere and above-average food make the search well worth the effort. Tube: Leicester Square.

**MAISON BERLEMONT, 49 Dean St., W.1. Tel. 071/437-2799.**

Better known as the French House, this pub is an exceptional reminder of Soho's ethnic past. Still run by a member of the Berlemont family, the pub was the unofficial headquarters of the French government in exile during World War II, and it continues to attract a fiercely loyal French-speaking clientele. Tube: Tottenham Court Road.

**THE OLD KING LUD, 78 Ludgate Circus, E.C.4. Tel. 071/236-6610.**

The "hook" of this pub is its location; it was built in 1855, on top of the dungeons of the old Fleet Prison. Although it does not offer it these days, the Old King Lud was the home of the original Welsh rarebit. Tube: Blackfriars.

**THE SHERLOCK HOLMES, 10 Northumberland St., off Trafalgar Square, W.C.2. Tel. 071/930-2644.**

In the upstairs dining room of this popular pub you will find a re-creation of Holmes's fictional living room at 221b Baker Street. The head of the hound of the Baskervilles and other relevant "relics" decorate the downstairs bar. Tube: Charing Cross.

**THE SUN, 63 Lamb's Conduit St., W.C.1. Tel. 071/405-8278.**

Popular not for its architecture or history, but for its truly remarkable selection of "real" ales and out-of-town brews. There are over 20 brands on tap, including rotating rare "guest" beers. Landlord Roger Berman will proudly show you his vaulted cellars during slow periods. Tube: Holborn or Russell Square.

**YE OLDE CHESHIRE CHEESE, Wine Office Court, 146 Fleet St., E.C.4. Tel. 071/353-6170.**

Open since 1667, this historical wooden pub is where Dr. Johnson took his tipple, and is a sightseeing attraction in its own right. Ducking through the low doors will transport you back in time, as the cracked black varnish, wooden benches, and narrow courtyard entrance give it authentic period charm. Meals here are delicious and filling, but expensive. Tube: St. Paul's.

### GAY PUBS

**BRIEF ENCOUNTER, St. Martin's Lane, W.C.2. Tel. 071/ 240-2221.**

Centrally located around the corner from Covent Garden Market, this extremely popular pub attracts a young, business-oriented crowd. Tourists—gay and straight alike—regularly drink at the pub's outdoor tables. Tube: Leicester Square.

**THE KING'S ARMS, 23 Poland St., W.1. Tel. 071/734-5907.**

A busy gay men's pub on two levels, with good food and a cheap double-measures bar upstairs. Tube: Oxford Circus.

## WINE BARS

Wine lovers will appreciate these welcome alternatives to pubs. Although not as ubiquitous as pubs, wine bars have become fairly common throughout London. Most have a good selection by both the glass and the bottle, and food is almost always served. Menus tend to have a continental flavor, with standards and prices that are higher than at most pubs. You don't have to eat, however, and a bottle of the house wine, usually costing £5 to £6 ($9–$10.80), shared between two or three people, may come out cheaper than a visit to a pub. Most wine bars keep pub hours.

**BRAHMS & LISZT, 19 Russell St., W.C.2. Tel. 071/240-3661.**

The name is Cockney rhyming slang for "pissed," which in British English means "drunk." Head downstairs for food, upstairs for rowdier times. The bar features live music nightly (see "The Club & Music Scene," above, for more information). Tube: Covent Garden.

**THE CORK AND BOTTLE WINE BAR, 44046 Cranbourne St., W.C.2. Tel. 071/734-7807.**

Located between Leicester Square and Charing Cross Road, this basement bar is in the heart of the theater district. The Cork and Bottle is known both for its gourmet food and extensive wine list. Tube: Leicester Square.

**THE EBURY WINE BAR, 139 Ebury St., S.W.1. Tel. 071/ 730-5447.**

The Ebury, a stone's throw from Victoria Station, is a typical no-nonsense wine bar. It is popular with younger office workers and executives from the nearby investment bank. Tube: Victoria or Sloane Square.

# 4. MORE ENTERTAINMENT

## MOVIES

If you want to see a first-run film, go to one of the megascreens, like the **Odeon** (tel. 071/930-6111) or **Empire** (tel. 071/734-7123), that ring Leicester Square. These grand old theaters show American blockbusters almost exclusively. Avoid the postage-stamp–size screens of the local multiplex. Most Leicester Square cinemas sell reserved seats at prices that range from £4.50 to £8 ($8.10–$14.40), depending on the seat's location.

### FOREIGN & INDEPENDENT

In addition to the Hollywood houses, London is blessed with several cinemas showing top foreign and independent films.

**THE PREMIERE, in the Swiss Center, Leicester Square. Tel. 071/439-4470.**

This comfortable, alternative movie house is heavy on French films, though films from other Western and Eastern European countries are routinely represented. Tube: Leicester Square.

**Tickets:** £4.50 ($8.10).

**GATE CINEMA, 87 Notting Hill Gate, W.11. Tel. 071/727-4043.**

The Gate alternates between offbeat English and foreign-language films, with double features on Sunday afternoons. Tube: Notting Hill Gate.

**Tickets:** £4.50 ($8.10); £3.50 ($6.30) for the first performance Mon–Fri and Sun.

### REPERTORY CINEMAS

Repertory cinemas of note include the **Scala,** 275-277 Pentonville Road, N.1 (tel. 071/278-0051; tube to King's Cross); and the **Everyman,** Hollybush Vale, N.W.3 (tel. 071/435-1525; tube to Hampstead). Both are known for their triple bills and prices that rarely top £4 ($7.20).

# CHAPTER 10

# EASY EXCURSIONS FROM LONDON

**1. GREENWICH**
**2. HAMPTON COURT PALACE**
**3. KEW GARDENS**
**4. WINDSOR**
**5. BATH**
**6. CAMBRIDGE**
**7. OXFORD**
**8. STRATFORD-UPON-AVON**

Even if you only have a short time in London, try to arrange a trip outside the city. Just a few miles from the metropolis there's an England that is strikingly different from the city. The air is cleaner, the people are friendlier, everything is cheaper. A visit to any of the destinations listed below may make you wish you never had to leave.

The **British Travel Centre,** 12 Regent St., W.1 (tel. 071/730-3400), just south of Piccadilly Circus, is definitely worth a visit before heading out. They offer free leaflets and advice, and can also book trains, buses, and tours for you.

For train journeys under 50 miles, the cheapest tickets are called "cheap day returns." Try to avoid day trips on Friday, when fares increase to catch the mass exodus of city-dwellers. For information on specific trains, contact the British Travel Center, **BritRail** (tel. 071/928-5100), or the departing station listed below.

**National Express** (tel. 071/730-0202), the country's primary long-haul bus line, operates coaches to almost every corner of Britain. Victoria Coach Station, located one block west of Victoria Rail Station, is the line's London hub.

## DAY TRIPS

Many of the following attractions are officially within the limits of Greater London. They are, however, sufficiently far from the tourist center to warrant a listing here. A tour of each can easily take up a full day but, if you are pressed for time, it is possible to get there and back in just a few hours.

# 1. GREENWICH

**GETTING THERE** **By Waterbus** Boats depart from Westminster Pier (tel. 071/930-4721) near Big Ben (tube to Westminster), or from the Tower of London Pier (tel. 071/488–0344; tube to Tower Hill). The waterbus operates daily from 10:30am to 4pm and takes from 25 to 45 minutes. Round-trip tickets cost £4 ($7.20) for adults, £2 ($3.60) for children under 15.

**By Docklands Light Railway** This futuristic train ride transports you through the Docklands, London's fastest-developing area. Trains depart every few minutes from the DLR Tower Hill Station (tel. 071/222-1234), located 1 block from Tower Hill Underground. The journey takes about 15 minutes and costs £1.50 ($2.70) each way.

Greenwich is only a few miles from Piccadilly Circus, but it feels like it's eons away. This famous Thames-side town is the place where Greenwich mean time is fixed, and you can take a picture of yourself straddling the meridian by the Royal Observatory.

## WHAT TO SEE & DO

The **Royal Naval College** (tel. 081/858-2154), beautifully designed by Sir Christopher Wren, was commissioned by William and Mary in 1695. The buildings are baroque masterpieces, in which the chapel and Painted Hall are particularly outstanding. Entrance to the college is free, and open to the public Friday through Wednesday from 2:30 to 5pm.

The ***Cutty Sark*** (tel. 081/853-3589) is also here, permanently in dry dock, and open as a museum. This most famous of clipper ships made regular tea runs to China covering almost 400 ocean miles per day. It's open April through September, Monday through Saturday from 10am to 6pm and on Sunday from noon to 6pm; October through March the museum closes one hour earlier. Admission is £1.60 ($2.90) for adults, and 80p ($1.45) for children under 15.

# 2. HAMPTON COURT PALACE

**GETTING THERE** **By Waterbus** Boat service operates in summer only. Waterbuses depart 4 times daily from Westminster Pier (tel. 071/930-4721) near Big Ben (tube to Westminster). The journey takes from 3 to 4 hours round-trip, depending on the tide. One-way tickets cost £5.50 ($9.90) for adults, £3.50 ($6.30) for children under 15.

**By Train** BritRail trains depart every half hour from Waterloo Station, and take about 30 minutes. Tickets cost £3 ($5.40) round-trip.

---

The grounds of Hampton Court Palace are some of the most beautiful in London, and are perfect for picnicking. Hampton Court Road divides the palace from Bushy Park, an uncrowded, rambling swath of plantations, ponds, and parkland, with herds of roaming deer, occupying 1,110 acres.

### WHAT TO SEE & DO

Hampton Court Palace was built in the 16th century by Cardinal Thomas Wolsey, and reluctantly given to King Henry VIII. Five of the king's six wives lived here, and today this mammoth Tudor structure, on 50 landscaped acres, offers visitors one of the most satisfying day trips outside London.

Entrance to the palace, courtyard, and cloister costs £4.50 ($8.10) for adults, £2.50 ($4.50) for children under 16. An additional token charge allows you to get lost in the famous garden maze. The palace is open from mid-March to mid-October, Monday through Saturday from 9:30am to 5pm, Sunday from 2pm to 7pm. The grounds are open year-round from dawn to dusk.

## 3. KEW GARDENS

**GETTING THERE** **By Tube** Take the Underground to Kew Gardens. It takes about half an hour and costs £2.10 ($3.80).

### WHAT TO SEE & DO

The **Royal Botanic Gardens,** better known as **Kew Gardens** (tel. 081/940-1171), is an important research facility with some of London's most beautiful indoor and outdoor gardens. The architectural splendor of the greenhouses and the 164-foot Chinese-style pagoda combine with chrysanthemums, rhododendrons, peonies, and the like to make a visit to Kew unforgettable. The gardens are open April to mid-September Monday through Saturday from

---

**IMPRESSIONS**

*Go down to Kew in lilac time*
*(it isn't far from London!)*
*And you shall wander hand in hand with love*
*in summer's wonderland.*
—Alfred Noyes

9:30am to 6:30pm, Sunday and bank holidays from 9:30am to 8pm; mid-September through October daily from 9:30am to 6pm. Admission is £1 ($1.80) for adults, 50p ($.90) for students and seniors.

---

# 4. WINDSOR

**GETTING THERE** **By Train** BritRail trains depart from Paddington Station (tel. 071/262-6767) and make the journey in about 30 minutes. Trains leave 13 times each day, and tickets cost £7.60 ($13.70) round-trip.

**By Bus** Green Line buses (tel. 071/668-7261) leave once an hour from London's Eccelston Bridge, behind Victoria Station. Tickets cost £4.50 ($8.10) round-trip.

---

Surrounded by gentle hills and lush valleys, this pretty riverside town is characterized by Victorian and Georgian houses looming over still-extant cobblestone streets. Windsor is old—it was known to ancient Britons as "Windlesore"—and today the town is famous for two things: a castle and a prep school.

## WHAT TO SEE & DO

**Windsor Castle** (tel. 0753/868286) claims to be the largest inhabited castle in the world, and it's on a site that has been a home to monarchs for over 900 years. Situated on a bend in the Thames about 20 miles from London, the castle is surrounded by 4,800 acres of lawn, woodlands, and lakes.

When royalty is away, the **State Apartments** are open for viewing. Fabulous paintings, including works by Rubens and Rembrandt, adorn the walls, while elegant antique furnishings include Gibbons carvings and Gobelin tapestries. Call before setting out to learn whether the apartments will be open.

The **Changing of the Guard** ceremony takes place May through August, Monday through Saturday at 11am; the rest of the year it takes place every other day, excluding Sunday. To see if the ceremony is taking place on the day you visit, call the castle number and ask for extension 252.

✪ **Queen Mary's Doll House** is the most spectacular you will ever see. It is crafted with exacting detail, and everything in it actually works, from the miniature plumbing to a tiny electric iron. Even the bottles in the wine cellar contain vintage wine of that era.

**St. George's Chapel** (tel. 0753/865538), founded in the late 15th century, has long been a favorite of English monarchs. There are many royal tombs here, including those of Henry VIII and his third wife, Jane Seymour. The chapel is usually open Monday through

Saturday from 10:45am to 3:45pm, Sunday from 2pm to 3:45pm. It is closed during services.

The exclusive **Eton College** (tel. 0753/863593) is across a cast-iron footbridge. The prep school's students attend classes in collars and tails; illustrious alumni include George Orwell and Aldous Huxley. Twenty-nine former prime ministers also call Eton their alma mater. The **Lower School** houses one of the oldest extant classrooms in the world, dating from 1443.

The school is open for visitors from Easter to the end of September daily from 2pm to 4:30pm. During summer holidays, hours are extended from 10:30am to 5pm.

## FARTHER AFIELD

The excursions listed below are close enough to London to be visited in a day trip from the capital, but each warrants a more thorough exploration; make an overnight visit if you have the time.

# 5. BATH

110 miles W of London

**GETTING THERE By Train** BritRail trains depart from London's Paddington Station (tel. 071/262-6767) every 90 minutes and make the trip in about 80 minutes. Round-trip standard-class tickets cost from £21 to £29 ($37.80–$52.20); SuperSaver Return tickets are cheapest.

**By Bus** National Express (tel. 071/730-0202) buses leave daily from London's Victoria Coach Station, and make the trip in about 3 hours. About twice as slow and half as expensive as the train, round-trip tickets cost £11.50 to £15 ($20.70–$27).

**By Car** From London, take the M4 motorway to exit 18.

**ESSENTIALS Orientation** Bath (pop. 83,000) is situated along the River Avon, which is traversed by two bridges: North Parade Bridge and Pulteney Bridge. Most of the city's main sights are crowded around the bridgeheads and the centrally located abbey. Both the bus (tel. 0225/464446) and train (tel. 0225/463075) stations are located at the end of Manvers Street, within easy walking distance to the city center.

**Information** Bath's **Tourist Information Centre,** the Colonnades Shopping Centre, Bath St. (tel. 0225/462831), opposite the Roman Baths, will provide information and help you find accommodations at any one of a number of local bed-and-breakfasts. The center is open May through October Monday through Saturday from 9:30am to 8pm, Sunday from 10am to 6pm; November through April Monday through Saturday from 9:30am to 5pm, Sunday from 10am to 4pm.

**Fast Facts** The **area code** is 0225. The main post office is on New Bond Street (tel. 0225/825211). The **American Express** office is located on Bridge Street (0225/444767). In case of **emergencies,** dial 999.

---

According to legend, Bath was founded by King Lear's father, Bladud, who was miraculously cured of leprosy after immersing himself in the town's legendary hot springs. In actuality, however, the warm waters of Bath have been a resort site since Roman times.

Although it was founded in A.D. 75, Bath didn't become popular with the moderns until the beginning of the 18th century, when Queen Anne made it fashionable. Once again, the resort became a social center for the leisure class.

Bath was heavily bombed by the Germans in 1942, the result of a misguided strategy to demoralize Britons by targeting urban centers and historical sites. Since that time, the city has been painstakingly restored to its Georgian splendor. Although the public is no longer permitted to bathe in the town's natural springs, Bath is an extraordinarily beautiful town, and one of the most popular excursions from London.

## WHAT TO SEE & DO

Begin your tour at the **Roman Baths and Museum** (tel. 0225/461111, ext. 2785). These well-preserved remains of the original Roman Baths are the town's primary tourist draw. Perhaps the finest Roman structures in Britain, the baths were originally dedicated to Sulis, a local Celtic goddess who is closely identified with the Roman goddess Minerva. Hot mineral water still gurgles into large pools and, although you can no longer bathe here, you can sip the spring water from an adjacent drinking fountain.

The museum contains some stunning finds from local digs, including a bronze head of Minerva, and a small mountain of Roman-era pennies, tossed into the baths for good luck by superstitious Ancients. It's open March through June and September through October daily 9am to 5:30pm; July through August daily 9am to 6:30pm; and November through February Monday to Saturday 9am to 5pm, Sunday 10am to 5pm.

The 18th-century **Pump Room,** which overlooks the baths, is a beautiful example of Victorian elegance. Created in 1703 by professional gambler Richard Beau Nash, the architecturally stunning meeting house helped make Bath a fashionable luxury resort. It is still a major tourist attraction, as well as a civilized place for lunch or tea. Meals are usually accompanied by the classical music of the Pump Room Trio. It's open Monday to Saturday from 10am to noon, and again from 2:45 to 5pm.

**Bath Abbey,** located opposite the Pump Room, is the town's most magnificent church, dating from the 15th century. Restored in 1574 at the behest of Queen Elizabeth I, the abbey's many windows have earned it the nickname "Lantern of the West." It's open Monday through Saturday 9am to 5:30pm. Sunday hours vary, depending on services.

**Royal Crescent House** (tel. 0225/428126), is a painstakingly restored town house, made to look the way it may have late in the 18th century. Period furnishings, kitchen implements, and paintings give the house an air of lived-in authenticity.

The house itself is located on one end of Bath's most elegant Georgian street. Even if you don't want to visit the museum, be sure to take a stroll along this remarkable street. It's open March through October, Tuesday through Saturday 11am to 5pm, Sunday from 2 to 5pm; November through February, Saturday and Sunday only from 11am to 3pm.

## WHERE TO STAY

The Tourist Information Centre (see "Information," above) offers an exceptionally efficient accommodations booking service. Reservations for local hotels and bed-and-breakfasts—in all price ranges—are made with a 10% deposit and a £2 ($3.60) booking fee.

The largest cluster of budget-priced B&Bs are located along Pulteney Road and Pulteney Gardens, just past the cricket grounds. Except during festival time, when hotels of all description are booked solid, you can usually get a room without prior reservations.

**LEIGHTON HOUSE, 139 Wells Rd., Bath, Avon BA2 3AL. Tel. 0225/314769.** 7 rms (all with bath). TV TEL

**$ Rates** (including English breakfast): £42 ($75.60) single, £52-£56 ($93.60–$100.10) double, MC, V.

Proprietors David and Kathleen Slape offer terrific value in their big 1870s Victorian. All rooms have private bath, direct-dial telephones, and coffee/teamaking facilities. The B&B is a 10-minute walk from the town center, and located directly on a bus route.

**ARDEN HOTEL, 73 Great Pulteney St., Bath, Avon BA2 4DL. Tel. 0225/466601.** 10 rms (all with bath). TV TEL

**$ Rates** (including English breakfast): £45–£50 ($81–$90) single, £58–£65 ($104.40–$117) twin. MC, V.

This pleasant 3-story hotel is located in a small Georgian building. Rooms are equipped with color TVs, coffee/teamaking facilities, and hair dryers. The higher, and smaller, rooms are priced lower than those down below. The Arden is well located, close to the major sights. From the train station, cross the North Parade Bridge and take North Parade Road past the cricket ground.

## WHERE TO DINE

**THE WALRUS AND THE CARPENTER, 28 Barton St. Tel. 0225/314864.**

**Cuisine:** CONTINENTAL. **Reservations:** Recommended

**$ Prices:** Meals £5–£9 ($9–$16.20). MC, V.

**Open:** Lunch Mon–Sat noon–2pm; dinner daily 6–11pm.

Complete with checked tablecloths and studied casualness, this budget burger bistro serves everything from steaks to salads. Daily vegetarian specials are also available.

**CRYSTAL PALACE, 11 Abbey Green. Tel. 0225/423944.**
**Cuisine:** ENGLISH. **Reservations:** Not required.
**$ Prices:** Meals £4–£8 ($7.20–$14.40). No credit cards.
**Open:** Mon–Sat 11am–11pm, Sun 11am–2:30pm and 6–11pm.
This large 18th-century pub/restaurant features traditional English fare, such as steak-and-kidney pie, and a variety of sandwiches served beneath wood-beamed ceilings. During winter, try to get a table beside the paneled fireplace. In summer, the best dining is al fresco, on the outdoor patio.

The Crystal Palace is one of the few places in England where you can order Thomas Hardy Ale, a strong brew claiming the highest alcohol content of any beer in the world.

# 6. CAMBRIDGE

55 miles N of London

**GETTING THERE By Train** BritRail trains depart from London's Liverpool Street (tel. 071/283-7171) and King's Cross (tel. 071/278-2477) stations every 20 minutes and make the trek in about an hour. The standard round-trip fare is £13.50 ($24.30). From Cambridge station, take the Cityrail link bus to Market Square, in the center of the city.

**By Bus** National Express (tel. 071/730-0202) buses leave from London's Victoria Coach Station 13 times each day, take an hour and 50 minutes, and cost from £8 to £10.50 ($14.40–$18.90) round-trip.

**By Car** From London, take the M11 motorway to exit 11.

**ESSENTIALS Orientation** There are two main thoroughfares in Cambridge (pop. 103,000). Trumpington Road, which becomes Trumpington Street, King's Parade, Trinity Street, and finally St. John's Street, runs parallel to the River Cam, and is close to several of the city's colleges. The main shopping street starts at Magdalene Bridge, and turns into Bridge Street, Sidney Street, St. Andrew's Street, and finally Regent Street.

**Information** The **Tourist Information Centre,** Wheeler St. (tel. 0223/322640), located behind Guildhall, offers transportation and sightseeing information, as well as maps and accommodations lists. The office is open November through March, Monday through Friday 9am to 5:30pm, Saturday 9am to 5pm; April through June and September through October, Monday through Friday 9am to 6pm, Saturday 9am to 5pm, Sunday 10:30am to 3:30pm.

**Fast Facts** The **area code** is 0223. The main post office is located at 9 St. Andrew's St. (tel. 0223/351212). The **American**

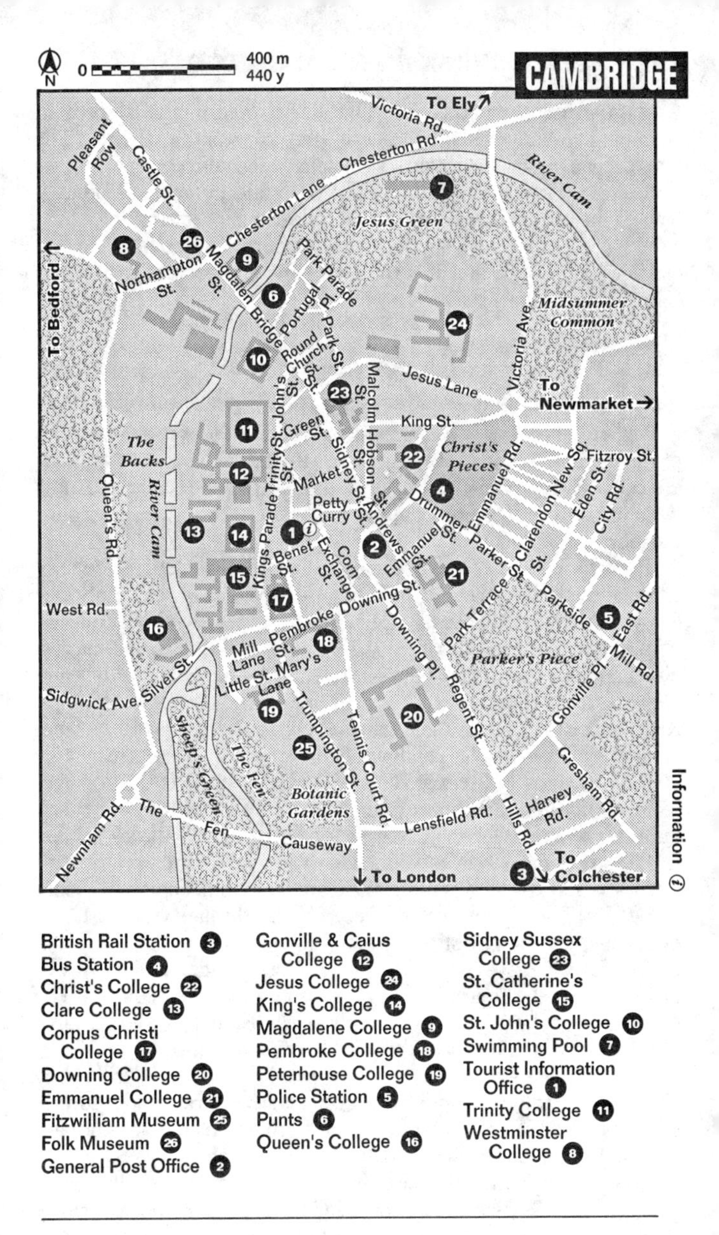


**Express** office is at 25 Sydney St. (tel. 0223/351636). In case of **emergencies,** dial 999.

---

Cambridge was settled by the Romans who bridged the River Cam, but the city did not begin to flourish until the 13th century, when the first teaching institution was founded here.

Cambridge competes with Oxford in everything. It loses in age—and usually in boat races—but it wins on charm. The magnificent town is dotted with spires and turrets, as well as drooping willows and daffodils. The romantically named Bridge of Sighs is the centerpiece of St. John's College, which itself is located in a town center that is devoid of cars. Most of the college buildings are clustered near here, and it is their stunning architecture that makes Cambridge worth a visit.

## WHAT TO SEE & DO

Encompassing 31 colleges, Cambridge University is one of the largest in England. It is one of the prettiest, too, packing over seven centuries of English architecture into a single square mile. The college grounds are open to the public year-round, though they are crammed only with tourists during summer months, when the schools are closed for vacation.

Even though you'll have to navigate through some dark cobblestone streets between stone buildings, the best way to see Cambridge is to do "the backs," a stroll along the riverside, behind the colleges.

**King's College Chapel** is a world-renowned Gothic masterpiece, and the town's most famous structure. Completed in the early 16th century, the chapel is one of the purest examples of early Renaissance architecture. It's fan-vaulted stone ceilings are complemented by magnificent windows, most of which were created by Flemish artisans between 1517 and 1531. A small exhibition hall features pictures and commentary on how and why the chapel was built. It's open during school term Monday through Saturday 9:30am to 3:45pm, Sunday 2 to 3pm and 4:30 to 5:45pm. During vacation it's open Monday through Saturday 9:30am to 5:45pm, Sunday 10:30am to 5:45pm. The chapel is closed December 26 through January 1, and occasionally without notice for recording sessions.

**Trinity College** (tel. 0223/338400) was founded by Henry VIII in 1546 and is the largest and wealthiest of Cambridge's colleges. The courtyard, or "quad," is particularly spacious, and includes a large fountain in which it is said the poet Byron used to bathe nude.

The college's particularly pretty **Wren Library** was designed by Sir Christopher himself and houses original works by famous former students. In addition to Byron, famous professors and alumni have included philosopher Bertrand Russell, poet John Dryden, author Andrew Marvell, and physicist Sir Isaac Newton.

**Queens' College** (tel. 0223/335511) is arguably the prettiest of all of Cambridge's colleges. The school was founded in 1448, and named for the wives of Henry VI and Edward IV. The Tudor courtyard is home to the half-timbered **President's Lodge,** which dates from the beginning of the 16th century.

"Punting," or pole-boating, on the River Cam is a Cambridge institution. So is **Scudamore's Boatyards,** Granta Place (tel. 0223/359750). This boatshop by the Anchor Pub has been renting punts, canoes, and rowboats since 1910. All boats rent for £5 ($9) per hour, and require a £30 ($54) refundable deposit. It's open during summer only, daily from 10am to 7pm.

## WHERE TO STAY

Some of the city's best B&Bs are clustered along Chesterton Road, not far from the train station.

**ASHLEY HOTEL, 74 Chesterton Rd., Cambridge, Cambridgeshire CB4 1ER. Tel. 0223/350059.** 16 rms (14 with shower). TV

**$ Rates** (including English breakfast): £23 ($41.40) single, £42 ($75.60) double. MC, V.

This good-quality bed-and-breakfast is located close to the city center, between the River Cam and Jesus Green. In addition to televisions, there are coffee/teamaking facilities in every room. If you can, make reservations, as there are only a handful of rooms here.

**FAIRWAYS, 141 Cherryhinton Rd., Cambridge, Cambridgeshire CB1 4BX. Tel. 0223/246063.** 14 rms (6 with bath). TV

**$ Rates:** £19 ($34.20) single without bath, £25 ($45) with bath; £32 ($57.60) double without bath, £36 ($64.80) with bath. MC, V.

The cozy rooms in this handsomely restored Victorian all have color TVs and coffee/teamaking facilities. A small lobby bar serves drinks, snacks, and light meals. Located about 1½ miles from the heart of the city.

**IHYF YOUTH HOSTEL, 97 Tenison Rd. Tel. 0223/354601.** 125 beds (none with bath). **Directions:** Walk straight from the train station, and turn right onto Tenison Road.

**$ Rates:** £10 ($18) per night with an IYHF Card.

Open year-round, Cambridge's conveniently located hostel is close to the train station and comfortable. Guests can use kitchen and laundry facilities and, if space permits, couples may share a room. The hostel is closed from 10am to 1pm, and curfew is at 11:30pm.

## WHERE TO DINE

**HOBBS PAVILION, Park Terrace. Tel. 0223/67480.**
**Cuisine:** CREPERIE. **Reservations:** Recommended.

**$ Prices:** £5–£8 ($9–$14.40). MC, V.
**Open:** Lunch Tues–Sat noon–2:30pm; dinner Tues–Wed and Fri–Sat 7–10pm, Thurs 8:30–10pm.

Located in a historic building, Hobbs is widely known for its imaginative crêpes. In fact, the menu features over 40 of these French-style pancakes, stuffed with everything from spicy ratatouille to black pudding. Soups and salads are also available.

**THE ANCHOR, Silver St. Tel. 0223/353554.**
**Cuisine:** ENGLISH. **Reservations:** Not required.

**$ Prices:** £3–£6 ($5.40–$10.80). No credit cards.

**Open:** Mon–Sat noon–11pm, Sunday noon–3pm and 7–10:30pm

One of the city's most popular riverside pubs, the Anchor serves traditional English specialties at either of two bars. Traditional hand-pulled "real" ales are also available, along with the usual selection of lagers and bitters.

## 7. OXFORD

57 miles NW of London

**GETTING THERE By Train** BritRail trains depart from London's Paddington Station (tel. 071/262-6767), and make the trip in about an hour. Standard-class tickets cost £13.20 ($23.75) round-trip.

**By Bus** Oxford Tube and Oxford CityLink (information from Victoria Coach Station, tel. 071/730-0202) run competing bus services departing from Victoria's Grosvenor Gardens. The journey takes about 90 minutes, and cost just £6 ($10.80) round-trip. Between the two services, buses leave 6 times per hour, 7 days per week.

**By Car** From London, take the M40 to the A40, to the A420 (or the A423, the scenic route via Windsor and Henley). Don't drive into the city center, however, as parking and traffic are horrific. Free **Park and Ride** car parks are located on the main approaches to the north, south, and west sides of the city, and are regularly served by buses that run into the heart of the city. These transport buses cost 80p ($1.45) and depart every 8 to 10 minutes.

**ESSENTIALS Orientation** Carfax, the city center, is surrounded by the colleges of Oxford, and intersected at right angles by Cornmarket Street, St. Aldates Street, Queen Street, and High Street. Magdalen Bridge lies past the east end of High Street, while the train and bus stations are located to the west.

**Information** The **Oxford Information Centre,** St. Aldate's Chambers, St. Aldate's (tel. 0865/726871), can provide you with maps, brochures, and accommodations information. They also have a lot of information on local sights and attractions. The office is open May through September, Monday through Saturday 9:30am to 5pm, Sunday 10:30am to 1pm and 1:30pm to 4pm: October through April, Monday through Saturday 9:30am to 5pm, closed Sunday.

The spires of Oxford may be dreamy, but the rest of the city is hustle and bustle. In addition to being home to the world's oldest English-speaking university, Oxford is also an active industrial city; its founding predates the school's by about two centuries.

Wedged between the Thames and Cherwell rivers, the city is

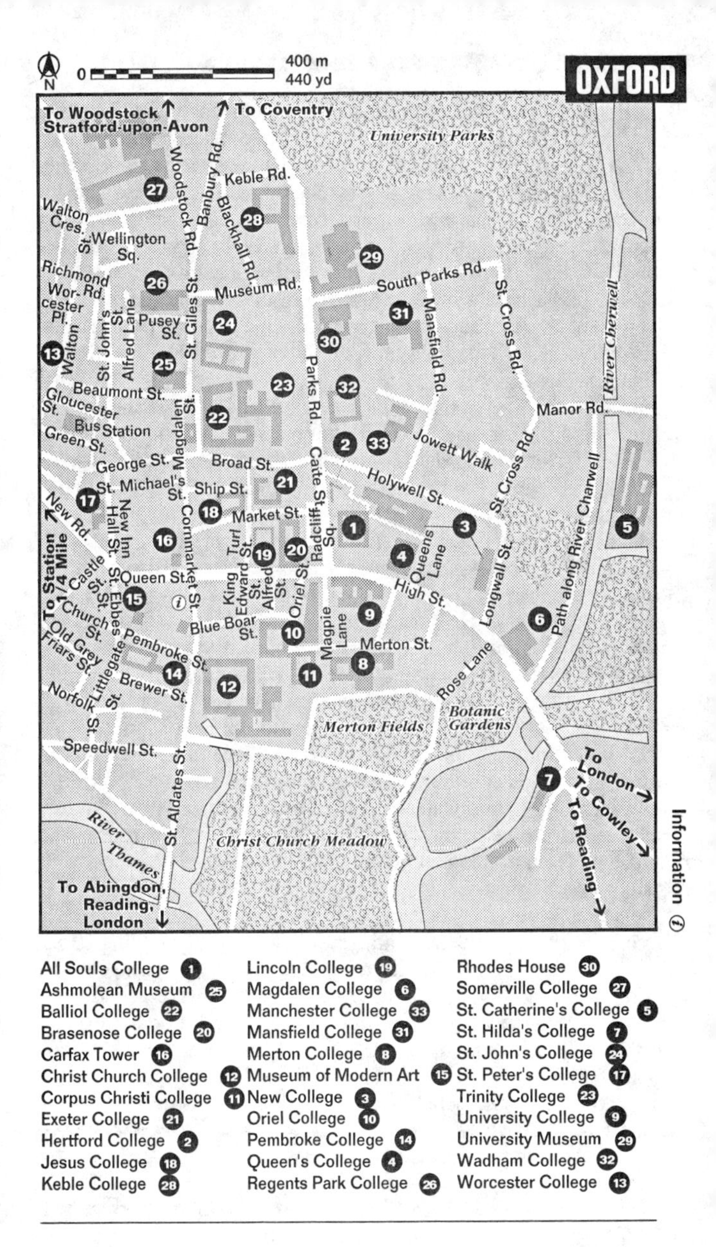


blessed with dozens of parks and gardens, and over 600 buildings listed for their historical or architectural interest.

## WHAT TO SEE & DO

Before setting out to see the city's sights, you might want to visit **The Oxford Story,** 6 Broad St. (tel. 0865/728822). Here you can learn about the history of Oxford and its university through a multimedia presentation. Visitors are transported Disney-style, on a moving coaster, through various tableaux, each depicting an important scene from the city's past. It's open July through August, daily 9:30am to 7pm; April through June and September through October, daily 9:30am to 5pm; November through March, daily 10am to 4pm.

Just 97 steps above Oxford, the top of Carfax Tower (tel. 0865/250239) is one of the best places to look out over the colleges. Get a map of adjacent rooftops from the attendant at the bottom. It's open March through October only, Monday through Saturday 10am to 6pm, Sunday 2 to 6pm.

Although students were congregating here as early as the beginning of the 12th century, Oxford University wasn't founded until 1167, when Henry II ordered it built. Like many urban schools, Oxford has no central campus; its 35 colleges are scattered throughout the city.

Magdalen (pronounced "maud-len") is one of the largest and most beautiful colleges in Oxford. The colorful flower-dotted grounds encompass one of the oldest botanic gardens in England. Begun in 1621, the garden originally grew plants for medicinal purposes. In addition to a meadow, a deer park, and a river (spanned by the famous Magdalen Bridge), the college is known for its Bell Tower. By tradition, the college choir sings from the top of the tower on May Day of each year. It's open daily from 2 to 6:15pm.

Known colloquially as The House, the college of Christ Church features the largest courtyard, or "quad," of any college in Oxford. The intimidating stone walls of **Tom Quad** enclose **Tom Tower** which, in turn, houses the Great Tom, an immense 18-thousand-pound bell. Each evening at 9:05pm, the bell strikes 101 times, as it has since 1682.

Dedicated to Oxford's patron saint, Frideswide, Christ Church's church is England's smallest cathedral. The current building dates from the 12th century, but its most distinguishing features—the vaulting over the choir, and the Norman pillars—were added over 300 years later. The cathedral is open in summer Monday through Saturday 9:30am to 6pm, Sunday 1 to 6pm; in winter Monday through Saturday 9:30am to 4:30pm, Sunday 1 to 4:30pm.

In addition to the schools mentioned above, **Merton, New College, St. John's, Trinity, Wadham,** and **Worcester** colleges all have pretty grounds and gardens that are definitely worth exploring.

The exciting **Museum of Modern Art** on Pembroke Street (tel. 0865/722733) is a well-planned counterpoint to Oxford's antiquity. It is also a leading center for contemporary visual arts. Exhibitions change regularly, and include sculpture, architecture, photography, video, and other media. Call for an exhibition schedule. It's open Tuesday through Saturday 10am to 6pm, Sunday 2pm to 6pm.

Founded in 1683, the **Ashmolean Museum,** Beaumont Street (tel. 0865/278000) is England's oldest public museum. In addition to housing a terrific archeology collection—with Egyptian mummies and casts of Greek sculptures—the galleries contain a Stradivarius violin, and works by da Vinci, Raphael, and Rembrandt. It's open Tuesday through Saturday 10am to 4pm, Sunday 2 to 4pm.

## WHERE TO STAY

Accommodations in Oxford are limited, especially during the school term. If you don't mind a healthy walk, however, the main roads out of town are lined with affordable bed-and-breakfasts.

In addition to the listings below, the **Oxford Information Centre,** St. Aldate's Chambers, St. Aldate's (tel. 0865/726871) can help you with accommodations information and make reservations for a £2 ($3.60) booking fee.

**LONSDALE GUEST HOUSE, 312 Banbury Rd., Summertown, Oxford, Oxfordshire OX2 7ED. Tel. 0865/54872.** 9 rms (7 with shower). TV **Bus:** 20, 21, or 22.

**$ Rates** (including English breakfast): £19 ($34.20) single without shower; £36 ($64.80) double with shower. No credit cards.

About 10 minutes by bus from the city center and one of the nicest B&Bs in town, Lonsdale offers comfortably furnished rooms, most with a private shower, down comforters, and central heating. Tennis courts, a heated indoor swimming pool, and a Laundromat are all a two-minute walk away.

**ADAMS GUEST HOUSE, 302 Banbury Rd., Oxford, Oxfordshire OX2 7ED. Tel. 0865/56118.** 22 rms (none with bath).

**$ Rates** (including English breakfast): £22 ($39.60) single, £34 ($61.20) twin. No credit cards.

Located in Summertown, 1¼ miles from Oxford, this is one of the best B&Bs around. Rooms are comfortable and cozy, and a bus runs every few minutes to the city center.

Adams is located opposite the Midland bank, in a quiet neighborhood with a number of restaurants, shops, and a laundry.

## WHERE TO DINE

**MUNCHY MUNCHY, 6 Park End St. Tel. 0865/245710.** **Cuisine:** INDONESIAN/MALAYSIAN. **Reservations:** Not required.

**$ Prices:** Lunch £5–£12 ($9–$21.60)

**Open:** Tues–Sat noon–2pm and 5:30–10pm. **Closed:** Three weeks in Aug and mid-Dec to mid-Jan.

Expect lines on weekends for the city's best Southeast Asian food. Dishes change daily according to the chef's mood and the availability of ingredients, but expect something creative and good. Bring your own beer or wine, as there is no liquor license. There is a 50p (90¢) per person corkage charge.

**BROWNS RESTAURANT, 5-9 Woodstock Rd. Tel. 0865/511995.**

**Cuisine:** ENGLISH/CONTINENTAL. **Reservations:** Not required.

$ **Prices:** £4–£6 ($7.20–$10.80) for burgers and sandwiches, £8–£11 ($14.40–$19.80) for full meals.

**Open:** Mon–Sat 11am–11:30pm, Sun noon–11:30pm.

Known for good, reliable food and generous portions, Browns is extremely popular with students, locals, and tourists alike. Spaghetti, salads, English pies, and a variety of meat sandwiches can satisfy even the most voracious of appetites.

**CHERWELL BOATHOUSE RESTAURANT, Bardwell Rd. Tel. 0856/52746.**

**Cuisine:** CONTINENTAL. **Reservations:** Recommended.

$ **Prices:** £15 ($27) for dinner; £10 ($18) for Sunday lunch.

**Open:** Dinner nightly 7:30–11pm; lunch Sun 12:30–2pm.

Perched on the riverbank, this romantic restaurant specializes in excellent fixed-price dinners and Sunday lunches. There are usually two price categories, the lower of which is always under £15 ($27). Meals are both delicious and filling, and the restaurant's wine list is one of the best in the city. It is truly worth the extra bucks.

## 8. STRATFORD-UPON-AVON

92 miles NW of London

**GETTING THERE By Train** BritRail trains make the trip from London's Paddington Station (tel. 071/262-6767) in about 90 minutes. Round-trip standard-class tickets cost from £19 to £25 ($34.20–$45). The **Shakespeare Connection** rail/bus link departs from Euston Station, and takes about 2 hours. This is the only transport offering evening service back to London after the Stratford theaters close. Tickets cost £23 ($41.40).

**By Bus** National Express (tel. 071/730-0202) buses run every two hours or so, and make the trip from London's Victoria Coach Station in about 3½ hours. Tickets cost £10 to £13.50 ($18–$24.30).

**By Car** From London, take the M40 motorway, then turn north on A34.

**ESSENTIALS Orientation** Stratford's simple layout—unchanged since the Middle Ages—is an important component of its charm. There are just three streets running parallel to the river, and three streets at right angles to it. Buses stop at the Travel Shop office (tel. 0789/204181), at the corner of Guild Street and Warwick Road.

**Information** **The Information Centre,** Judith Shakespeare's House, 1 High St. (tel. 0789/293127), offers tourist information, maps, and a helpful accommodations booking service. It's open April through October, Monday through Saturday 9am to 5:30pm, Sunday 2 to 5pm; November through March, Monday through Saturday from 10:30am to 4:30pm, closed Sunday.

**Fast Facts** The **area code** is 0789. The main post office is at 24 Bridge Street. **American Express** is located at 37 Wood Street (tel. 0789/293582). In case of **emergencies,** dial 999.

---

The Bard was born here. But even if Stratford-upon-Avon were not Shakespeare country, this beautiful and charming town would still be one of the most touristed towns in Britain. Picture-perfect half-timbered houses are shaded by statuesque chestnut and poplar trees, while lazy willows hang over one of the world's most romantic rivers. In spring and summer the town literally blooms with roses, and honeysuckle clambers over every wall.

## WHAT TO SEE & DO

Stratford's five most important restored sites are administered by the Shakespeare Birthplace Trust and collectively referred to as the "Shakespeare Properties." A money-saving ticket, good for admission to all five properties, can be purchased at any site for £5 ($9), £2 ($3.60) for children under 15.

Begin at the beginning, at Shakespeare's Birthplace, a three-gabled, half-timbered house, where the playwright was born on St. George's Day (April 23) in 1564. In addition to period furniture, the home supports a "life-and-times" exhibit of memorabilia, which includes a one-shilling fine for "unauthorized midden" (rubbish) in the street outside their home.

More than 660,000 annual visitors make their way through the narrow hallways and low doors of this charming home. Try to arrive before 11am, when the masses of day trippers arrive. It's open April through October, Monday through Saturday 9am to 6pm, Sunday 2 to 5pm; November through March, Monday through Saturday 9am to 6pm, Sunday from 1:30 to 4:30pm.

✪ **Anne Hathaway's Cottage,** pictured on tea trays, boxes of chocolates, and other souvenirs all around town, must be the prettiest cottage in England. Located 1 mile from Stratford in the hamlet of Shottery, Shakespeare's wife's childhood home is actually a country farmhouse, surrounded by lush gardens and orchards. A large open fireplace and massive beamed ceilings are preserved along with many original furnishings.

If the weather is good, walk to the cottage from Stratford, across the meadow, along the marked pathway from Evesham Place. Or take the bus from Bridge Street. The cottage keeps the same opening hours as Shakespeare's birthplace, above.

Shakespeare's daughter Susanna lived in **Hall's Craft** with her well-to-do husband, Dr. John Hall. The exceptional Tudor home, which is traditionally furnished with oak dressers and tables, also contains exhibits illustrating the medical practice in Elizabethan times. In back, a particularly beautiful walled garden is especially worth visiting. The adjoining Hall's Croft Club serves morning coffee, lunch, and afternoon tea. It's open April through October, Monday through Saturday 9am to 6pm, Sunday 2 to 5pm; November through March, Monday through Saturday 9am to 6pm, closed Sunday.

Thomas Nash married Elizabeth Hall, one of Shakespeare's granddaughters, and moved to **Nash's House,** a 16th-century home next to **New Place,** the Bard's place of retirement. When it was purchased by the prosperous playwright in 1597, New Place was one of Stratford's nicest homes. Unfortunately, only the foundations and gardens still stand.

The two houses are connected by **Knott Garden,** a tourist-filled Elizabethan green famous for its mulberry tree, said to be grown from a cutting of a tree planted by Shakespeare. The site is open April through October, Monday through Saturday 9am to 6pm, Sunday 2 to 5pm; November through March, Monday through Saturday from 9am to 6pm, closed Sunday.

Located in Wilmcote, 3 miles from Stratford, **Mary Arden's House** is said to have been home to Shakespeare's mother. Today, this large Tudor farmstead contains traditional furniture and utensils, while the adjacent barns house a farming museum.

The neighboring **Glebe Farm** is a working country farm, using techniques from Shakespeare's day. Both are open April through October, Monday through Saturday 9am to 6pm, Sunday 2 to 5pm; November through March, Monday through Saturday 9am to 6pm, closed Sunday.

Shakespeare is buried in **Holy Trinity Church,** his local parish church. His grave is marked with a small plaque with the words, ". . . and cursed be he who moves my bones." It's open April through October, Monday to Saturday 8:30am to 6pm, Sunday noon to 5pm; November through March, Monday through Saturday 8:30am to 4pm, Sunday 2 to 5pm.

The small **Stratford-upon-Avon Motor Museum,** 1 Shakespeare St. (tel. 0789/69413), has special-edition Rolls-Royces, Italian Bugattis, and classic Jaguars from the 1920s. There is also a bookshop where maintenance books on old models and vintage cars are for sale. It's open April through October, daily 9am to 6pm; November through March, daily 10am to 4pm.

## ATTENDING THE THEATER

The **Royal Shakespeare Company** (tel. 0789/295623) performs in two primary theaters in Stratford-upon-Avon.

The **Shakespeare Theatre** is located on the banks of the Avon and seats 1,500. This is the company's primary playhouse. About five different plays are staged each season, which runs from early April to late January.

To insure good seats, tickets should be purchased in advance, either from the theater box office, or in the United States through Keith Prowse, 234 W. 44th St., New York, NY 10036 (tel. 212/398-1430). You can sometimes get good matinee seats on the morning of a performance. Customer returns and standing-room tickets may also be available on the day of an evening performance. The **box office** is open Monday through Saturday 9:30am to 8pm.

**Backstage Tours** are offered Monday through Saturday at 1:30 and 5:30pm, and Sunday at 12:30, 2:15, 3:15, and 4:15pm. They are also offered after some evening performances. Tours cost £2.80 ($5.05), £2 ($3.60) for students and seniors.

Opened in 1986, the **Swan Theatre** seats just 430, and is primarily used for productions by post-Shakespearean playwrights. Built in a neo-Elizabethan style, the theater usually rotates a repertoire of five plays each season. The **box office** is open Monday through Saturday 9:30am to 8pm.

## WHERE TO STAY

Although there are many beds-and-breakfasts here, it is probably wise to call ahead for reservations during the summer.

**The Information Centre,** Judith Shakespeare's House, 1 High St., Stratford-upon-Avon, Warwickshire CV37 6AU (tel. 0789/293127), can book accommodations for you in any price range. The charge for this service is £2.65 ($4.75), payable in pounds sterling only. Rooms are confirmed with a 10% deposit, deducted from the final bill. You can write ahead to reserve accommodations. Be specific about price range, number of nights, and the number of beds required.

**THE HOLLIES, 16 Evesham Pl., Stratford-upon-Avon, Warwickshire CV37 6HT. Tel. 0789/266857.** 6 rms (1 with bath). TV

**$ Rates** (including English breakfast): £30 ($54) double without bath, £38 ($68.40) with bath. No credit cards.

Located in an old three-story schoolhouse, this spacious guesthouse offers comfortable rooms kept spotlessly clean by the mother-and-daughter resident proprietors. Coffee/teamaking facilities are in every bedroom, and the sunny breakfast room is decorated with hand-cut crystal.

**SALAMANDER GUEST HOUSE, 40 Grove Rd., Stratford-upon-Avon, Warwickshire CV37 6PB. Tel. 0789/205728.** 7 rms (3 with bath).

**$ Rates** (including English breakfast): £15 ($27) single without bath; £30 ($54) double without bath, £34 ($61.20) with bath. No credit cards.

Fronting a wooded park, this homey guesthouse is efficiently run by Maurice and Ninon Croft. Home-cooked dinners are available for £7 ($12.60). The B&B is a 5-minute walk from the town center.

**IYHF YOUTH HOSTEL, Hemmingford House, Wellesbourne Rd., Alverton. Tel. 0789/297093.** 170 beds.

$ **Rates:** £7 ($12.60) per night with an IYHF Card. MC, V. **Closed:** Jan–Feb.

Stratford's busy hostel is located 2 miles from the city center, in a large 200-year-old building with 20 rooms. Guests have full use of kitchen facilities. The hostel is closed from 10am to 1pm, and curfew is at 11:30pm.

## WHERE TO DINE

**BLACK SWAN, Southern La. Tel. 0789/297312.**
**Cuisine:** ENGLISH.
$ **Prices:** £5–£12 ($9–$21.60).
**Open:** Mon–Sat 11:30am–4pm and 5:30–11pm, Sun noon–2pm.

Affectionately known as the Dirty Duck, this popular pub has been a regular hangout for local actors since the 18th century. Autographed photos of patrons, including Lord Olivier, adorn the walls.

Unusual English specialties like braised kidneys are served next to more traditional country grills. During cold weather an open fire blazes. When it's nice out, you can dine in the front garden, overlooking the river.

**THE HORSESHOE BUTTERY AND RESTAURANT, 33 Greenhill St. Tel. 0789/292246.**
**Cuisine:** ENGLISH.
$ **Prices:** £3.50–£7 ($6.30–$12.60). No credit cards.
**Open:** Daily noon–2:30pm and 5–9pm.

Centrally located, opposite the Safeway supermarket, this simple café serves straightforward English food at reasonable prices. Grilled chicken and fish are usually available, as are a good selection of sandwiches, burgers, and snacks.

# APPENDIX

## A. METRIC MEASURES

### LENGTH

| | | |
|---|---|---|
| 1 millimeter (mm) | = | .04 inches (*or* less than 1⁄16 in.) |
| 1 centimeter (cm) | = | .39 inches (*or* just under ½ in.) |
| 1 meter (m) | = | 39 inches (*or* about 1.1 yards) |
| 1 kilometer (km) | = | .62 miles (*or* about ⅔ of a mile) |

**To convert kilometers to miles,** multiply the number of kilometers by .62. Also use to convert kilometers per hour (kmph) to miles per hour (m.p.h.).

**To convert miles to kilometers,** multiply the number of miles by 1.61. Also use to convert from m.p.h. to kmph.

### CAPACITY

| | | |
|---|---|---|
| 1 liter (l) | = | 33.92 fluid ounces = 2.1 pints = 1.06 quarts |
| | = | .26 U.S. gallons |
| 1 Imperial gallon | = | 1.2 U.S. gallons |

**To convert liters to U.S. gallons,** multiply the number of liters by .26.

**To convert U.S. gallons to liters,** multiply the number of gallons by 3.79.

**To convert Imperial gallons to U.S. gallons,** multiply the number of Imperial gallons by 1.2.

**To convert U.S. gallons to Imperial gallons,** multiply the number of U.S. gallons by .83.

### WEIGHT

| | | |
|---|---|---|
| 1 gram (g) | = | .035 ounces (*or* about a paperclip's weight) |
| 1 kilogram (kg) | = | 35.2 ounces |
| | = | 2.2 pounds |
| 1 metric ton | = | 2,205 pounds (1.1 short ton) |

**To convert kilograms to pounds,** mulitply the number of kilograms by 2.2.

**To convert pounds to kilograms,** multiply the number of pounds by .45.

### AREA

| | | | | |
|---|---|---|---|---|
| 1 hectare (ha) | = | 2.47 acres | | |
| 1 square kilometer ($km^2$) | = | 247 acres | = | .39 square miles |

**To convert hectares to acres,** multiply the number of hectares by 2.47.

**To convert acres to hectares,** mulitply the number of acres by .41.

**To convert square kilometers to square miles,** multiply the number of square kilometers by .39.

**To convert square miles to square kilometers,** mulitply the number of square miles by 2.6.

### TEMPERATURE

°C −18° −10 0 10 20 30 40

°F 0° 10 20 32 40 50 60 70 80 90 100

**To convert degrees Celsius to degrees Fahrenheit,** multiply °C by 9, divide by 5, and add 32 (example: 20°C × 9/1 + 32 = 68°F).

**To convert degrees Fahrenheit to degrees Celsius,** subtract 32 from °F, multiply by 5, then divide by 9 (example: 85°F − 32 × 5/9 = 29.4°C).

## B. SIZE CONVERSIONS

The following charts should help you to choose the correct clothing sizes in London. However, sizes can vary, so the best guide is simply to try things on.

### WOMEN'S DRESSES, COATS, AND SKIRTS

| American | 3 | 5 | 7 | 9 | 11 | 12 | 13 | 14 | 15 | 16 | 18 |
|---|---|---|---|---|---|---|---|---|---|---|---|
| Continental | 36 | 38 | 38 | 40 | 40 | 42 | 42 | 44 | 44 | 46 | 48 |
| British | 8 | 10 | 11 | 12 | 13 | 14 | 15 | 16 | 17 | 18 | 20 |

### WOMEN'S BLOUSES AND SWEATERS

| American | 10 | 12 | 14 | 16 | 18 | 20 |
|---|---|---|---|---|---|---|
| Continental | 38 | 40 | 42 | 44 | 46 | 48 |
| British | 32 | 34 | 36 | 38 | 40 | 42 |

### WOMEN'S STOCKINGS

| American | 8 | 8½ | 9 | 9½ | 10 | 10½ |
|---|---|---|---|---|---|---|
| Continental | 1 | 2 | 3 | 4 | 5 | 6 |
| British | 8 | 8½ | 9 | 9½ | 10 | 10½ |

### WOMEN'S SHOES

| American | 5 | 6 | 7 | 8 | 9 | 10 |
|---|---|---|---|---|---|---|
| Continental | 36 | 37 | 38 | 39 | 40 | 41 |
| British | 3½ | 4½ | 5½ | 6½ | 7½ | 8½ |

## MEN'S SUITS

| | | | | | | | | |
|---|---|---|---|---|---|---|---|---|
| American | 34 | 36 | 38 | 40 | 42 | 44 | 46 | 48 |
| Continental | 44 | 46 | 48 | 50 | 52 | 54 | 56 | 58 |
| British | 34 | 36 | 38 | 40 | 42 | 44 | 46 | 48 |

## MEN'S SHIRTS

| | | | | | | | | |
|---|---|---|---|---|---|---|---|---|
| American | 14½ | 15 | 15½ | 16 | 16½ | 17 | 17½ | 18 |
| Continental | 37 | 38 | 39 | 41 | 42 | 43 | 44 | 45 |
| British | 14½ | 15 | 15½ | 16 | 16½ | 17 | 17½ | 18 |

## MEN'S SHOES

| | | | | | | | |
|---|---|---|---|---|---|---|---|
| American | 7 | 8 | 9 | 10 | 11 | 12 | 13 |
| Continental | 39½ | 41 | 42 | 43 | 44½ | 46 | 47 |
| British | 6 | 7 | 8 | 9 | 10 | 11 | 12 |

## MEN'S HATS

| | | | | | | |
|---|---|---|---|---|---|---|
| American | 6⅞ | 7⅛ | 7¼ | 7⅜ | 7½ | 7⅝ |
| Continental | 55 | 56 | 58 | 59 | 60 | 61 |
| British | 6¼ | 6⅞ | 7⅛ | 7¼ | 7⅜ | 7½ |

## CHILDREN'S CLOTHING

| | | | | | |
|---|---|---|---|---|---|
| American | 3 | 4 | 5 | 6 | 6X |
| Continental | 98 | 104 | 110 | 116 | 122 |
| British | 18 | 20 | 22 | 24 | 26 |

## CHILDREN'S SHOES

| | | | | | | | | | |
|---|---|---|---|---|---|---|---|---|---|
| American | 8 | 9 | 10 | 11 | 12 | 13 | 1 | 2 | 3 |
| Continental | 24 | 25 | 27 | 28 | 29 | 30 | 32 | 33 | 34 |
| British | 7 | 8 | 9 | 10 | 11 | 12 | 13 | 1 | 2 |

# INDEX

## GENERAL INFORMATION

# SIGHTS AND ATTRACTIONS

## LONDON



**NOTE:** *indicates an Author's Favorite

## DAY-TRIP AREAS

### BATH



### CAMBRIDGE



### GREENWICH



### KEW GARDENS



### OXFORD



### STRATFORD-UPON-AVON



### WINDSOR



# ACCOMMODATIONS

## LONDON

### BAYSWATER AND PADDINGTON

## DAY-TRIP AREAS



**KEY TO ABBREVIATIONS:** *B&B* = Bed-and-Breakfast; *Hs* = Private Hostel; *W* = Worth the Extra Bucks; $ = Super Budget Choices; * = an Author's Favorite

# RESTAURANTS

## LONDON

### By Cuisine



## DAY-TRIP AREAS



**KEY TO ABBREVIATIONS:** *W* = Worth the Extra Bucks; * = an Author's Favorite

**TURN TO THE LAST PAGE OF THIS BOOK FOR ORDER FORM.**

**(TURN PAGE FOR ADDITONAL BOOKS AND ORDER FORM)**